Cultures in Contact

STUDIES IN CROSS-CULTURAL INTERACTION

INTERNATIONAL SERIES IN EXPERIMENTAL SOCIAL PSYCHOLOGY

Series Editor: Michael Argyle, University of Oxford

Vol 1. BOCHNER
Cultures in Contact

Vol 2. HOWITT
The Mass Media and Social Problems

Vol 3. PEARCE
The Social Psychology of Tourist Behaviour

A Related Pergamon Journal
LANGUAGE & COMMUNICATION*

An Interdisciplinary Journal

Editor: Roy Harris, *University of Oxford*

The primary aim of the journal is to fill the need for a publicational forum devoted to the discussion of topics and issues in communication which are of interdisciplinary significance. It will publish contributions from researchers in all fields relevant to the study of verbal and non-verbal communication.

Emphasis will be placed on the implications of current research for establishing common theoretical frameworks within which findings from different areas of study may be accommodated and interrelated.

By focusing attention on the many ways in which language is integrated with other forms of communicational activity and interactional behaviour it is intended to explore ways of developing a science of communication which is not restricted by existing disciplinary boundaries.

*Free specimen copy available on request.

NOTICE TO READERS

Dear Reader

An Invitation to Publish in and Recommend the Placing of a Standing Order to Volumes Published in this Valuable Series.

If your library is not already a standing/continuation order customer to this series, may we recommend that you place a standing/continuation order to receive immediately upon publication all new volumes. Should you find that these volumes no longer serve your needs, your order can be cancelled at any time without notice.

The Editors and the Publisher will be glad to receive suggestions or outlines of suitable titles, reviews or symposia for editorial consideration: if found acceptable, rapid publication is guaranteed.

ROBERT MAXWELL
Publisher at Pergamon Press

Cultures in Contact

STUDIES IN CROSS-CULTURAL INTERACTION

Edited by

STEPHEN BOCHNER

PERGAMON PRESS

OXFORD · NEW YORK · TORONTO · SYDNEY · PARIS · FRANKFURT

U.K.   Pergamon Press Ltd., Headington Hill Hall,
                        Oxford OX3 0BW, England U.S.A.

U.S.A.   Pergamon Press Inc., Maxwell House, Fairview Park,
                        Elmsford, New York 10523, U.S.A.

CANADA   Pergamon Press Canada Ltd., Suite 104, 150 Consumers
                        Road, Willowdale, Ontario M2J 1P9, Canada

AUSTRALIA   Pergamon Press (Aust.) Pty. Ltd., P.O. Box 544,
                        Potts Point, N.S.W. 2011, Australia

FRANCE   Pergamon Press SARL, 24 rue des Ecoles,
                        75240 Paris, Cedex 05, France

FEDERAL REPUBLIC   Pergamon Press GmbH, 6242 Kronberg-Taunus,
OF GERMANY   Hammerweg 6, Federal Republic of Germany

First edition 1982

Library of Congress Card No 82-3852

British Library Cataloguing in Publication Data
Cultures in contact.—(IESPI:1)
1. Intercultural communication
I. Bochner, Stephen
302.2 (expanded)   GN496
ISBN 0-08-025805-0 (Hardcover)
ISBN 0-08-028919-3 (Flexicover)

*Typeset in IBM Press Roman by Express Litho Service
(Oxford)
Printed in Great Britain by A. Wheaton & Co. Ltd.,
Exeter*

Introduction to the series

MICHAEL ARGYLE

SOCIAL psychology is in a very interesting period, and one of rapid development. It has survived a number of "crises", there is increased concern with external validity and relevance to the real world, the repertoire of research methods and statistical procedures has been greatly extended, and a number of exciting new ideas and approaches are being tried out.

The books in this series present some of these new developments; each volume contains a balance of new material and a critical review of the relevant literature. The new material consists of empirical research, research procedures, theoretical formulations, or a combination of these. Authors have been asked to review and evaluate the often very extensive past literature, and to explain their new findings, methods or theories clearly.

The authors are from all over the world, and have been very carefully chosen, mainly on the basis of their previous published work, showing the importance and originality of their contribution, and their ability to present it clearly. Some of these books report a programme of research by one individual or a team, some are based on doctoral theses, others on conferences.

Social psychologists have moved into an increasing number of applied fields, and a growing number of practitioners have made use of our work. All the books in this series will have some practical application, some will be on topics of wide popular interest, as well as adding to scientific knowledge. The books in the series are designed for advanced undergraduates, graduate students and relevant practitioners, and in some cases for a rather broader public.

We do not know how social psychology will develop, and it takes quite a variety of forms already. However, it is a great pleasure to be associated with books by some of those social psychologists who are developing the subject in such interesting ways.

Preface and overview

STEPHEN BOCHNER

INTERACTION between members of different ethnic groups is an increasingly common aspect of modern life, as more and more people study, work, play or settle in cultures other than their own. Not just the visitors, but also those indigenous to a given society can be profoundly affected by such contact. The aim of this book is to look closely at the processes and outcomes of cross-cultural encounters — to provide an account of what transpires and emerges when persons from different cultures meet.

The volume has been organized into three parts. The first section provides an overview of the field. The various types and purposes of contact are described, and the major empirical findings reviewed. A chapter with a historical perspective traces the development of research and thinking in this area from its beginnings at the turn of the century to the present day. A broad aim is to alert the reader to the main theoretical, practical and methodological issues that have been pursued in work on cross-cultural interaction.

The second section of the book deals with the processes underlying effective communication between culturally diverse persons. The topics cover the attribution of behaviour, language, and non-verbal communication including a special chapter on gestures. The discussion centres on those aspects of the communication process that may either enhance or hinder mutual understanding during cross-cultural interaction.

Whereas the first two sections of the book deal primarily with theories, concepts and processes, the last section is expressly concerned with the practical outcomes of culture contact, i.e. with the reactions of the persons engaged in the meeting. Clearly this is a vast field, since cross-cultural interaction takes many shapes and forms, and is engaged in for a variety of reasons. Nevertheless, several of the effects appear to generalize across different contact situations, and some conclusions can be drawn about how people are affected by unfamiliar environments. The two chapters in this section deal with overseas study and tourism respectively; both activities that literally millions of people participate in, and which have a profound impact on international relations. Even though these two areas constitute only a small sampling of contact situations occurring in the world, the problems encountered by overseas students and tourists (and their hosts), are typical of most varieties of cross-cultural encounters.

Each chapter is an original contribution by an acknowledged authority, and was written expressly for this book at the request of the editor. Most of the authors met at Oxford in June 1979 at a one-day Workshop which was specially convened for the purpose of presenting the papers to a select, invited audience. At the Workshop, the contributions were critically reviewed, and the final drafts were written in the light of that experience.

The Oxford Workshop had a second purpose — to celebrate Otto Klineberg's eightieth year and some six decades of pioneering work in the psychology of cross-cultural interactions. Klineberg has been one of the giants in the field, and practically all those working in the area today have been affected by his seminal ideas and studies. Klineberg's presence at the Workshop, made possible by a grant from the Cyril Foster Bequest, was a major inspiration to the editor, and greatly influenced the selection of topics and hence the shape of the book. Although Klineberg would be embarrassed at the thought that this volume is a *Festschrift* to him, all of the authors would like to pay tribute to his wisdom, scholarship, and to his unfailing support of younger workers, during his long and distinguished career.

About the contributors

Michael Argyle is Reader in Social Psychology in the Department of Experimental Psychology at Oxford University, and a Fellow of Wolfson College. He has been a visiting professor at universities in the U.S.A., Canada, Europe, Australia, Africa and Israel. He has carried out cross-cultural studies using subjects from Italy, Japan, and Hong Kong, and pioneered the use of social skills training in Britain. He is the author of numerous books and articles on social interaction.

Verner C. Bickley is the Director of the Culture Learning Institute of the East—West Center in Honolulu, Hawaii. Before that, he was the Language Officer of the British Council in Japan, and First Secretary of the British Embassy Cultural Department in Tokyo. He has taught linguistics and English in universities in Singapore, Burma, Indonesia and Japan, and has been active in broadcasting with the B.B.C., Radio Singapore, Radio Republik Indonesia, the Burma Broadcasting Service, and the NKH in Japan. He was awarded the M.B.E. in 1964.

Stephen Bochner is Senior Lecturer in Psychology at The University of New South Wales in Sydney. He has held visiting appointments at the University of Hawaii, the East—West Center, Rutgers University, and Oxford University. His special area of interest is cross-cultural psychology, and he has carried out field research in Southeast Asia and Central Australia. He has been on the editorial board of the *Journal of Cross-Cultural Psychology* since its inception, and has edited several books and published numerous articles on the subject of inter-cultural interaction.

Peter Collett is a Research Officer in the Department of Experimental Psychology at Oxford University. He is the editor of *Social Rules and Social Behaviour* and co-author of *Gestures: Their Origins and Distribution.* He is interested in the study of behavior in natural settings and has worked on ritual forms of interaction in different countries.

Adrian Furnham is a Lecturer in Psychology at University College, London. He completed his B.A. and M.A. degrees at the University of Natal. He subsequently earned a M.Sc. from the University of London, a further M.Sc. from the University of Strathclyde while on a Rotary International Fellowship and a D.Phil. at Oxford University. He has published several articles on cross-cultural differences in social behavior.

Miles Hewstone graduated from Bristol University with a B.Sc. in Psychology, and is currently completing a D.Phil. at the University of Oxford.

Jos Jaspars is a Lecturer in Psychology in the Department of Experimental Psychology at Oxford University, and a Fellow of St. Edmund Hall. He obtained his doctorate from Leiden University, and has studied with George Kelly and Raymond Cattell in the U.S.A. Prior to coming to Oxford, he was Professor of Social Psychology at the University of Nijmegen and the University of Leiden. He has been the Editor of the *European Journal of Social Psychology,* Chairman of the European Association of Experimental Social Psychology, and has published extensively in the area of social perception.

Otto Klineberg has degrees in psychology and medicine from McGill, Harvard and Columbia universities. His first publication appeared in 1927, and in his long and distinguished career he made many seminal contributions to knowledge. He has conducted empirical research in many parts of the world, and has been largely instrumental in showing that there is no scientific basis for the belief in a link between race and cognitive abilities. His writings have had a profound impact, not just on his professional colleagues, but on public opinion at large. He went beyond conventional scholarly publications to write for a broader audience, and was responsible for the UNESCO brochures on race and science.

After his retirement from Columbia in 1962, Klineberg embarked on a new career in Paris, where he holds a Chair and is the Director of the International Center for the Study of Intergroup Relations, that is when he is not travelling to various parts of the world to lecture on the psychology of race relations.

Klineberg has been the recipient of the Butler Medal, the Kurt Lewin Memorial Award, the New York Society of Clinical Psychologists Annual Award, a medal from the University of Liege, and the Annual Award of the International Society for Educational, Cultural and Scientific Interchanges.

Most recently, in 1979 he received the American Psychological Association Award for Distinguished Contributions to Psychology in the Public Interest.

Philip L. Pearce is a Lecturer in Psychology at the James Cook University of North Queensland. He did his undergraduate degree at the University of Adelaide, and completed a D.Phil. at Oxford University in the Department of Experimental Psychology. His research interests include cognitive mapping, and attitude changes associated with overseas travel.

Contents

PART I

Cross-cultural interaction: theory and definition of the field

STEPHEN BOCHNER

THIS section provides an introduction to the theories, concepts and issues prominent in research on inter-group contact. In the first chapter Bochner draws on the perspective of social psychology to account for the development of ethnic identity. He then lists some major variables of cross-cultural contact, such as whether it occurs within or between societies; its time span, purpose, type of involvement, frequency and the degree of intimacy and relative status of the participants. The discussion then shifts to an analysis of the in-group—out-group differentiation, and the implications of this categorization for inter-group behaviour. Various factors contributing to the distinction between "us" and "them" are explored, including hypotheses relating to deindividuation and territoriality.

An overview of the empirical literature on the effects of contact then follows, organized according to the four main classes of dependent variables that have been measured: attitudes, social perceptions, attributions, and behavioural indices. Bochner then offers a model of contact based on two ideas: (1) that behaviour settings can be characterized as either monocultural, bicultural, or multicultural; and (2) that individuals in multicultural settings will respond to the contact by either undergoing or resisting changes in their ethnic identities, in effect either becoming or remaining mono-, bi-, or multicultural persons. The implications of this theory for inter-group relations are explored, and the chapter concludes with a review of some empirical studies that were generated by the model.

Klineberg's chapter is based on the author's personal contribution, over six decades, to research on inter-ethnic contact. He reviews the literature in four areas. The first issue is whether some groups are genetically inferior to others, particularly in cognitive ability. At the turn of the century it was widely accepted that non-white peoples were less well endowed intellectually than whites. Klineberg shows how the position has changed over the years, the current view with a few exceptions being that there is no scientific basis for a doctrine of racial inferiority.

The second issue is the role played in group contact by ethnic stereotypes, and Klineberg reviews the classic studies in this area. He then looks at inter-group conflict, rejecting that it is inevitable. Finally, Klineberg surveys findings relating to the effect of contact on mutual understanding, concluding that three contact variables in particular improve inter-group attitudes: equal status, superordinate goals, and intimate relations between members of the two groups.

4

Taken together, the contributions in this section provide a general theoretical framework for an inquiry into cross-cultural interaction, identifying the main issues and giving some indication of the major research findings. Some of the issues will be explored in greater detail later in this book, particularly topics such as social perceptions, stereotypes, attribution, and the contact variables contributing to positive inter-group relations.

1

The social psychology of cross-cultural relations

STEPHEN BOCHNER

Introduction

THE AIM of this chapter is to review the main issues, concepts and theoretical models involved in the study of cross-cultural relations. The approach will be to regard cross-cultural contact as a problem in social psychology. This view holds that relations between culturally disparate individuals are largely determined by the groups to which these persons belong, and to the nature and quality of the relationships existing between the respective groups.

As a preliminary to the analysis of cross-cultural contact, there follows a brief discussion of how individuals, groups, societies, and cultures are patterned.

Individuals and groups

Human beings are social creatures (Aronson, 1972). They mature, work, play and generally live out their span as members of groups; and as countless studies in social psychology have shown, the groups that individuals belong to greatly affect their attitudes, values, perceptions of the world, and ultimately the person's very sense of identity, of who they are.

Two features of social life greatly complicate the relationship between the individual and the group. The first is that individuals usually belong to more than one group. The main groups that most persons belong to are the *family* (or families, if the person is married but also has parents who are living, or children who have left home); the *work*, occupational or professional group; *recreational* groups such as sporting clubs, bridge-playing companions, regular drinkers in a pub, stamp-collecting associations, and all the many leisure activities that people carry out in the company of others with similar interests; groups that provide a setting for spiritual activities such as *worship* and prayer; *artistic* groups for the expression of the self; and *political* groups (political parties, trade unions, pressure groups) enabling a person to influence events and exercise power. A problem arises when the person belongs to groups that place contra-

5

dictory demands on the individual. A good example is the working mother, who often finds it difficult to reconcile the requirements of her work group with the expectations of her family regarding her duties in the home.

The second noteworthy feature of human beings as social animals is that groups tend to be hierarchically organized, rather like Chinese boxes. The Scots provided a good example of this principle. A person belongs to a family, which in turn belongs to a clan, which in turn belongs to a region, which is either in the Highlands or the Lowlands, which together form Scotland, which is part of Great Britain. The individual's identity partakes variously in all of these group-ings, depending on which is salient at the time (Bochner and Perks, 1971). But the matter does not rest there; the Scot in the example could just as easily have been shown to belong to a local sailing club, the Scottish Sailing Association, and the World Yachting Federation; or as the local general practitioner with links to ever-wider bodies of medical and scientific societies.

The idea of hierarchical organization is the central feature of one of the most general theories in the natural and social sciences, namely open systems theory (Berrien, 1968; Emery, 1969). Open systems thinking provides a means of unifying the various sciences. For example, a biochemist may be interested in the structure of individual cells. When these form a cluster they become the concern of the physiologist, clusters of clusters are the province of anatomy, and so forth until we reach the level of the whole organism, the realm of the psychologist. Groups are regarded as social systems composed of persons who of course themselves are systems of systems. At a higher level of abstraction, the sociologist's unit of analysis is society, made up of the sub-systems such as social classes or occupational categories, these in turn being systems of groups. Further up the hierarchy the cross-cultural psychologists may be interested in whole cultures, for example Western culture as a system of societies united by common features that distinguish it from Eastern culture.

There are three main advantages in using a general open systems framework. Firstly, it provides theoretical support for the important idea that the various sciences and disciplines are connected and interrelated, that the microbiologist studying single cells and the demographer describing population trends are both concerned with the same topic, albeit at different levels of abstraction. Secondly, we are reminded that what happens in one part of the system ineluctably affects other units elsewhere no matter how remote, heightening awareness of the inter-dependence of biological and social units throughout the world. Such awareness influences how individuals and governments approach issues like pollution, conservation, the chemicalization of the environment, and all the other human activities that may have potentially damaging, global consequences. The third advantage of open systems thinking is that it enables us to speak about different groupings of individuals without getting too tangled up in interesting but basically unanswerable questions such as what is a group, society, or culture.

The concept of culture is a case in point. Kroeber and Kluckhohn (1952) reviewed over 150 definitions of culture, all of them plausible, and one could spend a great deal of time arguing about their relative merits without resolving the issue. Many analyses of culture never get beyond this point, and are paralysed as a consequence. In contrast, the open systems approach enables scholars to adopt as their unit of analysis whatever phenomenon they are interested in at any level of abstraction, as long as they explicitly acknowledge the existence of systems above, below, and beside the problem they have chosen to work on. That way, investigators can devote their energies to substantive research without getting sidetracked into pursuing existential definitions.

In summary, group membership is a major determinant of individual psychology. Most persons belong to more than one group; and group species tend to be hierarchically organized. Open systems theory provides a unifying and common framework for the natural and social sciences, underlines the interdependence of the systems that constitute the subject-matter of these sciences, and provides a means of delineating the unit of analysis.

Groups in societies

Societies differ in the extent to which they are *internally* homogeneous. Societies are complex systems with many facets, and the notion of homogeneity can be applied to any and all aspects of a society, such as its physical and geological features, class structure, linguistic practices, leisure patterns, and so on. In this chapter we are concerned with the cultural and ethnic dimensions of a society. To avoid fruitless disputes about the meaning of these terms, we propose to use the concept as referring to the ethnic and/or cultural *identity* of an individual (DeVos, 1980). Thus, the concept is grounded in the empirical operation of asking people what cultural group they belong to. For example, in Australia many persons of mixed Aboriginal and white descent are now publicly saying that they are Aborigines, although this is not obvious from their physical appearance. Nevertheless, it makes sense to classify such individuals as Aboriginal, irrespective of their light skin and previous identification with the white group in Australian society.

In culturally homogeneous societies practically all members have the same ethnic identification. Culturally heterogeneous societies contain many different ethnic groups. Using this principle it would be possible to empirically classify the world's societies along the continuum of cultural diversity. Although no society is completely homogeneous culturally, a country that comes rather close is Japan. At the other end, the United States has always seen itself as being very diverse culturally. Switzerland, with its three or four major groupings, might serve as an example of a country that is moderately heterogeneous.

Societies and cultures

Societies, in addition to differing internally with regard to cultural homogeneity, can also be compared *externally* with other societies, again on a variety of dimensions ranging from climate and geographical features, through economic resources to sociocultural features. There have been several attempts to find a yardstick on which the *cultural* aspects of different societies might be compared. Some of the more practical solutions have been schemes to classify cultures according to whether they are "simple" or "complex" (Freeman and Winch, 1957), "tight" or "loose" (Pelto, 1968), or the extent to which they are differentiated (Witkin and Berry, 1975). The actual solutions or categorizations do not concern us here. What is important is that although the conceptual and measurement problems have not been fully resolved, it is possible in principle to think and speak of such similarities and differences (Boldt, 1978; Boldt and Roberts, 1979). It is, for example, feasible to hypothesize that Great Britain and Sweden are culturally more similar than Great Britain and Saudi Arabia, because it is possible to think of measures and operations that could be used to test this hypothesis. The experiment described in Chapter 7 is an example of such an approach leading to fruitful empirical research.

In summary, societies differ internally in cultural homogeneity, indicated by the number and diversity of ethnic and cultural groups they contain; and societies differ externally from each other, as indicated by measures that reflect general dimensions of culture.

Dimensions of contact

As was stated at the outset of this chapter, the aim is to describe the concepts, issues, and theoretical models that lead to an understanding of the phenomenon of cross-cultural contact. The essential preliminaries have now been covered, and we can now proceed to the heart of the matter, which concerns the psychological effects of contact between culturally disparate individuals and groups. The first step will be to identify the main dimensions of cross-cultural relations, resulting in a general typology of contact situations.

The discussion in the preceding section suggests that a major variable is whether the contact occurs between culturally or ethnically disparate members of the same society (e.g. between black and white Americans); *or* whether the participants are from different societies (e.g. Australian tourists in Nepal). These particular examples have been chosen because they in turn suggest the other major dimensions of cross-cultural contact, including: (a) on whose territory the contact occurs; (b) the time span of the interaction; (c) its purpose; (d) the type of involvement; (e) the frequency of contact; and (f) the degree of intimacy, relative status and power, numerical balance, and distinguishable characteristics of the participants. The classification is presented in detail in Table 1.

The analysis suggests that there is a major difference regarding within-society and between-society cross-cultural contacts. Permanent members of multi-

TABLE 1 *Dimensions of cross-cultural contact and examples of each classification*

	Type of cross-cultural contact			
	Between members of the same society		Between members of different societies	
Contact variables	Type	Example	Type	Example
On whose territory	Usually joint	Black and white Americans	Home or foreign territory	Tourists Overseas students Immigrants and their respective hosts
Time-span	Long term	Black and white Americans	Short-term Medium-term Long-term	Tourists Overseas students Immigrants
Purpose	Make a life in	Black and white Americans	Make a life in Study in Make a profit Recreate	Immigrants Overseas students Workers Tourists
Type of involvement	Participate in society	Black and white Americans	Participate Exploit Contribute Observe	Immigrants Workers Experts Tourists
Frequency of contact	High	Black and white Americans	High Medium Low	Immigrants Overseas students Tourists
Degree of intimacy between participants	High to low social distance (variable)	Black and white Americans	High to low social distance (variable)	Immigrants Overseas students Tourists
Relative status and power	Equal to Unequal (variable)	Black and white Americans	Equal Unequal	Tourists Overseas students Immigrants
Numerical balance	Majority—minority Equal Distribution	White-Black Americans, Chinese, Japanese & Caucasian Hawaiians	Majority—minority	Host and students Immigrants Tourists
Visible distinguishing characteristics	Race Religion Language	Black and white Americans Ireland India Canada	Race Religion Language	Immigrants Overseas students Tourists

cultural societies tend to interact on public territories that are joint to both groups, and include streets, schools, transport, entertainment, the work place, and the legal administrative institutions. Their commitment is for ever, in the sense that the society that they belong to is the behaviour setting (Barker, 1968) for the conduct of their lives. Being full participants of that society for better or worse, they are unlikely to be able to segregate themselves from frequent contact with members of the other group. However, the degree of intimacy in contacts between the different factions is likely to be variable, ranging from the superficial to the close. Relative status will also vary, from equal to unequal status among the participants. Population distribution is another variable: although most multicultural societies have a numerically and politically dominant majority, as is the case in Australia and the U.S., there are countries such as South Africa where the dominant group are in the minority; and there are also societies that contain several different ethnic groups who are relatively equal in the wealth and power that they control, and in their numbers. Two societies that approximate this latter condition are Hawaii, which contains three dominant groups: the Japanese, Chinese, and Caucasians: and Fiji, where the Fijians and the Indians are roughly equal in population and political influence. It is interesting to note that in these two societies the various groups have developed specialized interests and spheres of influence. Thus in Hawaii the Japanese dominate the civil service, the Chinese are active in commerce, and the Caucasians in finance (Daws, 1968). In Fiji the Indians are influential in commerce and finance, and the Fijians in land-use and agriculture.

Finally, when individuals interact with persons from other cultures, the differences that separate the participants tend to become salient (Bochner and Ohsako, 1977; Bochner and Perks, 1971; Hartley and Thompson, 1967). The most important areas, and those that have been a major source of inter-group hostility in the past, are the highly visible characteristics of race, skin colour, language and religion (Klineberg, 1971). When we have dealings with members of other cultures, their physical appearance and language and/or accent provide inescapable cues to their ethnic origin, and by implication to their status as strangers. We immediately place such people into the category "they", distinguishing "them" from "us". Religion, although not as visible as race, can be inferred from a variety of cues, and is a highly salient aspect of inter-group perceptions (Bochner, 1976). Most of the world's conflicts are associated with differences in racial, linguistic and religious characteristics, although whether these differences provide both the necessary and sufficient conditions for inter-group hostility is unclear, and we shall return to this issue later in the chapter.

Turning now to encounters among people from dissimilar societies, the analysis reveals that between-society contacts differ both qualitatively and quantitatively from inter-group relations within a multicultural society. The major difference between inter- and intra-society cross-cultural contacts is related to the distinction between hosts and visitors. The social role of the visitor/stranger and its associated expectations and dispensations is a well-established finding in sociology (e.g. Schild, 1962), and the English language has many terms for such persons; for example, newcomer, immigrant, alien, guest, refugee. The Australian vernacular contains terms such as New Australian, new chum, remittance man, and refo; the Americans talk about resident aliens; and in Europe the phrase "guest arbeiter" has been coined to describe contract workers. All these individuals share the characteristics of having "come later", and are therefore to be distinguished from the established "owners" of the territory. Being a newcomer has many obvious problems, and laboratory studies in which subjects are cast into the position of a stranger, have confirmed that the role induces anxiety (Heiss and Nash, 1967; Nash and Wolfe, 1957; Rose and Felton, 1955).

In-groups and out-groups

A great many studies have shown that even relatively small differences between groups are very noticeable to the members of the respective societies, and that these differences are often exaggerated and distorted to provide a mutually negative image or stereotype (Allport, 1954; Katz and Braly, 1933; Campbell, 1967). Various explanations have been offered for this phenomenon, of which the most persuasive is Sherif's (1970) that inter-group conflict stems from the participants making an "us" and "them" differentiation, in effect a distinction between who belongs to the in-group and who is a member of the out-group. The categorization of the social world into "us" and "them" and the resultant hostility is due, according to Sherif, to competition for scarce resources, in particular competition for goals desired by both groups but only attainable by one of them. Conversely, harmonious inter-group relations occur when the parties share a superordinate goal, i.e. a goal that both groups want but can only attain if they cooperate, and neither can achieve if they compete. Presumably under these latter conditions the in-group—out-group distinction becomes blurred, people are less likely to categorize others as belonging either to "us" or to "them", and are more prone to identify the common predicament (Edney, 1980) and the interdependence of human beings.

Unfortunately for Sherif's elegant thesis, there is evidence that the *mere* division of people into groups, without any history of social conflict or hostility, is sufficient to trigger in-group—out-group distinctions and discriminatory behaviour (Tajfel, 1970). Tajfel explains this effect with reference to a generalized norm of hostility toward out-groups. The process goes deeper than forming negative value-judgements about a specific group and then behaving accordingly. Rather, Tajfel suggests that individuals construct a subjective social order based on the classification of "we" and "them", and learn that the appropriate attitude is to favour a member of the in-group and discriminate against a member of the out-group. If such a generic norm of behaviour towards out-groups does exist, it follows that individuals may discriminate against "them" even if there is nothing to be gained from the discrimination, either economically as suggested by Sherif and others (cf. the review by Chesler, 1976); or psychologically, as implied in the scapegoat theory of prejudice (Allport, 1954). Tajfel's work also implies that discrimination may occur in the absence of previously existing attitudes of hostility toward the out-group, and/or before any negative attitudes have been formed. The mere categorization of a person as an out-group member is sufficient to make that person a target for treatment that is less favourable than would be accorded to someone from the in-group, simply because that is the appropriate norm.

Not all the evidence supports this prediction. There are studies indicating that under some conditions strangers are treated more leniently and/or favourably, particularly when they transgress a local custom, on the grounds that they could not have learnt the appropriate norms of behaviour, and can therefore be excused from their *faux pas* (Feldman, 1968; Schild, 1962). Likewise, recent studies of the phenomenon of reverse discrimination (Dutton, 1971, 1973) have shown that under certain conditions minority members are given preferential treatment over members of the dominant majority (Bochner and Cairns, 1976), presumably on the grounds of reparation and the restoration of equity. Nevertheless, reverse discrimination studies tend to be the exception rather than the rule, and Tajfel's own research confirms that mere inter-group categorization, *per se,* leads to discrimination against the out-group. However, why this should be so is unclear. An appeal to a generalized norm is unsatisfactory since it does not explain why such a norm is learned, except by vague reference to some hypothesized bio-logically adaptive mechanism that enables us to recognize friends from foes. Nor is the problem solved by supposing that people generalize from individual hostile inter-group incidents to a universal norm of out-group suspicion, since this does not explain why the initial incidents should be hostile in the first place.

Perhaps the most promising development is recent research linking the concept of deindividuation (Zimbardo, 1969) to out-group discrimination. For example, Milgram (1974) has shown that the greater the anonymity of persons pretending to be victims, the more readily will subjects obey instructions to harm them. Thus subjects gave more severe electric shocks when the person was out of sight, than when they could either see or touch the victim. In simulated prison experiments, ordinary, well-adjusted individuals role-playing the part of guards behaved quite brutally towards subjects who had been deindividuated through being labelled as prison inmates (Hanney, Banks and Zimbardo, 1973; Lovibond, Mithiran and Adams, 1979). Jorgenson and Dukes (1976) compared the behaviour of students in a crowded university cafeteria (rendering the subjects relatively anonymous) with their responses when the place was only a quarter full, the individuated condition. Significantly more of the students in the deindividuated condition behaved irresponsibly, as measured by the percentage of food trays returned to the serving area. Numerous other studies have come up with similar results, indicating that persons who are deindividuated are likely to behave less responsibly, *and* are likely to be treated less favourably, than individuated persons.

The individuated—deindividuated distinction has important consequences for in-group—out-group relations, in particular suggesting the hypothesis that out-group members will be more deindividuated than members of the in-group. If true, the further hypothesis is implied that discrimination against out-group members could be reduced by individuating them. Recently Wilder (1978) conducted a series of experiments which support this hypothesis. For example, when the out-group was individuated by providing subjects with individual communications from out-group members, discrimination was reduced. The same happened when the out-group was individuated by making its members appear to have idiosyncratic rather than unanimous opinions.

The implication is that the "we" and "they" distinction may become blurred as a consequence of individuating "them". This may go some way towards explaining Tajfel's findings that mere categorization of persons into distinct groups is sufficient to produce a bias in favour of the in-group, since such categorization is usually confounded with individuation. Most persons have, or believe that they have, far greater information about "their own kind" than they do about strangers. They are therefore likely to make greater differentiations amongst their own members than among the out-group, and hence individuate the in-group more. However, to date this hypothesis awaits direct empirical confirmation.

Territoriality and the in-group—out-group distinction

Another possible explanation, not sufficiently explored in the literature, is that the in-group—out-group distinction may be linked to the territorial rights and aspirations of the interacting groups, territorial in the psychological rather than in the political or geographic sense. The concept of territoriality is an idea that has been extended from studies with animals (Eibl-Eibesfeldt, 1970; Wynne-Edwards, 1962, 1965) to human beings (Ardrey, 1966, 1970; Sommer, 1969). There is no doubt that human beings create territories for themselves, feel threatened if these are invaded, and will defend their territories against encroachment with a variety of means (Felipe and Sommer, 1966; Goffman, 1971; Sommer and Becker, 1969). Furthermore, there is clear evidence that what constitutes an act of invasion, and the appropriate defensive response, depends on who the transgressor is, and what is the relationship between the invader and the owner of the territory. As Hall (1966) has found, there are at least four zones of inter-personal distance.

The first is the intimate distance zone, ranging from zero to 18 inches, and is the characteristic spacing for people engaged in lovemaking, comforting, nursing and other intimate activities. Admission to this zone is reserved for spouses, lovers, and close friends. When strangers are forced into involuntary intimate distance, such as in lifts or crowded trains, they find the experience very stressful.

The second zone is the personal distance region, extending from 1½ to 4 ft away from the individual, and is the characteristic spacing for chatting, gossiping, playing cards, and generally interacting with friends and acquaintances. Discomfort is felt if strangers intrude into this space, and also if friends place themselves too far away, outside the limits of the zone.

Next is the social distance zone, 4 to 12 ft in extent, and is the characteristic spacing in formal settings such as the office; in the professional rooms of doctors, lawyers, accountants and other practitioners; and in shops, television interviews, and wherever people enact their formal roles. Again, discomfort occurs if the norm is broken, if the lawyer sits too close to the client or the shop assistant stands too close to the customer.

The last region is the public distance zone, ranging from 12 to 25 ft, and is the characteristic spacing of official, ceremonious occasions such as the formal dinner, church service, courtroom, parliament, political rally and the university lecture, particularly where there is a large status difference between the speaker and the audience. Embarrassment is often felt when there is an involuntary coming together of such personages with their clients, for example when a student meets a professor in the cafeteria, or a member of the public encounters the distinguished after-dinner speaker in the washroom.

The general principle of spacing is that the "correct" interpersonal distance depends on two things, the nature of the *activity* that the persons are engaged in, and the nature of the *relationship* existing between them. Neither of these conditions are necessarily fixed. For example strangers on a long train journey, thrown together in a crowded compartment, may redefine their mutual relationship by introducing themselves to each other. The enforced proximity will then become more appropriate and bearable, since it now exists between acquaintances rather than strangers.

This principle can be extended to the in-group—out-group distinction, and to cross-cultural contact in general: It is appropriate for members of the in-group (lovers and friends) to be physically much closer than members of the out-group (professional associates and strangers). Cross-cultural contact between members of different societies generally takes the form of a highly visible out-group, invading the well-delineated territory of an established in-group. Even if there are no obvious economic implications of such an invasion (as is presumably the case with overseas students) the newcomers nevertheless constitute an easily identifiable out-group, perceived as encroaching on the territory of the in-group. According to the psychology of personal space, this territorial invasion should trigger feelings of tension and anxiety, and defensive action in the original inhabitants, setting up a vicious cycle of mutually hostile behaviour. The greatest perceived threat will attach to those newcomers who have come to stay, the immigrants who are heavily involved in their new society, are in frequent contact with their hosts, and form a visible and cohesive minority group whose racial, religious and linguistic characteristics differ markedly from the host culture.

In theory, the conflict will continue until the newcomers are either repelled and the territorial imperative is re-established; *or* they are no longer seen as outsiders, but as members of the in-group, granted the same territorial rights and privileges as the original inhabitants. In practice, five ways of "resolving" the conflict exist: (1) the original owners of the territory are dispossessed and wiped out, as happened in the United States and Australia; (2) the newcomers are wiped out, as for example was the fate of the Jews in Nazi Germany; (3) the newcomers are assimilated so that they become ethnically indistinguishable from the original inhabitants after a few generations, a process that is exemplified by the 'melting pot' philosophy of the United States; (4) there is an attempt to carve up the territory and develop separate enclaves, a process sometimes called apartheid and practised formally in South Africa but unofficially in many parts of the world; and (5) there is an explicit endeavour to develop a pluralistic society, in which members of the out-groups are psychologically redefined to make them eligible for in-group status despite their racial, linguistic or religious differences. This process has been called integration, and more recently cultural mediation (Bochner, 1979). In a later section the five modes of inter-group conflict resolution will be discussed in greater detail.

Outcomes of contact

There is a large literature on the psychological effects of cross-cultural contact, but it suffers from being mostly a-theoretical. Typically, the studies consist of surveys, using what Brislin and Baumgardner (1971) have called "samples of convenience". The most numerous reports are undoubtedly those dealing with the attitudes of foreign students attending university in a western country. Thus an annotated bibliography compiled in 1964 (Parker, 1965) contained 915 entries, and a selected bibliography by Shields (1968) listed 495 items. A scan of the more recent literature indicates that the research output has not diminished in the intervening years. This is not surprising, since the presence in large numbers of foreign students on campus provides many opportunities for both pure and applied research. According to Edgerton (1976) the annual world-wide enrolment of foreign students is around 600,000, and quite a few of these seem to participate as subjects in psychological surveys.

A second large-scale research effort took place in the area of migration, with studies being conducted in the major countries receiving immigrants, such as the United States (Gordon, 1964), Great Britain (Watson, 1977), Canada (Kosa, 1957), and Australia (Taft, 1966; Stoller, 1966). These studies, too, consist mainly of surveys, usually of the adjustment of the migrants to their new surroundings.

A third literature has investigated the phenomenon of majority group—minority group relations, or what is now being openly labelled as racism. Most of these studies are concerned with the racist attitudes and behaviour of White towards Black Americans (e.g. Pettigrew, 1969; Katz, 1976). There is also a large body of literature emanating from Great Britain (e.g. Banton, 1967; Little, 1948), and a growing interest in Australia (e.g. Stevens, 1971, 1972).

There have been several major attempts to review and integrate the contact literature. An excellent early review is that of Cook and Selltiz (1955), and more recent well-known critical summaries are by Amir (1969, 1976), and Brein and David (1971). These reviews all conclude that, contrary to popular belief, inter-group contact does not necessarily reduce inter-group tension, prejudice, hostility and discriminatory behaviour. Yet one often hears politicians, church leaders and other public figures saying that if only people of diverse cultural backgrounds could be brought into contact with each other, they would surely develop a mutual appreciation of their points of view and grow to understand, respect and like one another (e.g. Fulbright, 1976). Unfortunately, the evidence does not support this hypothesis. Indeed, at times inter-group contact may increase tension, hostility and suspicion (e.g. Bloom, 1971; Tajfel and Dawson, 1965; Mitchell, 1968). It all depends on the conditions under which the contact occurs, in particular on factors such as those listed in Table 1. Research indicates that variables which tend to reduce prejudice include equal status of the participating persons or groups; intimate rather than casual or superficial relations; contact situations involving interdependent activity, inter-group cooperation, and superordinate goals; contact situations that are pleasant and rewarding; and most important, a social climate that favours inter-group contact and harmony. Conditions that tend to increase prejudice include unequal status of the participants, or where the contact lowers the status of one of the groups; unpleasant, involuntary, frustrating, or tension-laden contact; situations producing competition between the groups; contact between groups with diametrically opposed moral philosophies; and social norms that promote or approve of racial inequality.

Dependent variables and theoretical frameworks

Ethnic contact research cannot be said to have been conducted with a great deal of theoretical sophistication. The tendency has been to use lengthy and diffuse questionnaires and/or interviews that generate masses of unrelated information. These data are then typically treated by means of correlational and *post-hoc* analyses with little regard to testing or building a general model of inter-ethnic contact.

To the extent that some investigators have been influenced by theoretical considerations, three models have played a part in shaping research strategies.

The first is the psychoanalytic school, of which perhaps the best known product is *The Authoritarian Personality* (Adorno *et al.,* 1950), linking ethnocentrism to harsh, rigid and arbitrary child-rearing practices, and regarding prejudice largely as a venting of displaced aggression or scapegoating. The contact situation provides the behaviour setting that evokes such responses in prejudiced individuals. The second approach stems from the similarity-attraction paradigm, generated both by reinforcement and cognitive balance theories of inter-personal behaviour (e.g. Byrne, 1969; Heider, 1958; Newcomb, 1956) which all imply that similar people are more likely to get along than dissimilar ones. A special variant of this theory is Rokeach's belief-similarity hypothesis (Rokeach, 1960, 1961) which tries to account for inter-cultural disharmony in terms of the actual or assumed dissimilarity in the belief systems of the interacting groups. The same principle is evident in Triandis' concept of "subjective culture" (Triandis *et al.,* 1972), which implies that different ethnic groups have unique, idiosyncratic ways of perceiving their social environments. When members of such groups interact, their subjective cultures may not overlap either in content or structure (i.e. differentiation), leading to the participants making faulty attributions about one another's behaviour.

A third view is based on social learning principles, and regards culture as a naturally occurring and all-pervasive matrix of reinforcement schedules (Guthrie, 1975). Persons who have been placed in an unfamiliar cultural setting are suddenly faced with a totally new set of contingencies, and until and unless they have mastered these, will experience uncertainty, confusion and stress. The rather vague concepts of culture shock (Oberg, 1960), role shock (Byrnes, 1966), and role strain (Guthrie, 1966) can all be reduced to the confusion resulting from well-established habits no longer having their expected consequences, so that reinforcement becomes unpredictable and apparently non-contingent. Social learning theory has also been used to account for the development of racial awareness in the self and in others. Research has shown convincingly that children as young as 5 years of age are aware of their own ethnic identity, and are able to recognize the racial identification of other people (Pushkin and Veness, 1973). One explanation offered is that children learn racial attitudes by observation, modelling, and subtle reinforcement rather in the same way that they learn their "appropriate" sex role behaviour (Bem and Bem, 1973).

The dependent variable measures used in contact research have reflected these theoretical orientations. The responses fall into four major categories: (a) attitudes, (b) social perceptions, (c) attributions, and (d) behavioural indices.

Attitudes

Questionnaires and interviews have been used to assess the inter-group attitudes of a great variety of different types of subjects. An extremely well carried out example is that of Selltiz *et al.* (1963) studying the attitudes and social relations of foreign students in the United States. In addition, particular instruments have been widely used. A well-known technique is Bogardus' (1928) Social Distance Scale, in which subjects are asked whether they would be willing to admit members of a particular target group to increasingly close relationships (marriage, friendship, neighbour, my occupation, citizen in my country, visitor to my country, exclude from my country).

Social perceptions

Attitudes towards other people and groups are linked to the way in which the target persons are perceived. The nature of the link between perceptions, attitudes and behaviour has generated considerable debate, along three fronts. The first issue has been whether perceptions determine attitudes (we see someone as sly and dislike them for it); or whether attitudes influence perceptions (we dislike a person, and so tend to see that individual as sly). It is now generally agreed that this is a pretty futile debate, since attitudes and perceptions influence each other in a mutually reacting spiral, and it does not really matter which comes first.

The second issue concerns the veridicality of the perceptions, and is a much more interesting question. The term "stereotype" is used to refer to the images which persons or groups have of each other, the pictures in their heads (Klineberg, 1966) that they have of one another. The debate has been about the extent to which stereotypes accurately describe the character of the group which is the object of the perceptions, or whether instead stereotypes simply reflect the preoccupations of the perceiver. Those arguing for the "correctness" of stereotypes maintain that the very existence of these images must mean that they have a "kernel of truth" and a "well-deserved reputation" (Zawadski, 1948). Other writers have disagreed with this interpretation, basing their argument on evidence that stereotypes can and do develop without any basis in reality and are often completely false (e.g. Katz and Braly, 1933; LaPiere, 1936). According to this view, the out-group provides a "living inkblot" (Ackerman and Jahoda, 1950) onto which the beholders project their neurotic motives and concerns. Campbell (1967) has attempted to integrate this literature in terms of a figure-ground or contrast hypothesis stating that the greater the real differences between two groups, the more likely is it that those differences will appear in the stereotypes they hold of each other. According to Campbell, the real issue is not whether the content of the stereotypes is true or false, but the causal misperceptions that accompany them. An example is the belief held by many Whites that the poverty of Blacks is due to their racial characteristics, ignoring the environmental circumstances that are the root cause of low income among disadvantaged groups. The idea of causal misperceptions was subsequently taken up more systematically by attribution theory (Jones and Nisbett, 1971) and will be discussed in the next section.

Most stereotype studies have used a variant of the semantic differential method (Osgood, Suci, and Tannenbaum, 1957). Typically, subjects are given a set of bipolar scales (e.g. warm—cold, systematic—impulsive, reliable—unreliable, trustworthy—untrustworthy) and asked to rate a particular target group (e.g. Blacks) on these dimensions. More sophisticated studies also require the subjects to indicate which end of the scale is the desirable one; for example is it good to be systematic or impulsive. The method lends itself to a great many variations, of which 'some of the theoretically more interesting developments have included making comparisons between autostereotypes and heterostereotypes, i.e. how groups perceive themselves on the same traits they have used to describe the out-group; studies that compare reciprocal stereotypes, i.e. how selected groups perceive each other; and studies looking at the effect of contact on the favourableness and clarity of the stereotypes they hold about each other (Abate and Berrien, 1967; Berrien, 1969; Bronfenbrenner, 1961; Triandis *et al.*, 1972).

Attributions

When we interact with another person, we make inferences about the causes of the other's behaviour. We are likely to ask ourselves what was the reason, motive or intention of a particular act, especially if the behaviour is of a non-routine kind. Our feelings about the other person will be affected by the attributions we make in "explaining" the behaviour. However, most acts are to some extent ambiguous, in the sense that they may be perceived as having several alternative causes. For example, if a student is not doing well in school the teacher may attribute the poor performance to either insufficient ability, or to lack of motivation on the part of the pupil. In the first case, the teacher may feel sorry for the student, and perhaps try to help by employing remedial training strategies. In the second case, the teacher may feel angry and disappointed, and punish the student for being slack.

Attribution theory (Jones, 1976) starts off with the distinction between the *actor* and the *observer,* or more precisely self-observation versus other-observation. Thus when I observe my own behaviour and attribute reasons to it, I am the *actor;* when I observe another person and make attributions about that other person's behaviour, I am an *observer.* The theory then extends this dichotomy by distinguishing between two types of explanations of behaviour, analogous to the "within-skin" accounts of personality psychology on the one hand, and the "between-skin" accounts favoured by social psychology on the other (Mann, 1969). The within-skin approach attributes the causes of behaviour to internal aspects of the *person,* and therefore regards behaviour as being determined by the individual's personality traits, dispositions, character, habits, reflexes, genetic make-up, racial characteristics and other features inherent in the individual. By contrast, the between-skin approach locates the causes of behaviour in the person's *situation,* and therefore tends to regard behaviour as being primarily determined by the social context, and by the environmental, cultural and ecological influences that provide the setting for the act.

These distinctions gave rise to a hypothesis which stimulated a great deal of empirical research, and which has an important bearing on the social psychology of cross-cultural contact. The hypothesis states that actors and observers make radically different attributions about the causes of behaviour: actors see their own behaviour as primarily determined by the situation they find themselves in; whereas observers will attribute the same behaviour to the actor's dispositional characteristics. For example, actors caught with their hand in the till may explain their own behaviour in terms of the need for money in order to relieve the illness of a loved one, diminished responsibility due to alcoholic intoxication, or the inequity of the capitalist social system. Observers, on the other hand, may attribute the theft to the person's wicked, callous, immoral or sinful nature. It follows that the act will evoke quite different attitudes according to who makes the attribution, the actor feeling self-pity whereas the observer feels anger and hostility.

It has been suggested that the reason why observers are biased towards dispositional attributions is that they have less information about the actor than actors have about themselves. Observers therefore tend to explain the behaviour of others in simplistic dispositional terms — e.g. the other person is angry due to possessing an angry personality. Actors presumably have more information about themselves, in particular about how the setting can and does modify their behaviour. Actors are therefore more likely to invoke situational explanations for their actions.

Alternatively, it has been proposed that the differential attributions of actors and observers may be due to differences in the visual perspective from which they regard their own and another's behaviour. The suggestion is that actors concentrate on the task that they are engaged in, whereas observers attend more to the actor's behaviour. These differences in perspective should predispose observers to making dispositional rather than situational attributions.

The observer-bias towards dispositional attributions has general implications for inter-personal misunderstandings, since actors and observers seldom make completely isomorphic attributions (Triandis, 1975). However, a more specific prediction can also be derived, namely that the better we get to know other people the more do we come to regard them as we regard ourselves, i.e. in situational terms. This principle can be extended to the contact situation via the in-group—out-group distinction referred to earlier in this chapter: since individuals are more familiar with in-group than out-group behaviour, the actions of an in-group member are more likely to be assigned a situational attribution, whereas similar behaviour performed by out-group members will be attributed to their personalities. This effect may also account for the stability of out-group stereotypes, since the behaviour of out-group members would be seen as being determined by their stable personality, racial and national characteristics rather than as a response to changing circumstances.

There is an anecdote which illustrates cross-cultural misattributions. Allegedly, the reason why the Chinese have slanted eyes is that as children at meal times they turn to their mothers and complain: "Oh no, not rice again", putting their hands to their temples. In more serious vein, there have been a great many studies (e.g. Triandis, 1975) showing that members of different cultures often make non-isomorphic attributions about the causes of each other's behaviour, and that this difference in attributions can make the contact an embarrassing, confusing and even harrowing experience. However, it is not clear from these studies whether the non-isomorphic attributions occur mainly in the content of the perceptions, or whether they relate to the actor—observer distinction. A scan of the literature did not reveal any studies that have explicitly sought to establish an empirical link between the commonly found observer bias in favour of dis-positional explanations, and a possible similar bias regarding out-group attri-butions. This issue is discussed in greater detail in Chapter 6.

Behavioural indices

There is a great deal of evidence, summarized by Bochner (1980) that know-ingly enacting the role of a subject in a scientific inquiry markedly affects how individuals will respond to an experimental treatment. It has also been estab-lished that statements of attitude often do not accurately predict behaviour — people do not always do what they had intended doing, nor are their actions always consistent with their stated values and beliefs (e.g. Gaertner, 1973; Liska, 1974; Wicker, 1969). Consequently, a great many experiments have been conducted in natural settings. Typically, the independent variable is cultural or racial similarity/dissimilarity, and the dependent variable is some behavioural index of positive or negative regard, usually helping behaviour. A special feature of many of these studies is that they use the unobtrusive method (Webb *et al.*, 1966). The special characteristic of this method is that subjects are unaware that they are participating in a psychological experiment, and are therefore less likely to give responses distorted by the knowledge that they are being observed, measured, evaluated, and are expected to be making a contribution to science. Another advantage is that the investigator does not have to make inferences from the subjects' verbal responses about their subsequent behaviour, since it is possible to observe directly the interaction patterns in the contact situation being studied.

The literature is replete with ingenious and revealing experiments of cross-cultural contact in everyday life. For example, Bryan and Test (1967) placed a Salvation Army kettle on the footpath outside a large store. The kettle was attended either by a black or white woman dressed in the uniform of the Army. The results showed that more passers-by made a donation when the solicitor was white than when she was black. In Bochner's (1971) experiment a black (Australian Aboriginal) or white girl walked a small dog through a park in Sydney. The dependent variable was the number of times that members of the general public (all of whom were white) smiled, nodded at, or spoke to either girl during a specified period of time. It turned out that the white girl received almost three times as many encouragements as the black girl. In a subsequent study, Bochner (1972) inserted two advertisements in the "Wanted to Rent" classified columns of a large Sydney newspaper. One advertisement stated that the people seeking the flat were an Aboriginal couple; the other did not specify the racial identity of the couple. As expected, the Aboriginal applicants received significantly fewer offers of accommodation.

West, Whitney, and Schnedler (1975) used the "motorist in distress" procedure. The experiment is designed around a car that has stopped by the side of the road with its hood up, apparently broken down. Next to the disabled car stands the "victim", who is either a black or a white person. The dependent measure is the frequency and latency of help offered in each condition, and the race and sex of the good samaritans. These studies consistently show a bias towards same-race helping, i.e. whites tend to get helped by whites and blacks by blacks. The final example is the well-known Feldman (1968) study, in which passers-by were accosted by a stranger requesting assistance. The experiment was done in three cities — Paris, Athens, and Boston, and in each location the person making the request was either a compatriot (i.e. French, Greek, and American respectively) or a foreigner. The results showed that compatriots were treated more favourably than foreigners in Paris and Boston, and foreigners received better treatment than compatriots in Athens.

From these examples it is apparent that behavioural studies of cross-cultural contact have the advantage of directly showing the likely pattern of interaction. However, these studies are generally silent regarding the reasons why people did what they were observed to do, since the subjects are seldom asked to explain their actions. To get at the underlying dynamics other methods, such as those described earlier in this chapter, have to be used. In any case, as Campbell and Fiske (1959) have pointed out, it is highly desirable to approach a problem from as many directions as possible, with different procedures and by different investigators. Then, if all the data show a consistent pattern, they provide what Lykken (1968) called multiple corroboration for the phenomenon, and in such circumstances much greater confidence can be placed in the results.

The social psychology of the contact situation

Earlier, three theoretical models of the contact situation were alluded to: the psychoanalytic model, which regards the contact situation as a setting for the re-enactment of oedipal patterns established in childhood; the social-learning model, regarding the contact situation as an abrupt and massive shift in the reinforcement matrix; and the cognitive/perceptual model, regarding the contact situation as a source of dissonant or imbalanced cognitions and perceptions.

One limitation of all three models is that, despite some superficial aspects to the contrary, they offer basically a personalistic or within-skin account of cross-cultural contact; they tend to overlook, or at least fail to stress, that contact occurs, at a minimum, between two people and therefore constitutes a mutually influencing social system. This limitation is most obvious in the case of the psychoanalytic model, which explicitly emphasizes the intra-psychic processes of the individuals in contact rather than their inter-personal trans-actions. The same can be said of the social learning model, which is primarily concerned with the "habits" of the sojourner, student, peace corps worker or tourist; and it is also largely true of the cognitive/perceptual model with its emphasis on the subjective cultures, beliefs, and auto- and heterostereotypes of the participants.

The limitations in the existing theories due to their personalistic bias led the author and his colleagues (Bochner, 1981) to develop a model of the contact situation that explicitly takes its social psychology into account. The central idea of the model is to regard any individual as functioning in a behaviour setting that can vary from being monocultural to being multi- or heterocultural. In practice, it is possible to distinguish three types of settings: monocultural, bicultural, and multicultural. For example, a Japanese in Tokyo could be regarded as living in a monocultural environment; a Malay student at Oxford and living in one of the colleges would be in a bicultural setting, as would a child born in Australia of migrant parents born in say Yugoslavia; and a Thai student living in an International House at a western university, a United Nations employee, an international air line hostess, or a New York policeman could be regarded as moving about in a multicultural milieu.

The other main premise of the model is to assume that the cultural compo-sition of the setting has a direct influence on the individuals in it. In this regard the model is similar to the traditional contact hypotheses, which make the same assumption. However, the present approach differs in what it regards as being the crucial outcome of the contact. Most conventional research concentrates on the attitudes, perceptions and feelings of the persons in contact with members of other cultural groups. Our theory goes beyond this narrow view to take into account the more general changes that persons in contact are likely to undergo as a consequence of their exposure to multicultural influences. In other words, the model takes seriously the contention made by social psychologists such as Sherif (Sherif, Sherif and Nebergall, 1965) that it is quite misleading to regard attitude change merely as a shift along some continuum; rather, non-trivial attitude modification inevitably involves a re-ordering of the individuals' cognitive structures, making them in a very real sense different persons. In particular, the theory assumes that persons in contact will either undergo or resist changes in their cultural identities, in effect that they may either become or remain mono-, bi-, or multicultural individuals. Thus, the model assumes that the various cultural groups in the person's social environment will exert varying degrees of influence on the individual, that they will differ in the extent to which they serve as reference groups (Newcomb, 1943) for the person.

A further implication of the theory is that individuals do not passively repond to their environments, but react and if possible modify their surroundings. Thus, when we speak of migrants adapting to their new circumstances, we should also ask to what extent, if any, has the host community changed as a consequence of an influx of migrants. Very few studies adopt such a systematic approach to the contact phenomenon, and instead proceed as if the effect were unidirectional, impacting as it were on the newcomer only.

Finally, the model can also account for contact effects at the group level. Just as culturally disparate individuals influence each others' ethnicity, so do groups in contact likewise modify each others' social structures and value systems.

In the next section the theory will be explained in more detail, and this will be followed by a brief summary of some empirical research that was generated by the social psychological model of the contact situation.

Outcomes of cultures-in-contact at the group level

Table 2 presents the various possible outcomes for groups that are in contact with each other. The effects are general in the sense that they can apply to groups within the same society, or to two or more societies in contact with one another.

Genocide

Genocide occurs when one group, usually in the majority or technologically superior, kill all members of another group with whom they come into contact. There are many examples of attempted genocide in ancient as well as recent history, indicating that this method has some apparent attraction as a means of dealing with out-groups. Advocates of genocide usually argue that the groups being eradicated are not really human beings. This argument is not shared by those individuals against whom the process is directed. There can be nothing more terrifying than belonging to an ethnic group that is being systematically and ruthlessly exterminated by a numerically or technologically more powerful horde.

Assimilation

Assimilation occurs when a group or an entire society gradually adopt, or are forced into adopting, the customs, beliefs, folkways and lifestyles of a more dominant culture. At the intra-societal level, after a few generations of assimila-

TABLE 2   *Outcomes of cultural contact at the group level*

Contact outcomes	Between groups in the same society Examples	Between different societies Examples
Genocide of original inhabitants by outsiders	–	Australian Aborigines in Tasmania American Indians
Genocide of newcomers by insiders	Nazi Germany	–
Assimilation of out-groups by in-group	Migrants in "melting pot" societies	Diffusion of western innovations "Cocacolonization"
Segregation of out-groups by in-group	Pre-Second World War U.S.A. South Africa Imperial India	White Australia Immigration policy
Self-segregation of out-group	Tribal lands Enclaves in Alaska, the U.S. southwest, Australian Centre	East Germany during Cold War Mainland China during Cultural Revolution
Integration	Emerging pluralistic societies such as Australia, New Zealand, Hawaii	Emerging transnational institutions such as the United Nations, the East–West Center, and "third cultures"

tion, minority members become culturally and physically indistinguishable from the mainstream of national life. Thus a policy of assimilation results in the virtual disappearance of the minority culture. At the inter-societal level, differences between cultures become eroded, diversity in lifestyles is reduced, traditional patterns tend to disappear, and there is an irreversible push towards global homogeneity in cultural manifestations (Bochner, 1979). The term "Cocacolonization" (Lambert, 1966, p. 170) is sometimes used to refer to this process of one culture being swamped by another. Advocates of assimilation may or may not realize that the policy implies a superiority of the majority culture relative to the minority, often to the extent of denying any worth in the culture being absorbed. Groups undergoing assimilation do not find the process psychologically satisfying, because of connotations of inferiority, self-rejection, and in extreme instances, self-hatred (Bettelheim, 1943; Lewin, 1941).

Segregation

Segregation is a policy of separate development. At the intra-societal level, the impetus can come from the dominant majority, as was the case in the southern regions of the United States, and is the case in South Africa; or the minority groups can actively seek separatism, with demands for separate states, cultural enclaves, special schools, land tenure based on ethnic background, reserves, sanctions against intermarriage, boycotts, and other similar devices. At the inter-societal level the impetus comes from protectionist policies aimed at keeping unwanted people, ideas and influences out, either by preventing their entry or by disallowing indigenous persons from becoming contaminated through travel abroad.

In practice, segregation usually does not work very well, whether the enforced or the self-imposed kind. The main reason is that the world is an interdependent place, particularly for people who live in close physical proximity to each other. Apartheid cannot work in South Africa because the dominant minority need a large labour force, and separatism will not work in the U.S.A. because too many blacks want to participate in the fruits of a wealthy industrial society. Non-white immigrants are being admitted to Australia because of world pressure, western influences have penetrated the Iron Curtain, and East Germans have crossed the Berlin Wall despite major efforts to prevent their leaving.

Groups and individuals who have been segregated by a dominant or power- ful culture do not find the process psychologically satisfying, because they perceive their freedom to be curtailed (Richmond, 1973); self-segregated groups may find their status initially exhilarating, with a newfound sense of pride, identity and worth. It remains an empirical question whether such enthusiasm can be sustained, in the face of the self-imposed but nevertheless real shrinkage in the economic, social and cultural opportunities available. In any case the undercurrent of hostility and the siege mentality, implicit in a self-segregated situation, are unlikely to be psychologically healthy for the group or individuals adopting such a lifestyle as a permanent arrangement.

Integration

Integration occurs when different groups maintain their cultural identity in some respects, but merge into a superordinate group in other respects. The term "integration" is sometimes wrongly used as interchangeable with "assimilation", but the technical sense refers to a situation of cultural pluralism. In fact, cultural pluralism exists widely, but only within the dominant sector of most com- munities. All the different special-interest groups that exist in a complex society attest to the existence and feasibility of cultural pluralism. Differences in form of worship, political philosophy, recreational preferences, occupational activity, and many other aspects of life all coexist within the broader framework of a unified identity and a shared set of broad values, rules and goals. In multiracial societies operating on the principle of cultural pluralism, different racial groups would maintain their distinct identities and cultures, within a framework of equal opportunity and mutual tolerance. It remains an empirical question whether such societies exist or can be created.

There is a suggestion that countries such as Australia (Throssell, 1981) and New Zealand (Ritchie, 1981) are emerging as pluralistic societies, and that Hawaii is another successful example of integration (Daws, 1968). However, the evidence is by no means conclusive, and is often contested. The evidence is stronger in regard to the emergence of what the Useems have called "third cultures" (Useem and Useem, 1967, 1968; Useem, Useem and Donoghue, 1963; Useem, Useem and McCarthy, 1979). "Third cultures" consist of individuals who live, work in and are identified with different societies around the world, but at the same time participate in a global community from which they derive their goals, values and rewards. The scientific communities fit this pattern, as do the employees of multinational companies, and those working for the various international agencies such as the World Health Organization, UNESCO, or the East—West Center.

Outcomes of cultures-in-contact at the individual level

Table 3 presents the various possible psychological outcomes for individuals who are in contact with persons from other cultures. As was stated earlier, the

TABLE 3   *Outcomes of cultural contact at the individual level: psychological responses to "second culture" influences*

Response	Type	Multiple group membership affiliation	Effect on individual	Effect on society
Reject culture of origins embrace second culture	"Passing"	Culture I norms lose salience Culture II norms become salient	Loss of ethnic identity Self-denigration	Assimilation Cultural erosion
Reject second culture, exaggerate first culture	Chauvinistic	Culture I norms increase in salience Culture II norms decrease in salience	Nationalism Racism	Intergroup friction
Vacillate between the two cultures	Marginal	Norms of both cultures salient but perceived as mutually incompatible	Conflict Identity confusion Over-compensation	Reform Social change
Synthesize both cultures	Mediating	Norms of both cultures salient and perceived as capable of being integrated	Personal growth	Intergroup harmony Pluralistic societies Cultural preservation

general principle is that such individuals can either become or resist becoming multicultural. An analogy can be drawn from the field of second language learning (Taft, 1981). Persons brought up in a linguistically homogeneous society will learn that country's language as their first tongue. If they then travel to other countries, or go to university abroad, or marry a person from another linguistic group, they may or may not acquire a second, third or nth language. Some people are born into a multilingual society or setting; for example, the Swiss, Belgians, and Dutch all speak several different (although related) languages; and persons born into multicultural settings include offspring of mixed marriages and second generation immigrants. Bilinguals may or may not retain both their languages, learn further languages, or gradually become monolingual in one of their tongues, shedding the others for practical or psychological reasons.

In the psychological domain, what can happen when a person is plunged into a multicultural setting, either through birth or circumstances? As is evident from Table 3, the alternatives parallel the group effects discussed in the previous section. It should be emphasized again that the conceptual bases for the categories are not the perceptions, attitudes or feelings of the participants about each other. In this particular analysis the concern is not with whether foreign students, migrants, tourists and other sojourners come to like, understand or respect the host country. Rather, the core theoretical idea is based on the notion of social influence, specifically the extent to which the participants emerge from the contact having rejected or exaggerated their first culture, rejected or exaggerated their "second" culture, vacillated between the two, or synthesized them.

Evidence for the existence of each type of outcome is available. A great variety of persons tend to reject their culture of origin and embrace a new culture. This has become a particular problem for international educational exchange schemes, with countless overseas students unwilling to return home from abroad after the completion of their studies because they have become acculturated to the society in which they attended university. A more subtle version of the same process can be seen at work in those overseas trained persons who uncritically apply the knowledge, techniques and solutions they have learned overseas to local problems, without modifying the exogenous procedures to make them culturally appropriate. Alatas (1972, 1975), writing about Asia, has called this the "captive mind" syndrome, which ". . . is the product of higher institutions of learning, either at home or abroad, whose way of thinking is dominated by Western thought in an imitative and uncritical manner" (Alatas, 1975, p. 691). Examples abound also in the areas of ethnic and race relations. In earlier times "passing" has been a major preoccupation of racists, demographers, novelists, and some sociologists and psychologists. Thus Stonequist (1937) devoted an entire chapter of *The Marginal Man* to passing. More contemporary writers talk about the assimilation, say, of migrants (e.g. Taft, 1973) but are in fact referring to their "passing" or attempted passing into the wider community.

There is also ample evidence for the occurrence of the response that is the direct opposite of "passing". A great many individuals, after coming into contact with a second culture, reject that culture and become militant nationalists and chauvinists. There must be at least as many western-educated professionals in Asia and Africa who cordially detest the country that gave them their education, as there are "captive minds", if reports like those by Morris (1960), Tajfel and Dawson (1965) and Terhune (1964) are any indication. Similarly, in the area of race relations, inter-group friction sometimes increases directly with the amount of contact (cf. Amir's 1976 review; Mitchell, 1968).

The marginal syndrome has been studied extensively, since the introduction of the idea to the literature by Park (1928) and Stonequist (1937). Despite some criticisms about the concept of marginality (e.g. Mann, 1973), the phenomenon certainly exists: there are a great many men and women who are members of, or aspire membership in, two racial or cultural groups that have mutually incompatible norms, values or entrance qualifications. Stonequist used the term "marginal" in connection with the inability of such individuals to become or remain full members of either group, therefore finding themselves on the margin of each. Such persons, unless they can resolve their conflict, are doomed to vacillate between their two cultures, unable to satisfy the contradictory demands that their two reference groups make upon them. This is poignantly illustrated by a passage from the autobiography of one of the world's most famous marginal men, J. Nehru: "I have become a queer mixture of the East and the West, out of place everywhere, at home nowhere. . . . I am a stranger and alien in the West. I cannot be of it. But in my own country also, sometimes, I have an exile's feeling" (1936, p. 596).

Finally, there is evidence that some individuals can select, combine and synthesize the appropriate features of different social systems, without losing their cultural cores or "myths" (Ritchie, 1981). Bochner (1981) had called such individuals mediating persons, people who have the ability to act as links between different cultural systems, bridging the gap by introducing, translating, representing and reconciling the cultures to each other.

In the preceding discussion the various possible outcomes of cross-cultural contact have been described. However, so far we have only touched on the crucial question of what determines the various types of responses, i.e. why do some individuals become marginal while others become mediating persons, or why do some become chauvinists while others attempt to "pass" into a second culture. Most existing research is unable to answer this question, except perhaps in a *post-hoc* fashion. The social psychological model being developed here does suggest a general principle which may account for the various contact outcomes listed in Tables 2 and 3. The theory implies that individuals should respond according to the relative social supports (Chu, 1968) that their settings provide for the various alternative solutions. The practical consequences of this idea are that a desirable outcome may be achieved by creating or controlling the social climates of particular settings. Potentially, there are many situations whose social climates are amenable to at least partial influence, including such diverse institutions as university dormitories, the armed forces, schools, churches, television programmes, employment policies, and a political system that values, respects and defends cultural pluralism (Greenberg and Mazingo, 1976; Hirschhorn, 1976; Throssell, 1981).

Empirical studies of the social psychology of the contact situation

This chapter concludes with a brief review of some studies conducted by the author and his group, illustrating the kind of research that the model generates. The studies were conducted in two domains of cross-cultural contact, the overseas student sojourn and second-generation migrant children areas respectively. The aim of the research has been to establish systematic links between the subjects' social and environmental conditions, and the likelihood of adopting a chauvinistic, "passing", marginal or mediating resolution. The particular hypothesis guiding the research is that the style of response will depend to a large extent on the nature of the subjects' friendship and acquaintance patterns, and on the psychological functions that these relationships serve.

Overseas students

Bochner (1973) interviewed 69 returned Thai, Pakistani and Philippine students after their re-entry, in Bangkok, Karachi and Manila respectively. All of the students had attended universities in the U.S.A. The interviews covered three time-periods, the students' pre-sojourn, during-sojourn, and their current (i.e. post-sojourn) lives. The interview explored the subjects' social relationships during each of these periods, in particular the norms, values and traditions of the groups they referred themselves to, and the occupational, recreational, familial and other roles that they enacted in their respective groups. The results indicate that prior to their sojourn the students were largely monocultural. The modal sojourn experience was bicultural, i.e. the students belonged to two social networks while overseas, a compatriot peer group of fellow nationals and a group drawn from members of the host culture. After their return home the students reverted to a mainly monocultural lifestyle, as would be expected, since their work, social and family environments were peopled mostly by individuals who were monocultural, and who had little or no experience of other societies. The study thus confirmed the importance of the peer group, as in each of the three phases of the academic sojourn it exerted a major influence on the cultural orientation of the students. It should be noted that students rejecting their home culture were probably under-represented in this study, as they would have either not returned home in the first place, or emigrated soon after re-entry.

The Bochner (1973) study was conducted in the post-sojourn phase, and its finding that in retrospect the students reported that they had belonged to two distinct social networks while abroad, requires direct confirmation, with current students describing their present friendship patterns. The literature in this area is contradictory. Some investigators (e.g. Chu, 1968; Gullahorn and Gullahorn, 1963) have found that overseas students do make frequent, non-superficial and lasting contacts with the host culture, whereas other authors (e.g. Miller *et al.*, 1971) have found that foreign students tend to "stick to their own kind". We have now conducted three studies which can reconcile this apparent contradiction, and which throw light on the underlying processes. All three studies (Bochner, Buker and McLeod, 1976; Bochner, McLeod and Lin, 1977; Bochner and Orr, 1979), show that the compatriot group is the most important social network of sojourning overseas students. However, overseas students do not engage exclusively with their cultural cohorts. Rather, they form associations with different categories of individuals for different and predictable reasons. Their primary network is monocultural, and consists of bonds between compatriots. The main function of the conational network is to provide a setting in which ethnic and cultural values can be rehearsed and expressed. The secondary network of foreign students is bicultural, and consists of bonds with host nationals. The main function of this network is to instrumentally facilitate the academic and professional aspirations of the sojourner.

Some implications can be drawn from these studies for the management of the academic contact situation. It is clear that the bonds with conationals serve a very important function, and should therefore not be administratively interfered with, regulated against, obstructed, or sneered at. The bicultural bonds, i.e. the relationships with members of the host culture, which may initially be entered into for some pragmatic or instrumental purpose, are capable of being expanded to include a warm and personal dimension. This often happens spontaneously, for example when an academic advisor becomes a friend, and ways and means should be found to capitalize on this tendency. The function of educational administrators and members of the helping professions is to structure the experience so that the students can belong to these two important social worlds without strain, and gain support from each network for the respective functions each network serves. Unfortunately, however, only too often the two networks seem to exert contradictory demands on the students, stressing rather than helping them to achieve their professional and cultural goals.

Second-generation migrants

The children of persons born overseas are faced with exactly the same alternatives as overseas students: they can reject the culture of origin and become completely assimilated; they can remain aggressively "ethnic" and find fault with everything in their new country; they can become marginal, at home in neither group; or they can integrate their two cultures, and become bicultural mediating persons. Recently, students under the author's supervision at the University of New South Wales conducted two studies exploring second-genera-tion migrant—host country relationships.

The first study, by Novakovic (1977) was done with second-generation Yugoslav migrant children, i.e. children born in Australia of parents born in Yugoslavia. These children are caught between the traditional culture of their parents and the Australian culture of their contemporary school and social environment. The two cultures differ significantly, particularly in regard to the social role of the adolescent, since Yugoslav and Australian expectations about what is and is not appropriate teenage behaviour are quite different and often incompatible. In effect, such children are faced with the difficult alternative of either accepting or rejecting their culture of origin, or finding some compromise. We were interested in exploring the determinants of this choice, i.e. why some children lean towards the Australian culture, whereas others tend to remain more oriented towards the culture of their parents. There is a considerable literature to indicate that the peer group is second only to the family in serving as a reference group for growing children, and by adolescence may even outweigh parental influence as a socializing agent (Stone and Church, 1968). We reasoned that the nature of the child's peer group, in particular the ethnic composition of that group, would affect whether they retained their Yugoslav culture or adopted the Australian culture. To test this hypothesis. Novakovic asked large numbers of Yugoslav children who their three best friends were, and what the ethnic identity of these best friends was. From this large group of respondents Novakovic selected three groups of Yugoslav children. One group of subjects had three best friends who were all Australian. Another group had mixed best friends, some Australian and some Yugoslav. The third group's best friends were all second-generation Yugoslavs. Age of subjects was systematically varied, from 9 to 16, and an equal number of boys and girls served in each condition. We next devised a test measuring acceptance or rejection of Yugoslav customs and traditions, such as food and language preferences, national identification, rules for social interaction and the like. Novakovic then administered this test to her subjects, predicting that as the children became older they would increas-ingly reject their parental culture, due to the cumulative influence of the dominant Australian cultural environment. But the degree of rejection should not be uniform, since it would be affected by influences emanating from the peer group. Consequently, we predicted that subjects with all Australian friends would have the highest rejection rate; subjects with all Yugoslav friends would have the lowest rejection rate; and subjects who have friends from both cultures would be intermediate between the two other groups. Figure 1 shows this pre-dicted relationship.

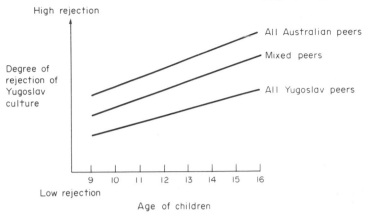

FIG. 1.

The hypothesis was confirmed, in that the data fell precisely into the pattern depicted in Figure 1. Of special interest are the implications of the data from the middle group, where the subjects had peers from both cultures. This group did not totally reject their parental culture, but neither did they accept it without question. It would seem as if these children have achieved a degree of biculturality, and are being supported in their bicultural stance by their bicultural peer group.

In the second study Crowley (1978) took the other side of the coin and looked at the effect of multicultural friendships on third-generation Australians. There is evidence that Australian culture is characterized by a degree of chauvinism and ethnocentrism (Stevens, 1971). These attitudes are transmitted by parents to their children, and by a variety of subtle and sometimes not so subtle societal influences. Until quite recently, assimilation was the official policy in regard to migration, and it is only in the last few years that the Government has openly provided support for the development of a multicultural society (Throssell, 1981). In effect, the children descended from the older pioneering stock are exposed to two competing influences: they can either continue the xenophobic tradition of their parents, or they can become part of the movement towards a multicultural Australian society. Again we reasoned that the ethnic composition of the children's peer group would affect their attitudes towards cultural diversity. To test this hypothesis Crowley employed the same technique as Novakovic (1977). He asked a large number of third-or-more-generation Australian children from British—Irish stock who their best friends were, and what the ethnic identity of these best friends was. From this large group of respondents Crowley selected two groups. One group of subjects had three best friends who were all Australians. The second group consisted of subjects who had at least one best friend who was a second-generation immigrant of southern European stock. Age of subjects was systematically varied from 10 to 15, and an equal number of boys and girls served in each condition. Crowley then administered a test measuring tolerance for and appreciation of cultural differences. The test was adapted from Sampson and Smith (1957), and Crowley labelled the continuum world-mindedness—ethnocentrism. We predicted that as the children got older they would become more world-minded due to the cumulative effect of multicultural influences from sources outside of the parental home. However, the acquisition of world-mindedness would not be uniform for all children, but would depend on the ethnic composition of their peer group: children who had at least one close migrant friend should be more aware and appreciative of cultural differences than children with only Australian friends. Figure 2 shows this predicted relationship, and the hypothesis was confirmed, as the results fell precisely into the pattern depicted.

FIG. 2.

Taken together, the two Australian studies showed the importance of multicultural contact under intimate conditions. The peer group in adolescence is probably the most cohesive group that people ever belong to, not excluding marriage. Because of its high cohesiveness, the group is able to maintain strict conformity in its members. Adolescence is also the time when most attitudes are formed, including the attitude of cultural mediation. The overseas student studies continue the same theme into post-adolescence, showing the continuing influence of the friendship network on cultural attitudes.

Summary and conclusion

Cross-cultural contacts take many forms. The people who engage in transactions with members of other cultures include travellers such as students, migrants and tourists; or they could be residents of ethnically or racially diverse societies. The purposes of these different categories of "persons-in-contact" differ greatly, as do their experiences and what they take away with them from the contact. At first blush, the literature on inter-cultural interaction presents a bewildering diversity of findings, ideas, concepts and speculations. However, there are some common themes underlying the apparent confusion, and one of the aims of this chapter has been to identify these points of reference, and integrate them into a general framework that will give some unity to the area.

The main elements of the model can now be summarized:

(1) Contact is always between a minimum of two people. Overseas students interact with host students, migrants with host members in the factories and offices where they work, tourists with local citizens, black Americans with white, and technical experts with indigenous counterparts. Thus contact always constitutes an encounter and therefore falls within the general principles of social psychology, to be understood in terms of concepts such as reference group membership, attribution, in-group—out-group differentiation, territoriality, contradictory demands and mutual influence.

(2) When two people interact they do not merely respond to each other as individuals but as members of their respective groups. The actors behave according to the norms of the group they belong to, and they ascribe to the target person qualities that are supposed to be characteristic of that person's group. In cross-cultural interactions the respective group affiliations are usually highly visible due to differences in racial characteristics, skin colour, linguistic forms, customs and religious practices.

(3) The larger the differences between groups in contact with each other, irrespective of whether these differences are real or imagined, the greater will be the tendency for the participants to make a distinction between in- and out-group membership. The distinction takes the form of categorizing people as belonging either to "us" (my family, my friend, my country) or to "them" (strangers, enemies, foreigners). The evidence indicates that out-group members are less favourably treated than in-group members, simply because of their out-group classification, even when everything else is equal. This suggests that the principles of deindividuation and territoriality may be operating. Deindividuated persons tend to be treated less favourably than individuated ones, and the interaction distance for strangers is greater than the distance for intimates. Strangers, until they become intimates, intrude into the personal space of those they are interacting with by their mere presence in that person's territory. Such intrusions generate anxiety and defensive reactions including hostility, derogation and withdrawal. Many cross-cultural contacts constitute a territorial invasion by a highly visible deindividuated out-group. Unless this out-group is redefined as belonging in some sense to the in-group, or given a special status placing it outside the

in-group—out-group dichotomy, the contact is unlikely to be harmonious. Redefining the out-group in some way is quite a common occurrence. For example, after the Second World War British migrants to Australia were more welcome than European settlers because they came from "common stock"; and despite the White Australia Policy, Asian students were admitted on the grounds that they were temporary visitors who would return to their countries of origin after completing their studies (Wicks, 1972).

(4) The tendency has been to measure only the superficial outcomes of cross-cultural contact, such as the extent to which the participants like, approve of, or understand each other. This approach is based on the narrow and misleading view that attitude change constitutes a shift along some belief continuum. Non-trivial change in beliefs almost always involves a reordering of the person's cognitive structure. In cross-cultural contact the participants mutually exert influence on each others' ethnicity. Four broad outcomes of this "struggle" were identified: intensified nationalism, "passing", marginality and mediation. It was proposed that the psychological dimension underlying these responses to contact, and used in measuring the outcomes of cross-cultural interaction, was the extent to which people remain or become mono- or heterocultural, and an analogy was drawn between second-culture learning and second-language learning.

(5) It was suggested that there is a connection between culture learning and personal growth, the assumption being that persons who are comfortably at home in more than one culture, lead intellectually and emotionally more satisfying lives than monocultural individuals. This assumption is extremely difficult to test empirically, and only indirect evidence in its favour is available. For example, many experiments show that children brought up in rich, complex and variegated environments subsequently perform better on a whole range of intellectual and cognitive tasks, than children brought up in dull and limited nursery surroundings (Mussen, Conger and Kagan, 1969; Stone and Church, 1968), an effect that has also been observed in rats (Forgus, 1954; Hebb, 1949; Hymovitch, 1952). Studies of bilingual children have shown that they perform significantly better than unilingual children on various cognitive measures (e.g. Bain, 1975; Ben-Zeev, 1977; Cummins, 1978; Feldman and Shen, 1971; Ianco-Worrall, 1972; Peal and Lambert, 1962). There is also a suggestion that a link may exist between ethnocentrism and unilingualism, which if confirmed may have practical implications for reducing prejudice. Finally, from an adaptive point of view, the more skills persons have the greater the range of contingencies with which they can cope. It follows that multicultural people are going to be more effective than monocultural individuals in dealing with the ever-growing number of cross-cultural encounters facing human beings in the future, as the world continues to shrink.

(6) Certain implications can be drawn for action to reduce prejudice and ethno-

centrism. Cross-cultural conflict has two major causes. A great deal of disharmony is based on realistic conditions such as an imbalance in power, economic exploitation, or genuine and irreconcilable differences in the goals and aspirations of the groups, an example of the latter being the conflict between those in favour and those against nuclear power. However, even greater friction stems directly from causes that are not realistically based in the above-mentioned sense, but which reside in the minds of the participants, and in the social psychology of the contact. The consideration of the first set of factors is in the province of lawyers, economists and the political process. The second set of factors belongs in the realm of social and cross-cultural psychology, and this chapter has devoted itself exclusively to these psychological rather than economic and political ingredients of the contact situation.

Clearly no amount of psychological engineering is going to make poverty-stricken ethnic groups inclined to welcome or even accept interactions with representatives of wealthy or powerful cultures. Nor are members of the better-placed cultures likely to feel comfortable in the presence of persons from grossly disadvantaged societies. However, psychology can make a contribution in instances where there is a minimum of realistic conflict, and yet a great deal of mutual distrust, hostility and even violence.

Cross-cultural contact can be either a threatening or an enhancing experience. It will be threatening if the other person is regarded as a deindividuated outsider intruding on a group's established territory, undermining the values and diluting the cultural identity of its members. The contact can also be enhancing, if the other person is regarded as a different but interesting individual, whose presence does not constitute a territorial infringement but instead an opportunity to learn something about the world at large. Clearly, a prerequisite for successful intercultural contact is that both parties must be sensitive to the impact they have on each other. Persons who find themselves in the "outsider" role must behave less intrusively, and "insiders" must become less defensive in relation to members of obviously different groups. The most direct way to accomplish this is for each group to learn the other group's culture, or at least for there to develop a critical mass of bicultural persons who can mediate between the two groups. However, the evidence indicates that mere cognitive learning is insufficient to bring about such changes (Bochner, Brislin, and Lonner, 1975; Guthrie, 1975). Simply providing general information about an exotic society does not constitute culture learning as the term is being used here, because such material does not generalize to everyday life situations and, if anything, exacerbates the "us" and "them" differentiation.

To blur the distinction between "us" and "them" requires that people become partially "them", i.e. incorporate some of "their" characteristics without however losing their own ethnic identity. It seems a tall order, to make the distinction without making it, and yet it is constantly being achieved quite easily in other, similar spheres. In universities, for instance, there is a clear-cut distinction made between staff and students. In some universities this leads to bitter relationships and mostly separate existences; in other universities, particularly those performing as a community of scholars, staff and students share a great many goals, perspectives, values, activities and facilities, and yet are still able to distinguish between those formally designated as staff and those formally designated as students. Exactly the same principle is evident in industrial organizations that have adopted a participative style of decision-making, which reduces but does not obliterate the distinction between managers and employees (Bochner, Ivanoff, and Watson, 1974).

The great challenge facing applied social and cross-cultural psychology is to devise training procedures capable of teaching people second cultures without at the same time undermining their first culture. A promising approach is the extension of the social skills training paradigm to culture learning, a topic discussed in greater detail in Chapter 7. Other methods include setting up special institutions such as multicultural living halls and International Houses, that teach and practise cultural relativism. The problem is that such places attract persons already sympathetic to cultural pluralism, and therefore tend to preach to the converted (Bochner, Lin and McLeod, 1979). To date, no practical psychological methods have been devised that could make a significant impact in the area of greatest need, those sectors of society where there is a high degree of ethnocentrism and chauvinism. The American solution has been to employ legislation and political pressure to change mass attitudes and practices (Katz, 1976; Rogers, 1972), and other countries such as Australia have followed suit (Berndt, 1971). Nevertheless, it remains for applied psychology to provide techniques and procedures that can be used to make legal and political action in this sphere more effective and acceptable.

References

ABATE, M. and BERRIEN, F. K. (1967) Validation of stereotypes: Japanese versus American students. *Journal of Personality and Social Psychology,* 7, 435–8.

ACKERMAN, N. W. and JAHODA, M. (1950) *Anti-Semitism and Emotional Disorder.* Harper, New York.

ADORNO, T. W., FRENKEL-BRUNSWIK, E., LEVINSON, D. J. and SANFORD, R. N. (1950) *The Authoritarian Personality.* Harper, New York.

ALATAS, S. H. (1972) The captive mind in development studies: some neglected problems and the need for an autonomous social science tradition in Asia. *International Social Science Journal,* 24, 9–25.

ALATAS, S. H. (1975) The captive mind and creative development. *International Social Science Journal,* 27, 691–700.

ALLPORT, G. W. (1954) *The Nature of Prejudice.* Doubleday Anchor, Garden City, N.Y.

AMIR, Y. (1969) Contact hypothesis in ethnic relations. *Psychological Bulletin,* 71, 319–42.

AMIR, Y. (1976) The role of intergroup contact in change of prejudice and ethnic relations. *Towards the Elimination of Racism* (Edited by KATZ, P. A.). Pergamon, New York.

ARDREY, R. (1966) *The Territorial Imperative.* Dell, New York.

ARDREY, R. (1970) *The Social Contract.* Dell, New York.

ARONSON, E. (1972) *The Social Animal.* W. H. Freeman, San Francisco.

BAIN, B. (1975) Toward an integration of Piaget and Vygotsky: bilingual considerations. *Linguistics,* **160,** 5–20.

BANTON, M. (1967) *Race Relations.* Tavistock, London.

BARKER, R. C. (1968) *Ecological Psychology: Concepts and Methods for Studying the Environment of Human Behaviour.* Stanford University Press, Stanford, Calif.

BEM, S. L. and BEM, D. J. (1973) Homogenizing the American woman: the power of an unconscious ideology, *Psychology for Our Times: Readings* (Edited by ZIMBARDO, P. and MASLACH, C.). Scott, Foresman, Glenview, Ill.

BEN-ZEEV, S. (1977) The influence of bilingualism on cognitive development and cognitive strategy. *Child Development,* **48,** 1009–18.

BERNDT, R. M. (1971) The concept of protest within an Australian Aboriginal context, *A Question of Choice: An Australian Aboriginal Dilemma* (Edited by BERNDT, R. M.). University of Western Australia Press, Nedlands, W.A.

BERRIEN, F. K. (1968) *General and Social Systems.* Rutgers University Press, New Brunswick, N.J.

BERRIEN, F. K. (1969) Familiarity, mirror imaging and social desirability in stereotypes: Japanese vs Americans. *International Journal of Psychology,* **4,** 207–15.

BETTELHEIM, B. (1943) Individual and mass behaviour in extreme situations. *Journal of Abnormal and Social Psychology,* **38,** 417–52.

BLOOM, L. (1971) *The Social Psychology of Race Relations.* Allen & Unwin, London.

BOCHNER, S. (1971) The use of unobtrusive measures in cross-cultural attitudes research, *A Question of Choice: An Australian Aboriginal Dilemma* (Edited by BERNDT, R. M.). University of Western Australia Press, Nedland, W.A.

BOCHNER, S. (1972) An unobtrusive approach to the study of housing discrimination against aborigines. *Australian Journal of Psychology,* **24,** 335–7.

BOCHNER, S. (1973) *The Mediating Man: Cultural Interchange and Transnational Education.* Culture Learning Institute, East–West Center, Honolulu.

BOCHNER, S. (1976) Religious role differentiation as an aspect of subjective culture. *Journal of Cross-Cultural Psychology,* **7,** 3–19.

BOCHNER, S. (1979) Cultural diversity: implications for modernization and international education, *Bonds Without Bondage: Explorations in Transcultural Interactions* (Edited by KUMAR, K.). The University Press of Hawaii, Honolulu.

BOCHNER, S. (1980) Unobtrusive methods in cross-cultural experimentation, *Handbook of Cross-cultural Psychology: Methodology,* vol. 2 (Edited by TRIANDIS, H. C. and BERRY, J. W.). Allyn & Bacon, Boston.

BOCHNER, S. (Editor) (1981) *The Mediating Person: Bridges Between Cultures.* Schenkman, Cambridge, Mass.

BOCHNER, S., BRISLIN, R. W. and LONNER, W. J. (1975) Introduction. *Cross-cultural Perspectives on Learning.* (Edited by BRISLIN, R. W., BOCHNER, S. and LONNER, W. J.). Wiley, New York.

BOCHNER, S., BUKER, E. A. and MCLEOD, B. M. (1976) Communication patterns in an international student dormitory: a modification of the "small world" method. *Journal of Applied Social Psychology,* **6,** 275–90.

BOCHNER, S. and CAIRNS, L. G. (1976) An unobtrusive measure of helping behaviour toward Aborigines, *Aboriginal Cognition: Retrospect and Prospect* (Edited by KEARNEY, G. E. and MCELWAIN, D. W.). Australian Institute of Aboriginal Studies, Canberra.

BOCHNER, S., IVANOFF, P. and WATSON, J. (1974) Organization development in the A.B.C. *Personnel Practice Bulletin,* **30,** 219–33.

BOCHNER, S., LIN, A. and MCLEOD, B. M. (1979) Cross-cultural contact and the development of an international perspective. *Journal of Social Psychology,* **107,** 29–41.

BOCHNER, S., MCLEOD, B. M. and LIN, A. (1977) Friendship patterns of overseas students: a functional model. *International Journal of Psychology,* **12,** 277–94.

BOCHNER, S. and OHSAKO, T. (1977) Ethnic role salience in racially homogeneous and heterogeneous societies. *Journal of Cross-Cultural Psychology,* **8,** 477–92.

BOCHNER, S. and ORR, F. E. (1979) Race and academic status as determinants of friendship formation: a field study. *International Journal of Psychology*, **14**, 37–46.

BOCHNER, S. and PERKS, R. W. (1971) National role evocation as a function of cross-national interaction. *Journal of Cross-Cultural Psychology*, **2**, 157–64.

BOGARDUS, E. S. (1928) *Immigration and Race Attitudes*. Heath, Boston.

BOLDT, E. D. (1978) Structural tightness and cross-cultural research. *Journal of Cross-Cultural Psychology*, **9**, 151–65.

BOLDT, E.D. and ROBERTS, L. W. (1979) Structural tightness and social conformity: a methodological note with theoretical implications. *Journal of Cross-Cultural Psychology*, **10**, 221–30.

BREIN, M. and DAVID, K. H. (1971) Intercultural communication and the adjustment of the sojourner. *Psychological Bulletin*, **76**, 215–30.

BRISLIN, R. W. and BAUMGARDNER, S. R. (1971) Non-random sampling of individuals in cross-cultural research. *Journal of Cross-Cultural Psychology*, **2**, 397–400.

BRONFENBRENNER, U. (1961) The mirror image in Soviet–American relations: A social psychologist's report. *Journal of Social Issues*, **17**, 45–56.

BRYAN, J. H. and TEST, M. A. (1967) Models and helping: naturalistic studies in aiding behaviour. *Journal of Personality and Social Psychology*, **6**, 400–7.

BYRNE, D. (1969) Attitudes and attraction, *Advances in Experimental Social Psychology*, vol. 4 (Edited by BERKOWITZ, L.). Academic Press, New York.

BYRNES, F. C. (1966) Role shock: an occupational hazard of American technical assistants abroad. *Annals of the American Academy of Political and Social Science*, **368**, 95–108.

CAMPBELL, D. T. (1967) Stereotypes and the perception of group differences. *American Psychologist*, **22**, 817–29.

CAMPBELL, D. T. and FISKE, D. W. (1959) Convergent and discriminant validation by the multitrait–multimethod matrix. *Psychological Bulletin*, **56**, 81–105.

CHESLER, M. A. (1976) Contemporary sociological theories of racism, *Towards the Elimination of Racism* (Edited by KATZ, P. A.). Pergamon, New York.

CHU, G. C. (1968) Student expatriation: a function of relative social support. *Sociology and Social Research*, **52**, 174–84.

COOK, S. W. and SELLTIZ, C. (1955) Some factors which influence the attitudinal outcomes of personal contact. *International Social Science Bulletin*, **7**, 51–8.

CROWLEY, M. (1978) *The other side of the integration coin: Level of worldmindedness of third generation Australian children as a function of ethnic composition of friendship group, age, ethnic density of school and sex.* Unpublished honours thesis, School of Psychology, University of New South Wales.

CUMMINS, J. (1978) Bilingualism and the development of metalinguistic awareness. *Journal of Cross-Cultural Psychology*, **9**, 131–49.

DAWS, G. (1968) *Shoal of Time: A History of the Hawaiian Islands.* The University Press of Hawaii, Honolulu.

DEVOS, G. A. (1980) Ethnic adaptation and minority status. *Journal of Cross-Cultural Psychology*, **11**, 101–24.

DUTTON, D. G. (1971) Reactions of restaurateurs to blacks and whites violating restaurant dress requirements. *Canadian Journal of Behavioural Science*, **3**, 298–302.

DUTTON, D. G. (1973) Reverse discrimination: the relationship of amount of perceived discrimination toward a minority group on the behaviour of majority group members. *Canadian Journal of Behavioural Science*, **5**, 34–45.

EDGERTON, W. B. (1976) Who participates in education exchange? *The Annals of the American Academy of Political and Social Science*, **424**, 6–15.

EDNEY, J. J. (1980) The commons problem: alternative perspectives. *American Psychologist*, **35**, 131–50.

EIBL-EIBESFELDT, I. (1970) *Ethology: The Biology of Behaviour.* Holt, Rinehart & Winston, New York.

EMERY, F. E. (Editor) (1969) *Systems Thinking.* Penguin, Harmondsworth.

FELDMAN, C. and SHEN, M. (1971) Some language-related cognitive advantages of bilingual five-year-olds. *Journal of Genetic Psychology*, **118**, 235–44.

FELDMAN, R. E. (1968) Response to compatriot and foreigner who seek assistance. *Journal of Personality and Social Psychology*, **10**, 202–14.

FELIPE, N. J. and SOMMER, R. (1966) Invasions of personal space. *Social Problems*, **14**, 206–14.

FORGUS, R. H. (1954) The effect of early perceptual learning on the behavioural organization of adult rats. *Journal of Comparative and Physiological Psychology*, **47**, 331–6.

FREEMAN, L. C. and WINCH, R. F. (1957) Societal complexity: an empirical test of a typology of societies. *American Journal of Sociology*, **62**, 461–6.

FULBRIGHT, J. W. (1976) The most significant and important activity I have been privileged to engage in during my years in the Senate. *The Annals of the American Academy of Political and Social Science*, **424**, 1–5.

GAERTNER, S. L. (1973) Helping behaviour and racial discrimination among liberals and conservatives. *Journal of Personality and Social Psychology*, **25**, 335–41.

GOFFMAN, E. (1971) *Relations in Public*. Basic Books, New York.

GORDON, M. M. (1964) *Assimilation in American Life*. Oxford University Press, London.

GREENBERG, B. S. and MAZINGO, S. L. (1976) Racial issues in mass media institutions, *Towards the Elimination of Racism* (Edited by KATZ, P. A.). Pergamon, New York.

GULLAHORN, J. T. and GULLAHORN, J. E. (1963) An extension of the U-curve hypothesis. *Journal of Social Issues*, **19** (3), 33–47.

GUTHRIE, G. M. (1966) Cultural preparation for the Philippines, *Cultural Frontiers of the Peace Corps* (Edited by TEXTOR, R. B.). M.I.T. Press, Cambridge, Mass.

GUTHRIE, G. M. (1975) A behavioral analysis of culture learning, *Cross-cultural Perspectives on Learning* (Edited by BRISLIN, R. W., BOCHNER, S. and LONNER, W. J.). Wiley, New York.

HALL, E. T. (1966) *The Hidden Dimension*. Doubleday, Garden City, N.Y.

HANEY, C., BANKS, W. C. and ZIMBARDO, P. G. (1973) Interpersonal dynamics in a simulated prison. *International Journal of Criminology and Penology*, **1**, 69–97.

HARTLEY, E. L. and THOMPSON, R. (1967) Racial integration and role differentiation. *Journal of the Polynesian Society*, **76**, 427–43.

HEBB, D. O. (1949) *The Organization of Behavior*. Wiley, New York.

HEIDER, F. (1958) *The Psychology of Interpersonal Relations*. Wiley, New York.

HEISS, J. and NASH, D. (1967) The stranger in laboratory culture revisited. *Human Organization*, **26**, 47–51.

HIRSCHHORN, E. (1976) Federal legal remedies for racial discrimination, *Towards the Elimination of Racism* (Edited by KATZ, P. A.). Pergamon, New York.

HYMOVITCH, B. (1952) The effects of experimental variations on problem solving in the rat. *Journal of Comparative and Physiological Psychology*, **45**, 313–21.

IANCO-WORRALL, A. (1972) Bilingualism and cognitive development. *Child Development*, **43**, 1390–1400.

JONES, E. E. (1976) How do people perceive the causes of behaviour? *American Scientist*, **64**, 300–5.

JONES, E. E. and NISBETT, R. E. (1971) The actor and the observer: divergent perceptions of the causes of behavior, *Attribution: Perceiving the Causes of Behavior* (Edited by JONES, E. E. *et al.*). General Learning Press, Morristown, N.J.

JORGENSON, D. O. and DUKES, F. O. (1976) Deindividuation as a function of density and group membership. *Journal of Personality and Social Psychology*, **34**, 24–9.

KATZ, D. and BRALY, K. (1933) Racial stereotypes of one hundred college students. *Journal of Abnormal and Social Psychology*, **28**, 280–90.

KATZ, P. A. (Editor) (1976) *Towards the Elimination of Racism*, Pergamon, New York.

KLINEBERG, O. (1966) *The Human Dimension in International Relations*. Holt, Rinehart & Winston, New York.

KLINEBERG, O. (1971), Black and white in international perspective. *American Psychologist*, **26**, 119–28.

KOSA, J. (1957) *Land of Choice*. University of Toronto Press, Toronto.

KROEBER, A. L. and KLUCKHOHN, C. (1952) Culture: A critical review of concepts and definitions. *Papers of the Peabody Museum*, **47**, (whole no. 1).

LAMBERT, R. D. (1966) Some minor pathologies in the American presence in India. *Annals of the American Academy of Political and Social Science*, **368**, 157–70.

LAPIERE, R. T. (1936) Type-rationalizations of group antipathy. *Social Forces*, **15**, 232–7.

LEWIN, K. (1941) Self-hatred among Jews. *Contemporary Jewish Record,* **4,** 219–32.

LISKA, A. E. (1974) Emergent issues in the attitude–behavior consistency controversy. *American Sociological Review,* **39,** 261–72.

LITTLE, K. (1948) *Negroes in Britain.* Routledge & Kegan Paul, London.

LOVIBOND, S. H., MITHIRAN, and ADAMS, W. G. (1979) The effects of three experimental prison environments on the behaviour of non-convict volunteer subjects. *Australian Psychologist,* **14,** 273–85.

LYKKEN, D. T. (1968) Statistical significance in psychological research. *Psychological Bulletin,* **70,** 151–9.

MANN, J. (1973) Status: the marginal reaction – mixed-bloods and Jews, *Psychology and Race* (Edited by WATSON, P.). Penguin, Harmondsworth.

MANN, L. (1969) *Social Psychology.* Wiley, Sydney.

MILGRAM, S. (1974) *Obedience to Authority: An Experimental View.* Tavistock, London.

MILLER, M. H., YEH, E. K., ALEXANDER, A. A., KLEIN, M. H., TSENG, K. H., WORKNEH, F. and CHU, H. M. (1971) The cross-cultural student: lessons in human nature. *Bulletin of the Menninger Clinic,* **35,** 128–31.

MITCHELL, I. S. (1968) Epilogue to a referendum. *Australian Journal of Social Issues,* **3,** (4), 9–12.

MORRIS, R. T. (1960) *The Two-way Mirror.* University of Minnesota Press, Minneapolis.

MUSSEN, P. H., CONGER, J. J. and KAGAN, J. (1969) *Child Development and Personality,* 3rd edition. Harper & Row, New York.

NASH, D. and WOLFE, A. (1957) The stranger in laboratory culture. *American Sociological Review,* **22,** 149–67.

NEHRU, J. (1936 – reprinted 1958) *An Autobiography.* The Bodley Head, London.

NEWCOMB, T. M. (1943) *Personality and Social Change.* Holt, Rinehart and Winston, New York.

NEWCOMB, T. M. (1956) The prediction of interpersonal attraction. *American Psychologist,* **11,** 575–86.

NOVAKOVIC, J. (1977) *The assimilation myth revisited: Rejection of home culture by second generation Yugoslav immigrant children as a function of age, friendship group and sex.* Unpublished honours thesis, School of Psychology, University of New South Wales.

OBERG, K. (1960) Cultural shock: adjustment to new cultural environments. *Practical Anthropology,* **7,** 177–82.

OSGOOD, C. E., SUCI, G. J. and TANNENBAUM, P. H. (1957) *The Measurement of Meaning.* University of Illinois Press, Urbana, Ill.

PARK, R. E. (1928) Human migration and the marginal man. *American Journal of Sociology,* **33,** 881–93.

PARKER, F. (1965) Government policy and international education: a selected and partially annotated bibliography, *Government Policy and International Education* (Edited by FRASER, S.). Wiley, New York.

PEAL, E. and LAMBERT, W. E. (1962) The relation of bilingualism to intelligence. *Psychological Monographs,* **76** (whole no. 546).

PELTO, P. J. (1968) The difference between 'tight' and 'loose' societies. *Transaction,* **5,** 37–40.

PETTIGREW, T. F. (1969) Racially separate or together? *Journal of Social Issues,* **25,** (1), 43–69.

PUSHKIN, I. and VENESS, T. (1973) The development of racial awareness and prejudice in children, *Psychology and Race* (Edited by WATSON, P.). Penguin, Harmondsworth.

RICHMOND, A. H. (1973) Race relations and behaviour in reality, *Psychology and Race* (Edited by WATSON, P.). Penguin, Harmondsworth.

RITCHIE, J. E. (1981) Tama tu, tama ora: mediational styles in Maori culture, *The Mediating Person: Bridges Between Cultures* (Edited by BOCHNER, S.). Schenkman, Cambridge, Mass.

ROGERS, G. W. (1972) Cross-cultural education and the economic situation: the Greenland and Alaska cases, *Education in the North* (Edited by DARNELL, F.). University of Alaska, Fairbanks.

ROKEACH, M. (1960) *The Open and Closed Mind*. Basic Books, New York.

ROKEACH, M. (1961) Belief versus race as determinants of social distance: comment on Triandis' paper. *Journal of Abnormal and Social Psychology*, **62**, 187–8.

ROSE, E. and FELTON, W. (1955) Experimental histories of culture. *American Sociological Review*, **20**, 383–92.

SAMPSON, D. L. and SMITH, H. P. (1957) A scale to measure world-minded attitudes. *Journal of Social Psychology*, **45**, 99–106.

SCHILD, E. O. (1962) The foreign student, as stranger, learning the norms of the host culture. *Journal of Social Issues*, **18** (1), 41–54.

SELLTIZ, C., CHRIST, J. R., HAVEL, J. and COOK, S. W. (1963) *Attitudes and Social Relations of Foreign Students in the United States*. University of Minnesota Press, Minneapolis.

SHERIF, C. W., SHERIF, M. and NEBERGALL, R. E. (1965) *Attitude and Attitude Change: The Social Judgment–Involvement Approach*. W. B. Saunders, Philadelphia.

SHERIF, M. (1970) *Group Conflict and Co-operation: their Social Psychology*. Routledge & Kegan Paul, London.

SHIELDS, J. J. (1968) A selected bibliography, *Problems and Prospects in International Education* (Edited by SCANLON, D. G. and SHIELDS, J. J.). Teachers College Press, New York.

SOMMER, R. (1969) *Personal Space: The Behavioral Basis of Design*. Prentice-Hall, Englewood Cliffs, N.J.

SOMMER, R. and BECKER, F. D. (1969) Territorial defense and the good neighbor. *Journal of Personality and Social Psychology*, **11**, 85–92.

STEVENS, F. S. (Editor) (1971) *Racism: The Australian Experience, vol. 1: Prejudice and Xenophobia*. Australia and New Zealand Book Company, Sydney.

STEVENS, F. S. (Editor) (1972) *Racism: The Australian Experience, vol. 2: Black versus White*. Australia and New Zealand Book Company, Sydney.

STOLLER, A. (Editor) (1966) *New Faces: Immigration and Family Life in Australia*. Cheshire, Melbourne.

STONE, L. J. and CHURCH, J. (1968) *Childhood and Adolescence: A Psychology of the Growing Person*, 2nd edition. Random House, New York.

STONEQUIST, E. V. (1937) *The Marginal Man*. Scribner, New York.

TAFT, R. (1966) *From Stranger to Citizen*. Tavistock, London.

TAFT, R. (1973) Migration: problems of adjustment and assimilation in immigrants, *Psychology and Race* (Edited by WATSON, P.). Penguin, Harmondsworth.

TAFT, R. (1981) The role and personality of the mediator, *The Mediating Person: Bridges Between Cultures* (Edited by BOCHNER, S.). Schenkman, Cambridge, Mass.

TAJFEL, H. (1970) Experiments in intergroup discrimination. *Scientific American*, **223** (5), 96–102.

TAJFEL, H. and DAWSON, J. L. (Editor) (1965) *Disappointed Guests*. Oxford University Press, London.

TERHUNE, K. W. (1964) Nationalism among foreign and American students: an exploratory study. *Journal of Conflict Resolution*, **8**, 256–70.

THROSSELL, R. P. (1981) Towards a multi-cultural society: the role of government departments and officials in developing cross-cultural relations in Australia. *The Mediating Person: Bridges Between Cultures* (Edited by BOCHNER, S.). Schenkman, Cambridge, Mass.

TRIANDIS, H. C. (1975) Culture training, cognitive complexity and interpersonal attitudes. *Cross-cultural Perspectives on Learning* (Edited by BRISLIN, R. W., BOCHNER, S. and LONNER, W. J.). Wiley, New York.

TRIANDIS, H. C., VASSILIOU, V., VASSILIOU, G., TANAKA, Y. and SHANMUGAM, A. V. (1972) *The Analysis of Subjective Culture*. Wiley, New York.

USEEM, J. and USEEM, R. H. (1967) The interfaces of a binational third culture: a study of the American community in India. *Journal of Social Issues*, **23** (1), 130–43.

USEEM, J. and USEEM, R. H. (1968) American-educated Indians and Americans in India: a comparison of two modernizing roles. *Journal of Social Issues*, **24** (4), 143–58.

USEEM, J. USEEM, R. H. and DONOGHUE, J. (1963) Men in the middle of the third culture: the roles of American and non-Western people in cross-cultural administration. *Human Organization,* **22,** 169–79.

USEEM, J. USEEM, R. H. and MCCARTHY, F. E. (1979) Linkages between the scientific communities of less developed and developed nations: a case study of the Philippines, *Bonds Without Bondage: Explorations in Transcultural Interactions* (Edited by KUMAR, K.). The University Press of Hawaii, Honolulu.

WATSON, J. L. (Editor) (1977) *Between Two Cultures: Migrants and Minorities in Britain.* Blackwell, Oxford.

WEBB, E. J. CAMPBELL, D. T. SCHWARTZ, R. D and SECHREST, L. (1966) *Unobtrusive Measures: Nonreactive Research in the Social Sciences.* Rand McNally, Chicago.

WEST, S. G. WHITNEY, G. and SCHNEDLER, R. (1975) Helping a motorist in distress: the effects of sex, race, and neighborhood. *Journal of Personality and Social Psychology,* **31,** 691–8.

WICKER, A. W. (1969) Attitudes versus actions: the relationship of verbal and behavioral responses to attitude objects. *Journal of Social Issues,* **25** (4), 41–78.

WICKS, P. (1972) Diplomatic perspectives, *Overseas Students in Australia* (Edited by BOCHNER, S. and WICKS, P.). The New South Wales University Press, Sydney.

WILDER, D. A. (1978) Reduction of intergroup discrimination through individuation of the out-group. *Journal of Personality and Social Psychology,* **36,** 1361–74.

WITKIN, H. A. and BERRY, J. W. (1975) Psychological differentiation in cross-cultural perspective. *Journal of Cross-Cultural Psychology,* **6,** 4–87.

WYNNE-Edwards, V. C. (1962) *Animal Dispersion in Relation to Social Behavior.* Hafner, New York.

WYNNE-EDWARDS, V. C. (1965) Self-regulating systems in populations of animals. *Science,* **147,** 1543–8.

ZAWADSKI, B. (1948) Limitations of the scapegoat theory of prejudice. *Journal of Abnormal and Social Psychology,* **43,** 127–41.

ZIMBARDO, P. G. (1969) The human choice: individuation, reason, and order versus deindividuation, impulse, and chaos, *Nebraska Symposium on Motivation* (Edited by ARNOLD, W. J. and LEVINE, D.). **17,** 237–307.

2

Contact between ethnic groups: a historical perspective of some aspects of theory and research

OTTO KLINEBERG

Introduction

THE PUBLISHED material dealing with contact between ethnic groups would fill a substantial library, and it is obviously impossible to do it justice in a relatively brief paper. What I have tried to do, therefore, is to select certain aspects for particular attention, and to indicate in connection with them some of the research findings which appear to me to be specially relevant to our contemporary understanding of inter-group contacts. Such a selection will certainly reflect my own personal bias, but since I have been involved in this area of investigation for a very long time it is difficult if not impossible for me to avoid using my own frame of reference. In any case I am sure that any significant lacunae in my presentation will be more than adequately filled by the other contributors to this volume.

The aspects of the problem to which I shall now turn include:

(1) the issue of inborn or genetic psychological differences between ethnic groups;
(2) the role of stereotypes regarding ethnic groups and the possibility of replacing them by a more adequate understanding of cultural characteristics;
(3) conflict associated with contact and the question of its inevitability; and
(4) the consequences of contact between ethnic groups, and the problem of the potential contribution of such contact to the improvement of inter-group relations.

Genetic differences

In connection with the first issue, it can hardly be doubted that contact between ethnic groups will be profoundly affected when accompanied by the belief that one group is innately inferior to the other. When I first became interested in this problem in the 1920s, the general impression was that most psychologists (largely as the result of the application of tests of intelligence) were convinced that such innate differences did exist; and that most anthropologists (as a consequence of their field experience with individuals in different cultures) took the opposite view. My own first research was conducted in 1926 and 1927 and published in 1928, and provided me with an unexpected finding, which was to influence all my further work in this area. I applied a number of performance (non-language) tests to American Indian children on the Toppenish Reservation in the state of Washington, with the usual instruction to complete the tasks "as quickly as possible". To my surprise, these children worked exceedingly slowly, no matter how often I repeated the instruction; they saw no advantage in completing a task in 55 rather than in 82 seconds. They were much slower, though on the whole more accurate, than the White comparison group. This difference disappeared in the case of American Indian children attending regular schools with White teachers in the usual White American setting, so it was pretty certain that culture rather than race was responsible.

Subsequent research in this field has been reviewed so frequently that I shall not attempt anything similar at this point. Instead I shall limit myself to a few general comments on what seem to me to be important developments. I have been particularly struck, for example, by the number of investigators who have changed their minds on this issue, moving from a "racial" to a "cultural" explanation of group differences. In 1910, for example, Howard W. Odum, a distinguished American sociologist at the University of North Carolina and at one time President of the American Sociological Society, published a book entitled *Social and Mental Traits of the Negro,* in which the constitutional inferiority of Blacks was presented as a definitive conviction. In 1936, however, he wrote an article entitled "The errors of sociology", which included as one such "error" the "assumption that races are inherently different rather than group products of differentials due to the cumulative power of folk-regional and cultural environment" (p. 338). In 1926 Florence L. Goodenough, professor of Psychology at the University of Minnesota, applied her Draw-A-Man Test, which she regarded as "culture-free", to a number of ethnic groups in the United States, and reported differences in the level of "intelligence" due to innate factors. Subsequent studies with the same test indicated the degree to which drawing a man was subject to previous experience and in an article published in 1950 together with Dale Harris, she wrote that "the search for a culture-free test, whether of intelligence, artistic ability, personal—social characteristics, or any other measurable trait is illusory". Referring to her own earlier study, she says that it is "certainly no exception to the rule" and adds "the writer hereby apologizes for it".

As a final example in this series may be mentioned the book by Professor C. C. Brigham of Princeton University, published in 1923 with the title *A Study of American Intelligence*. His analysis of the test scores obtained by soldiers of different ethnic origins serving in the American Army led him to the conclusion that there was clear evidence for the innate intellectual superiority of Whites over Blacks, and of North Europeans (or Nordics) over Alpines and Mediterraneans among subjects of European origin. This study was severely criticized, particularly by physical anthropologists, and this encouraged me, thanks to a National Research Council Fellowship, to study the test performance of boys in France, Germany and Italy, using rigorous anthropometric techniques in the selection of subjects to represent the various European "races". This investigation was conducted from 1927 to 1929, and published in 1931. On my return to the United States in September 1929 I met Professor Brigham, and started to tell him about my investigation (in which, incidentally, the only significant difference I found was between urban and rural children), which touched upon the same issues with which his book had dealt. He startled me by stating "I don't stand by a word in that book"! In the following year, 1930, he published an article in which he stated that all the studies which had appeared to demonstrate "racial" differences by means of tests of intelligence, including his own, fell completely to the ground.

These honest and courageous admissions of error, together with a significant amount of further research conducted after 1930, both contributed to and reflected a changed atmosphere among psychologists in the United States and elsewhere who now, with rare exceptions, agreed that there was no acceptable scientific basis for the conclusion that "races" or ethnic groups differed psychologically because of their heredity. It took longer for this position to be accepted by the general public. Gunnar Myrdal, the principal author of the classic *An American Dilemma* (1944), stated that in no other field was there so wide a gap between popular impressions and the conclusions reached by biological and social scientists. He called for an educational offensive to reduce that gap.

Later he came to feel that this particular battle had been won, perhaps in part because public opinion surveys in the United States showed that this gap had indeed been reduced. When persons representing a sample of White Americans were asked the question "In general, do you think that Negroes are as intelligent as White people — that is, can they learn things just as well if they are given the same education and training?", the proportion answering in the affirmative increased from 50 per cent in 1942 to almost 80 per cent in 1964 (Hyman and Sheatsley, 1964). Myrdal himself said at a Nobel Symposium in 1969, published in 1970, that "the racial inferiority doctrine has disappeared, which is an undivided advance, since it has no scientific basis".

As far as psychology is concerned, however, the disappearance turned out not to be complete. In the same year as the Symposium at which Myrdal spoke there appeared the monograph by A. R. Jensen in the *Harvard Educational Review*, which effectively reopened the issue; this was followed in 1971 by Hans Eysenck's book, *Race, Intelligence and Education,* which took the same line, although in somewhat more extreme form. For these authors there is indeed a genetic "social" hierarchy, with Whites definitely superior to Blacks.

It would take me too far afield at this point to enter into a detailed analysis of Jensen's position. As I have written elsewhere (1975):

> Jensen has been severely criticized on a number of counts, including the neglect of many of the research findings that throw doubt on his thesis, and the fact that a good deal of his argument is really irrelevant to the subject of race differences. He makes a strong case, for example, in favour of the role of genetic factors in determining variations among individuals and families; most psychologists would agree that heredity does play an important part in connection with such individual variations, without, however, accepting his inference that this implies ethnic differences as well. On this latter point the conclusion is still "Not proven".

From this point of view, the furore over Sir Cyril Burt's twin studies is entirely irrelevant to the position taken by Jensen with regard to the alleged genetic inferiority of Blacks, since no conclusion can be drawn from individual to ethnic genetic differences. In any case the overlapping between groups on every psychological measure which has been applied makes it unjustifiable to generalize to all members of any ethnic community.

Ethnic stereotypes

The second issue which seems important to me refers to the role played in group contact by ethnic stereotypes, those "pictures in our heads" that give us the impression that we know what "they" are like even before we have actually met them. One of the continuing arguments in this field is between those who believe that the existence and nature of the stereotypes determine our perception and judgement of others, and those who regard the content of such stereotypes as epi-phenomena, consequences rather than causes of existing inter-group relations. As an example of this second position, reference is made to the manner in which Russians were portrayed in the mass media of the West before, during and after the Second World War; the hairy, violent Bolshevik was replaced by the loyal ally, so similar to us in so many ways, only to regress to the earlier image during the Cold War, although presented with somewhat greater sophistication. There is no doubt in my mind that stereotypes are indeed shaped by social, economic, political and historical antecedents, and that they are used in order to justify the subjugation, exploitation and even elimination of others. They then serve as rationalizations of the *status quo*, permitting those in a position of power to persuade themselves, as Hooton (1937) puts it, that "the act of grabbing is somehow noble and beautiful", and they "can rape in righteousness and murder in magnanimity".

This does not mean, however, that once the stereotypes are there, for whatever reason, they play no part in determining the nature of inter-group contact. We have here, in my opinion, the familiar situation of a circular relationship, with stereotypes as both consequences and causes. In the well-known study by Wallace Lambert and his colleagues at McGill University (1960), students were the subjects of an experiment presented to them as a test of ability to judge character, intelligence and other qualities, from the sound of the voice. The results showed that those who spoke in French (Canadian) were usually judged to be inferior to those who spoke English; although unknown to the judges, it was the same bilingual speakers who were heard in both languages. This occurred even when the judges were themselves French Canadians, and the inferiority disappeared when the French accent was Parisian rather than Canadian. Granted that the stereotype arose because of the inferior economic and social position of the Francophones in Canadian communities, the fact remains that the images of the English and French groups did affect the perceptions and judgement, and presumably also the attitudes and actions related to inter-group contact. Many other examples could be given of this circular phenomenon. Lambert's technique has been applied by Tajfel and others in the case of bilingual communities in the United Kingdom, in general with similar results.

Here too we are faced with a complex phenomenon, which has been approached in a number of ways, and I shall have to limit my presentation to what seem to me to be significant but relatively neglected aspects. I have already referred to the manner in which stereotypes arise within a society; I should like now to add some comments as to how they are learned by individual members of that society. As already indicated, the mass media play a part, and it is striking to note the changes that have occurred in recent years in the portrayal of ethnic minorities in the cinema and television. With regard to the portrayal of Blacks in the United States, for example, there has been in general a move from the stereotyped lazy, superstitious and ignorant "Darky" to the Black gentleman of immaculate taste and high achievement, gradually giving way to an attempt at a more balanced presentation of Blacks of all varieties and all levels of attainment. What we do not know with any certainty, however, is the extent to which the portrayal of ethnic groups in the mass media influences the content of the stereotypes held and accepted by members of the audience.

The same question arises as to other potential sources of stereotypes. Many if not most languages contain a variety of expressions which suggest the presence of specific psychological traits in particular ethnic groups. English appears to be particularly well endowed in this respect; a sample of such expressions includes Dutch treat, Chinese puzzle, Jew him down, Nigger in the woodpile, to take French leave. (The French say *filer à l'anglaise* under the same circumstances.) My query is: do we think of the ethnic referent when we use these expressions? Or have they come to be used without necessarily pointing to the ethnic groups concerned? I tried this out with several groups of French students, using such expressions as *fort comme un Turc*, and *saoul comme un Polonais* (which is more or less the equivalent of the British "drunk as a lord"). Most of my subjects reported that they did *not* think of Turks or Poles when these expressions were used, but there were some who did. There was some agreement that "drunk as a Pole" suggested a burly, noisy Polish labourer, very boisterous, definitely lower class. This example is particularly striking because it was first used with a very favourable implication. Some French officers complained to Napoleon that the Polish soldiers under his command were frequently drunk. Napoleon was so pleased, however, with the performance of his Polish troops in battle that he suggested that it might be a good idea if everybody in his army became "drunk as a Pole".

Ethnic jokes or anecdotes may also play a part in reinforcing, if not creating, stereotypes, although just how important that part may be is difficult to determine. It does seem likely that the many stories told about the parsimony of the Scots (the French tell similar stories about the Auvergnats), the formality of the English, the pugnacity of the Irish, or (in Brazil) the simple-mindedness and naïveté of the Portuguese, will shape our expectations regarding their behaviour, and that examples to the contrary may be dismissed as examples.

The role of stereotypes in inter-group contact would probably be reduced if the following considerations were more widely appreciated. Stereotypes may sometimes contain "a kernel of truth", but research has demonstrated, for example by the early study of Armenians in California by LaPiere (1936), that they may be completely false. They may change with time and as a consequence of changes in the external situation; Schrieke (1936) describes the favourable image of the Chinese in the United States when they were needed as labourers, and the unfavourable characteristics applied to them when they were no longer wanted. The historian Hans Kohn (1944) has noted that 100 years ago the descriptions of the British and the French were almost diametrically opposed to the images of today. The Irish, now regarded as always ready for a fight, were in the past considered to be stolid and unimaginative, due according to Feuerbach to the consumption of immense quantities of potatoes! In the United States and Canada there appears to be a widespread conviction that the English lack a sense of humour, whereas in France the phrase "with typical British humour" is definitely regarded as a compliment. Stereotypes are sometimes regarded as inevitable, but the tendency to apply them indiscriminately might be reduced if the information available, some of it admittedly anecdotal but in other cases based on careful research, were incorporated in the educational process at various levels.

Even more significant educationally would be the replacement of stereotypes by more accurate knowledge about the psychological characteristics of ethnic groups. Jacques Barzun (1937), in a review of a book dealing with the English, wrote: "Of all the books that no one can write, those about nations and national character are the most impossible." This may be true for whole nations, complex and internally variable, changing in character throughout history, and for the study of which no adequate methodology has yet been discovered. However, research by anthropologists, and more recently by psychologists as well, has revealed a number of sources of misunderstanding which can be reduced by direct knowledge of cultural and sub-cultural patterns of behaviour. What seems to me important to realize is that there are both similarities as well as differences in such behaviour, and as a consequence that the exclusive emphasis either on "the psychic unity of mankind" as some anthropologists have expressed it, or on the predominant importance of cultural relativity, does violence to the reality of human behaviour. To take a recent example, C. E. Izard, in his book *Human Emotions* (1977) states that the fundamental emotions "have the same expressions and experiential qualities in widely different cultures from virtually every continent of the globe". He adds almost in the next sentence, however, that people of different social backgrounds and different cultures may learn quite different facial movements for modifying what he considers to be innate expressions (p. 6). What this means in practice with regard to contact with members of other cultural groups is that we must be prepared to find variations from our own forms of expression as well as certain similarities. Failure to keep both of these in mind as possibilities may create serious misunderstanding. A number of examples of this phenomenon are treated in subsequent chapters of this volume, particularly by Collett and Argyle.

Contact and conflict

The next issue which I shall consider is that of conflict associated with interethnic contact, and the question of its inevitability. Once again my comments will be brief, and will touch on only certain aspects of what is obviously a very complex phenomenon. As in the case of stereotypes, conflict which takes the form of prejudice and discrimination is due to a variety of causes – historical, political, economic, psychological. There is a continuing argument in the United States and elsewhere between sociologists and psychologists as to whether social or psychological factors are responsible. The classic study by Adorno and his colleagues (1950) has been severely criticized because of its neglect of a social approach, even though the authors clearly specify that they recognized the importance of that approach but were themselves more interested in an understanding of the psychological component. The argument between the two groups of proponents – or opponents – is in any case unrealistic, since both approaches are needed for a fuller understanding of the issue.

Any reader of contemporary newspapers must be struck by the variety of characteristics which serve either as causes or as symbols of group conflict. Differences in language as in Belgium or Canada; in religion as in Ireland or with reference to the Jews; in race as in South Africa or the United States; in national origin and the attempt to restore a former national identity as in the case of Basques, Corsicans, Kurds, and many others – this list could be extended almost indefinitely. It is also over-simplified since these symbols of differentiation may act in combination, may be influenced by cultural differences, and may also be complicated by a history of economic competition and exploitation. This evident pervasiveness of group conflict, for one apparent reason or another, has led many observers to conclude that group conflict, either within nations or between them, is inevitable and that any hope of its elimination is Utopian. This position is often linked to the theory of the universality and innateness of aggression, with group conflict − including war − seen as an expression of this instinctive need. This argument has never seemed to me to be convincing, since even the advocates of the biological basis of aggression speak of the possibility of sublimating or redirecting it into various non-violent forms of behaviour, such as sport, peaceful competition, achievement of success in science or industry, which would also satisfy the aggressive impulse (for example, Lorenz, 1966).

There are other powerful reasons for rejecting the hypothesis of the inevitability of group conflict. In the first place, it is by no means truly universal; some individuals and some nations show a great deal of it, others very little. Language differences may be used in some countries as a basis for hostility, but not in others. There is, for example, very little conflict between linguistic groups in Switzerland, probably because language is not associated with an economic or social hierarchy, and also because decisions are taken on a basis of consensus rather than according to the will of the majority. Secondly, there are many examples of minority groups at one time subject to discrimination but now almost completely accepted. This is true of the Quakers in the United Kingdom and the United States. In the latter country the former hostility against the Irish, who at one time were described in the mass media in the most violently negative terms, has for all practical purposes disappeared. As a symbol of this change one may compare the passage of an ordinance of the General Court of Massachusetts in 1720 directing that "certain families recently arrived from Ireland be warned to move off" (Feldman, 1931, p. 89) with the recent emergence of the Kennedy family as leaders in the political life of the nation. Jews in the United States have experienced considerable discriminations in the fairly recent past, but in the current programmes of "affirmative action" designed to improve the occupational and social level of minority groups, Jews are not included. They are no longer regarded as having the status of a minority, in comparison with groups like the Blacks, the Chicanos, or women. These improvements in the position of at least some minorities give some basis for the hope that discrimination may be reduced if not eliminated.

In a recent study which my colleagues in Paris and I conducted among students in eleven countries (Klineberg et al., 1979), we asked them if they agreed with the following statement: "Any discrimination against a person because of his race, religion, or color should be considered a crime." This rather extreme formulation was approved by a substantial majority of students in all countries, the percentages ranging from 81 to 96. These results would give us reason to be optimistic regarding the future, if we could be sure that such negative reactions against racism would persist into later life, rather than being replaced by a more conservative "Establishment" position with increasing years.

Consequences of contact

I turn now in conclusion to the last of the four issues listed at the beginning of this chapter; that is, the consequences of contact between members of two different ethnic groups. There is a view, widely but rather naively accepted, that conflict and prejudice arise mainly because of lack of acquaintance, and that bringing people of different backgrounds together will develop understanding and mutual acceptance. Gordon Allport (1954) reminds us that all depends on the kind of contact, and the situation in which contact occurs. He suggests that casual, superficial contacts may often do more harm than good, but that contact accompanied by true acquaintance usually does lessen prejudice. His conclusion is that the favourable effect of contact is greatly enhanced if there is "equal status contact between majority and minority groups in the pursuit of common goals" (p. 281). With regard to this latter point, Sherif *et al*. (1961) in their important investigation prefer to speak of "superordinate" rather than "common" goals. The goals must indeed be common to both groups, but the effect is enhanced if success is dependent on cooperation, with each group requiring the help of the other in reaching the desired goal and solving the problems which are important to both of them.

This formulation — equal status and superordinate goals — seems to me to be very fruitful as indicating the major factors contributing to better relations between members of two ethnic groups in contact. It has been applied successfully, for example, to the case in which Black and White soldiers in the same unit of the American Army develop friendlier attitudes to each other in carrying out a joint *successful* operation. To my knowledge, however, no-one has as yet examined the consequences when the operation is unsuccessful. Will solidarity be increased as the result of a shared frustration and unhappiness, or will the experience be followed by mutual recrimination?

There are situations in which equal status can be (more or less) assured, but where superordinate goals are difficult to introduce. I refer in particular to an area with which my good friend Stephen Bochner, the editor of this volume, and I have been concerned for a good many years; namely, international educational exchange. There are of course many different goals involved in creating opportunities for our students and scholars to work abroad, or for foreigners to attend or to teach at our universities. One of the major motivations, however, which is used to justify the effort and expenditure involved, and which explains in part the extensive programmes sponsored by national governments, international organizations and private foundations, is undoubtedly the hope that the resulting contacts will improve international relations. Extensive research in this area has not always yielded results which indicate that this hope has been realized. In any case, factors other than equal status or superordinate goals are involved.

Frank Hull and I have recently (Klineberg and Hull, 1979) published the results of an investigation of foreign students in eleven different countries which included questions regarding their attitudes toward the host country, and some of the experiences which appeared to be related to such attitudes. Our data unfortunately gave little support to the view that study abroad contributes substantially to a more favourable opinion of the country of sojourn. Attitudes were on the whole friendly on arrival, but became slightly less so in nine of the eleven countries studied. Since some other investigators have reported more positive results, I shall content myself at this point with the negative statement that confidence in a favourable outcome with regard to inter-group (in this case international) understanding is not always justified. Our study enabled us to identify a number of sources of problems and difficulties encountered by foreign students, leading them in many cases to feel discouraged and dissatisfied in relation to the whole experience. What is striking in this connection is that it was precisely in relation to *contact with the local population* that major frustration was encountered. Previous studies had shown that satisfaction with the foreign sojourn in general is closely related to the success in making friends locally, and our own results go in the same direction, with the added demonstration that the factor of personal contact is intertwined with almost all aspects of the foreign experience. Details varied from country to country, but disappointment with regard to social contacts with the local population was a major factor everywhere. While many of the visitors did make "good friends" in the sojourn country, a majority stated that their "best friend" was either a fellow-national or another foreign student.

It may therefore be appropriate to add one more variable to the two — equal status and superordinate goals — regarded as responsible for the success of contact in improving inter-group attitudes. Contact is more successful in bringing about this effect when it satisfies the social needs of the individual and is free of discrimination on the one hand and condescension on the other. It is too much to expect those responsible for international student exchange programmes to "create" friendships, but it may be possible for them to create an atmosphere in which the development of friendship is facilitated.

I am conscious of the fact that this brief account deals too summarily with a complex area. That is one reason why I entitled this chapter an overview of *some aspects* of theory and research. I am also aware that most of my bibliographical references are to publications that appeared a good many years ago. This I have done deliberately, convinced as I am that too many books and articles today seem to find it unnecessary to cite any item which is more than 5, or at the most 10, years old. Someone has said that originality consists in not knowing what anyone else has said or written before you. In that sense I cannot claim to be original. I can only hope that a moderate degree of historical perspective will not be out of place in this volume.

References

ADORNO, T. W., FRENKEL-BRUNSWIK, E., LEVINSON, D. J. and SANFORD, R. N. (1950) *The Authoritarian Personality*. Harper, New York.

ALLPORT, G. W. (1954) *The Nature of Prejudice*. Addison-Wesley, Cambridge, Mass.

BARZUN, J. (1937) *Race: A Study in Modern Superstition*. Harcourt Brace, New York.

BRIGHAM, C. C. (1923) *A Study of American Intelligence*. Princeton University Press, Princeton.

BRIGHAM, C. C. (1930) Intelligence tests of immigrant groups. *Psychological Review*, 137, 158–65.

EYSENCK, H. J. (1971) *Race, Intelligence and Education*. M. T. Smith, London.

FELDMAN, H. (1931) *Racial Factors in American Industry*. Harper, New York.

GOODENOUGH, F. L. (1926) Racial differences in the intelligence of school children. *Journal of Experimental Psychology*, 9, 388–97.

GOODENOUGH, F. L. and HARRIS, D. B. (1950) Studies in the psychology of children's drawings. *Psychological Bulletin*, 47, 369–433.

HOOTON, E. A. (1937) *Apes, Men and Morons*. Putnam, New York.

HYMAN, H. and SHEATSLEY, P. B. (1964) Attitudes towards desegregation. *Scientific American*, 211, 16–23.

IZARD, C. E. (1977) *Human Emotions*. Plenum, New York.

JENSEN, A. R. (1969) How much can we boost I.Q. and scholastic achievement? *Harvard Educational Review*, 39, 1–123.

KLINEBERG, O. (1928) An experimental study of speed and other factors in 'racial' differences. *Archives of Psychology*, whole no. 93.

KLINEBERG, O. (1931) A study of psychological differences between 'racial' and national groups in Europe. *Archives of Psychology*, whole no. 132.

KLINEBERG, O. (1975) Race and psychology, *Race, Science and Society* (Edited by KLINEBERG, O.). UNESCO, Paris.

KLINEBERG, O. and HULL, W. F. (1979) *At a Foreign University: An International Study of Adaptation and Coping*. Praeger, New York.

KLINEBERG, O., ZAVALLONI, M., LOUIS-GUERIN, C. and BENBRIKA, J. (1979) *Students, Values, and Politics: A Cross-cultural Comparison*. Free Press, New York.

KOHN, H. (1944) *The Idea of Nationalism*. Macmillan, New York.

LAMBERT, W. E., HODGSON, R. C., GARDNER, R. C. and FILLENBAUM, S. (1960) Evaluational reactions to spoken languages. *Journal of Abnormal and Social Psychology*, 66, 44–51.

LAPIERE, R. T. (1936) Type-rationalizations of group antipathy. *Social Forces*, 15, 232–7.

LORENZ, K. (1966) *On Aggression*. Methuen, London.

MYRDAL, G. (1944) *An American Dilemma*. Harper & Row, New York.

MYRDAL, G. (1970) Biases in social research. *The Place of Value in a World of Facts* (Edited by TISELIUS, A. and NILSSON, S.). Almqvist and Wiksell, Stockholm.

ODUM, H. W. (1910) *Social and Mental Traits of the Negro*. Columbia University Press, New York.

ODUM, H. W. (1936–37) The errors of sociology. *Social Forces*, 15, 327–42.

SCHRIEKE, B. (1936) *Alien Americans*. Viking, New York.

SHERIF, M., HARVEY, O., WHITE, B., HOOD, W. and SHERIF, C. (1961) *Inter-group Conflict and Cooperation: The Robbers' Cave Experiment*. Institute of Group Relations, Norman, Oklahoma.

PART II

Processes in cross-cultural interaction

STEPHEN BOCHNER

THE AIM of this section of the book is to describe the main processes of cross-cultural interaction. Process analyses are inherently difficult to conduct, since they deal by definition with on-going, often fleeting and ephemeral phenomena that may not have readily distinguishable empirical or operational referents. In the present book, the conceptual and methodological problems relating to process analysis have been minimized by regarding the essence of the transaction between culturally diverse persons as an exchange of information, including the transmission and receipt of affect, instructions, and so forth. By conceptualizing the processes underlying inter-cultural contact as a special variant of information exchange, one can then extend the constructs and findings of general communication theory to an analysis of cross-cultural transactions. That is in effect what the contributors in this section have done.

The first chapter, by Argyle, provides an overview of the main sources of communication difficulty in inter-cultural contacts. These are language fluency, polite usage, and sequencing; non-verbal signals, including facial expression, eye gaze, spatial behaviour, touching, posture, and gesture; and rules and patterns for the regulation of inter-personal conduct. Since all of these features of social life tend to vary from culture to culture, persons unfamiliar with the "correct" patterns are likely to misunderstand and be misunderstood. Argyle reviews various training methods that have been developed to overcome these obstacles, and improve inter-cultural communication.

The second chapter, by Collett, deals specifically with one source of cross-cultural misunderstanding, the misuse of gestures. Collett concentrates on hand movements, distinguishing between *mimic signals*, which convey their meaning directly, such as running a finger across one's throat to indicate death; *emblems*, which bear only an arbitrary relationship to their meaning, in that they possess no obvious connection between the gesture and its intention; and *batons*, those manual movements that beat time to the spoken word. Emblems show the greatest degree of cross-cultural variation, and there are many instances of two societies attaching quite different meanings to the same gesture, providing a fertile ground for misunderstanding when such an emblem is used by a member of one of the societies in the presence of members of the other culture.

The following chapter, by Bickley, provides an unusual treatment of language showing that in many cases languages serve as a bridge between cultures in addition to their conventional function as mediums of communication. For example, in multicultural nations such as Indonesia, India, or the U.S.S.R., a great many mutually unintelligible languages are spoken by the ethnically diverse

59

population. Often the only channel of communication between the different groups is a "third" language or *lingua franca* that all of the people speak to varying degrees. The culturally mediating function of language raises issues such as the ethnic and status connotations of the various tongues; the varieties that a particular language like English has developed; the various cultural contexts in which these different "languages" are appropriately used; and the extent to which certain languages serve as links between diverse cultural groups. Participants in a cross-cultural encounter where language has a mediating function, may be misunderstood if they do not use, or know how to use, the linguistic forms appropriate to that type of encounter.

The final chapter in this section, by Jaspars and Hewstone, extends attribution theory into the realm of cross-cultural interaction. One of the central features of attribution theory is the distinction made between how actors and observers perceive the causes of behaviour. The theory predicts that actors will attribute their own behaviour to situational circumstances, but assume that the behaviour of others stems from internal aspects such as their personality traits, character, or genetic make-up. The actor—observer difference in attribution style may have a parallel in how the behaviour of members of different groups is "explained", particularly in-group and out-group members. Thus if attribution theory can be generalized to inter-group relations, it would follow that the behaviour of in-group members is more likely to be seen as determined by situational factors, whereas the behaviour of out-group members will be attributed to their personalities, particularly if the behaviour is also regarded as having negative connotations. Jaspars and Hewstone explore this possibility, in the context of a detailed review of the attribution literature and the related topic of stereotype formation.

The four chapters in this section provide a detailed account of the main processes that characterize cross-cultural encounters: the rules governing inter-personal conduct in a particular context; the social-psychological connotations of the language employed; the non-verbal codes of the respective cultures; and the inferences that persons make about the causes of their own and others' behaviour. All of these processes may take quite different forms in different cultures. When there is a meeting of cultures, mutual misunderstanding and inter-group hostility may occur if the societies differ with respect to the processes underlying inter-personal communication and conduct. Preventive action depends on recognizing that such differences exist, and training persons in the social and communication skills of the unfamiliar culture.

3

Inter-cultural communication

MICHAEL ARGYLE

Introduction

MANY PEOPLE have to communicate and work with members of other cultures, and social skills training is now being given to some of these who are about to work abroad. Inter-cultural communication (I.C.C.) is necessary for several kinds of people:

(1) Tourists are probably the largest category, though they stay for the shortest periods, and need to master only a few simple situations – meals, travel, shopping, taxis, etc. To a large extent they are shielded from the local culture by the international hotel culture.

(2) Business, governmental and university visitors, on short business trips, have to cope with a wider range of problems, but are often accommodated in hotels or somewhere similar, and looked after by other expatriates. They, too, are somewhat shielded from the local culture, they rarely learn the language, and are given a great deal of help.

(3) Businessmen, or others on longer visits of up to 5 years, students who stay from 1 to 3 years, and members of the Peace Corps and Voluntary Service Overseas who stay for 2 years. This is much more demanding, involving living in a house or apartment, coping with many aspects of the local culture and learning at least some of the language.

(4) Immigration may take place as a deliberate move, or as a gradual process while a visit becomes extended. This requires mastery of the new culture, as well as changes of attitude and self-image.

(5) Those who stay at home may meet visitors from abroad, and may need to work effectively with them. They may also have to deal with refugees, those from other racial groups and other social classes. However these contacts are usually limited to meals and work settings.

A number of category schemes have been produced to describe the main modes of response of visitors to different cultures. The principal alternatives are: (1) detached observers, who avoid involvement; (2) reluctant and cautious

61

participants in the local culture; (3) enthusiastic participants, some of whom come to reject their original culture; and (4) settlers (Brein and David, 1971). The different kinds of visitor responses are discussed further in Chapter 1.

How can inter-cultural effectiveness be assessed? An important minimal criterion is whether an individual manages to complete the planned tour or whether he packs up and returns home early. For some British firms as many as 60 per cent of those posted to Africa or the Middle East fail to complete their tours, at great cost to the firms. For those who succeed in staying the course there are several possible indices of success:

(1) Subjective ratings of comfort and satisfaction with life in the other culture (e.g. Gudykunst, Hammer and Wiseman, 1977).
(2) Ratings by members of the host culture of the acceptability or competence of the visitor (e.g. Collett, 1971).
(3) Ratings by the field supervisor of an individual's effectiveness at the job, as has been used in Peace Corps studies. The effectiveness of salesmen could be measured objectively, and this applies to a number of other occupational roles.
(4) Performance in role-played inter-cultural group tasks, as used by Chemers *et al.* (1966).

Hammer, Gudykunst and Wiseman (1978) analysed ratings by returned visitors to other cultures and found that they recognized three dimensions of inter-cultural competence (I.C.C.): (a) ability to deal with psychological stress, (b) ability to communicate effectively, and (c) ability to establish interpersonal relations.

Competent performance as a visitor to another culture, or in dealing with members of another culture, can be regarded as a social skill, analogous to the skills of teaching, interviewing and the rest. I.C.C. is different in that a wide range of situations and types of performance are involved, together with a variety of goals. Inter-cultural skills may include some quite new skills, where quite different situations or rules are involved, such as bargaining, or special formal occasions. It may be necessary to perform familiar skills in a modified style, e.g., a more authoritarian kind of supervision, or more intimate social relationships. There are often a number of themes or modes of interaction in a culture, which are common to a wide range of situations. I suggest that these themes can be the most useful focus of training for I.C.C. In the next section we shall examine the main themes of this kind.

There is a special phenomenon here which has no clear equivalent among other social skills, i.e. "culture shock". Oberg (1960) used this term to refer to the state of acute anxiety produced by unfamiliar social norms and social signals. Others have extended the notion to include the fatigue of constant adaptation, the sense of loss of familiar food, companions, etc., rejection of the host population or rejection by it, confusion of values or identity, discomfort at violation of values, and a feeling of incompetence at dealing with the environment (Taft, 1977). These issues are discussed further in Chapter 7, which also contains an account of a recent empirical study which studied culture shock from the point of view of social skills deficit.

Some degree of culture shock is common among those living abroad for the first time, especially in a very different culture, and it may last 6 months or longer. Those going abroad for a limited period, like a year, show a U-shaped pattern of discomfort: in the first stage they are elated, enjoy the sights and are well looked after. In the second stage they have to cope with domestic life, and things get more difficult; they keep to the company of expatriates and are in some degree of culture shock. In the third phase they have learnt to cope better and are looking forward to returning home. There may be problems when they do return home, and many people experience problems of re-entry, due for example to a loss of status, or a less exciting life (Brein and David, 1971).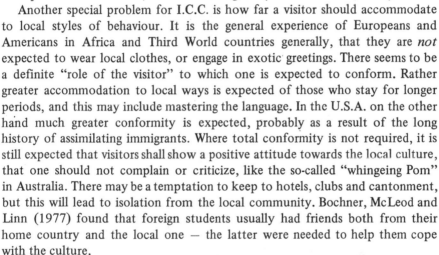

Another special problem for I.C.C. is how far a visitor should accommodate to local styles of behaviour. It is the general experience of Europeans and Americans in Africa and Third World countries generally, that they are *not* expected to wear local clothes, or engage in exotic greetings. There seems to be a definite "role of the visitor" to which one is expected to conform. Rather greater accommodation to local ways is expected of those who stay for longer periods, and this may include mastering the language. In the U.S.A. on the other hand much greater conformity is expected, probably as a result of the long history of assimilating immigrants. Where total conformity is not required, it is still expected that visitors shall show a positive attitude towards the local culture, that one should not complain or criticize, like the so-called "whingeing Pom" in Australia. There may be a temptation to keep to hotels, clubs and cantonment, but this will lead to isolation from the local community. Bochner, McLeod and Linn (1977) found that foreign students usually had friends both from their home country and the local one — the latter were needed to help them cope with the culture.

In this chapter I shall examine some of the areas of difference between cultures, which can give rise to communication problems. Any successful form of social skills training (S.S.T.) for I.C.C. should take account of these differences. Then I shall discuss the main forms of training which have been developed for this purpose.

Cultural differences in social interaction

Language

This is one of the most important differences between many cultures, and one of the greatest barriers. The person who has learnt a language quite well can still make serious mistakes, as with the Dutchman on a ship who was asked if he was a good sailor and replied indignantly that he was not a sailor but a manager.

Several studies have shown that language fluency is a necessary condition for the adjustment of foreign students in the U.S.A., though there is also evidence that confidence in the use of language regardless of ability is just as important (Gullahorn and Gullahorn, 1966). Often there are variations in accent, dialect, or grammar — as in Black American English, or in the actual language used — as in multilingual communities. An individual may indicate a positive or negative attitude to another by shifting towards a more similar or less similar speech style (Giles and Powesland, 1975). Visitors to another culture should be aware of the impression they are creating by the speech style which they use. While efforts to speak the language are usually well received, this is not always so; the French dislike the inaccurate use of their language. Taylor and Simard (1975) found that lack of interaction between English and French Canadians was less due to lack of language skills than to attitudes; language helped to preserve ethnic identity.

Most cultures have a number of forms of polite usage, which may be misleading. These may take the form of exaggeration or modesty. Americans ask questions which are really orders or requests ("Would you like to . . .?). In every culture, in many situations, there are special forms of words, or types of conversation, which are thought to be appropriate — to ask a girl for a date, to disagree with someone at a committee, to introduce people to each other, and so on. Americans prefer directness, but Mexicans regard openness as a form of weakness or treachery, and think one should not allow the outside world to penetrate their thoughts. Frankness by Peace Corps volunteers in the Philippines leads to disruption of smooth social relationships (Brein and David, 1971).

There are cultural differences in the sequential structure of conversations. The nearly-universal question—answer sequence is not found in some African cultures where information is precious and not readily given away (Goody, 1978). In Asian countries the word "no" is rarely used, so that "yes" can mean "no" or "perhaps". Saying "no" would lead to loss of face by the other, so indirect methods of conveying the message may be used, such as serving a banana (an unsuitable object) with tea to indicate that a marriage was unacceptable (Cleveland, Mangone and Adams, 1960). The episode structure of conversations varies a lot: Arabs and others have a "run-in" period of informal chat for about half an hour before getting down to business.

Some of these differences are due to different use of non-verbal signals. Erickson (1976) found that White Americans interviewing Blacks often thought the interviewee wasn't attending or understanding, and kept rewording questions in simpler and simpler forms. In several cultures "thank you" is signalled non-verbally; in China this is done at meals by rapping lightly on the table.

Non-verbal communication (N. V.C.)

It is now known that N.V.C. plays several essential parts in social interaction

— communicating attitudes to others, e.g., of like—dislike, expressing emotions, and in supporting speech by elaborating on utterances, providing feedback from listeners, and managing synchronizing. Although non-verbal signals are used in similar ways in all cultures, there are also differences and these can easily produce misunderstanding (Argyle, 1975). Triandis, Vassiliou and Nassiakou (1968) observed that friendly criticism may be interpreted as hatred, and very positive attitudes as neutral, by someone from another culture. Several studies have found that if people from culture A are trained to use the non-verbal signals of culture B (gaze, distance, etc.), they will be liked more by members of the second culture (e.g., Collett, 1971).

The face is the most important source of N.V.C. Similar basic emotional expressions are found in all cultures, and are at least partially innate. However, Chan (1979) has found that the Chinese express anger and disgust by narrowing the eyes, the reverse of that found in the U.S.A. There are also different display rules, prescribing when these expressions may be shown, where one may laugh, cry, and so on (Ekman, Friesen and Ellsworth, 1972). We carried out an experiment on the inter-cultural communication of inter-personal attitudes, in which judges decoded videotapes, the main cues being face and voice. As Table 4 shows, Japanese subjects found it easier to decode British and Italian than Japanese performers, probably because Japanese display rules forbid use of negative facial expressions (Shimoda, Argyle and Ricci Bitti, 1978). This shows that the Japanese are indeed relatively "inscrutable", but it is not yet known whether they make use of alternative channels, such as posture, for transmitting information normally conveyed by the face. There are also some variations of facial expression within cultures, between different regions and social classes. Seaford (1975) reports the use of a "pursed smile" facial dialect in the state of Virginia.

Gaze also is used in a similar way in all cultures but the amount of gaze varies quite widely. Watson (1970) studied the gaze of pairs of students from different countries. The highest levels of gaze were shown by Arabs and Latin Americans, the lowest by Indians and northern Europeans. When people from different

TABLE 4   *Accuracy of recognition of non-verbal cues for emotions and inter-personal attitudes by English, Italian and Japanese, expressed in percentages*

Judges	Performers			
	English	Italian	Japanese	Average
English	60.5	55	36	50
Italian	52	61.5	29	47
Japanese	54	56	43	51
Average	56	57	36	

From Shimoda, Argyle and Ricci Bitti, 1978.

cultures met, if the other had a low level of gaze he was seen as not paying attention, impolite, or dishonest, while too much gaze was seen as disrespectful, threatening or insulting. Some cultures have special rules about gaze, such as not looking at certain parts of the body, or at certain people. Gaze may have a special meaning, as when old ladies with squints are believed to have the evil eye (Argyle and Cook, 1976).

Spatial behaviour varies between cultures. Watson and Graves (1966) confirmed earlier observations that Arabs stand much closer than Americans (or western Europeans), and found that they also adopt a more directly facing orientation. When an Arab and an American meet it would be expected that the American would move backwards, turning, in a backwards spiral, closely followed by the Arab. An elaborate set of rules about distance is found in India, prescribing exactly how closely members of each caste may approach other castes. There are also rules for spatial behaviour in different situations — far greater crowding is allowed in lifts and buses, football matches, and parties. There are other cultural differences in the use of space. Americans establish temporary territorial rights in public places, but Arabs do not consider that people have such rights, e.g., to the seat they are sitting on.

Bodily contact is widely practised in some cultures, but allowed only under very restricted conditions in others. "Contact" cultures include Arab, Latin American, south European, and some African cultures, and they also have high levels of gaze. In non-contact cultures, bodily contact is confined to the family, apart from greeting and parting, and various professional actions, like those of doctors and tailors. Bodily contact outside these settings is taboo, and a source of considerable anxiety.

Gestures, bodily movements and posture vary widely between cultures. There are few if any universal gestures. Some gestures are used in one culture, not in others; there are probably more gestures in Italy than anywhere else; and the same gesture can have quite different meanings in different cultures. For example the V-sign, showing the back of the hand, which is a rude sign in Britain, simply means "2" in Greece. The pursed hand means a question in Italy, "good" in Greece and "fear" in northern Europe (Morris *et al.*, 1979). Many gestures are distinctive to a particular culture or cultural area and it is possible to construct "gesture dictionaries" giving the local meanings of such gestures (e.g. Saitz and Cervenka, 1972). Graham and Argyle (1975) found that Italian subjects could communicate spatial information (complicated shapes) more readily when able to use their hands; for British subjects adding the hands made less difference. Greeting is performed in a great variety of ways, including the Japanese bowing, the Indian placing of the hands together, and more exotic performances in pre-industrial societies (Krout, 1942). Disagreement is signalled by a head-shake in western countries, but a head-toss in Greece and southern Italy. Some cultures use special postures; where furniture is uncommon, various kinds of squatting, kneeling, or leaning on spears are common (Hewes, 1957).

Non-verbal aspects of vocalization vary between cultures. Arabs speak loudly, and give the impression of shouting. Americans speak louder than Europeans and give the impression of assertiveness. Speech style, especially accent, varies within cultures, and is an important clue to social class. The Japanese use the sound "hai" a lot, meaning literally "yes" but usually indicating understanding rather than agreement.

Rules

The existence of different rules in another culture is one of the main areas of difficulty in I.C.C. As we showed earlier, rules arise to regulate behaviour so that goals can be attained and needs satisfied. Systems of rules create behaviour patterns which are functional, but different sets of rules can emerge to do the same job. Here are some examples:

"BRIBERY"

In many parts of the world it is normal to pay a commission to civil servants, salesmen or professional people who have performed a service, although they are already receiving a salary. Sometimes there is a regular fee, e.g., 1—3 per cent of sales. This is regarded locally as a perfectly normal exchange of gifts, but in Europe and north America it is often illegal and unethical. Various devices are resorted to in overseas sales, such as paying a "sales commission" to an intermediary who uses some of the money for a bribe.

"NEPOTISM"

In Africa and other countries people are expected to help their relatives, and this is the local equivalent of social welfare. Sometimes relatives have contributed to an individual's education; when he gets a good job as a result they expect some return. If he is a civil servant or manager, such favours are regarded by others as nepotism and greatly disapproved of. In fact there are usually local rules which limit the forms which these favours can take.

GIFTS

In all cultures it is necessary to present relatives, friends or work colleagues with gifts on certain occasions, but the rules vary greatly. The Japanese spend a great deal of money on gifts, which must be bought from standard gift shops so that their value can be ascertained and a gift of the same value returned. The gift is not opened in the presence of the giver and a small token present is given immediately, in return (Morsbach, 1977).

BUYING AND SELLING

There are several alternate sets of rules here — barter, bargaining, fixed-price sales and auction. In cultures where bargaining is used it is normal to establish a relationship first, perhaps while drinking tea, and there are conventions about how the bargaining should proceed.

EATING AND DRINKING

One of the main problems is that there are rules in all cultures about what may not be eaten or drunk, especially certain kinds of meat — pork, beef, dog, etc., and alcohol. There may be very strong sanctions for breaking these rules, for example for consuming alcohol in some Arab countries. There are rules about how the eating is performed — knife and fork, chopstick, right hand, etc.; and there are extensive rules about table manners — when to start eating, how much to leave, how to obtain or refuse a second helping and so on.

RULES ABOUT TIME

How late is "late"? This varies greatly. In Britain and North America one may be 5 minutes late for a business appointment, but not 15 and certainly not 30 minutes late, which is perfectly normal in Arab countries. On the other hand in Britain it is correct to be 5–15 minutes late for an invitation to dinner. An Italian might arrive 2 hours late, an Ethiopian later, and a Javanese not at all — he had accepted only to prevent his host losing face (Cleveland, Mangone and Adams, 1960). A meal in Russia at a restaurant normally takes at least 3 hours. In Nigeria it may take several days to wait one's turn at a government office, so professional "waiters" do it for you.

SEATING GUESTS

In Britain, in middle-class circles at least, there are rules about seating people at table, when there are 6, 8 or other numbers present. In the U.S.A. there appear to be no such rules, and British visitors are commonly surprised to see familiar rules broken. In China the tables are circular and the seating rules are different again, and similar to the British though the most important person faces the door. In Japan different seating positions in a room have different status. There may also be rules about who should talk to whom, as in the "Boston switch" — hostess talks to person on her right during first course, switches to person on her left for the next course, and everyone else pairs off accordingly.

RULES BASED ON IDEAS

Sometimes the rules of another culture are quite incomprehensible until one understands the ideas behind them. In Moslem countries there are strict rules based on religious ideas, such as fasting during Ramadan, saying prayers five times each day, and giving one-fortieth of one's money as alms (Roberts, 1979). In order to visit some kinds of Australian Aboriginals it is necessary to sit at the edge of their land and wait to be invited further: to move closer would be regarded as an invasion of territory. It is necessary for them to have smoking fires (without chimneys) for religious reasons, despite possible danger to the health of those inside (O'Brien and Plooij, 1977).

In addition to different rules for the same or similar situations, there may also be new situations. Black American youths play the "dozens" (ritual insulting of the other's mother), other Americans go on picnics, Chinese families go to pay respect to their ancestors, Oxford dons drink port and take a special form of dessert. There may be special ceremonies connected with engagement, marriage, childbirth and other rites of passage.

Cultures also vary in the extent to which behaviour is a function of situations, as a result of their rules and other properties. Argyle, Shimoda and Little (1978) found that Japanese were more influenced by situations, while the British behaved more consistently, i.e., as a function of personality. This means that it is more difficult to infer the properties of personality from instances of behaviour for the Japanese.

Within cultures in developing countries there are often two sets of rules and ideas, corresponding to Traditional and Modern attitudes. Inkeles (1969) found similar patterns of modernization in different countries, centred round independence from parental authority, concern with time, involvement in civil affairs and openness to new experience. Dawson, Whitney and Lan (1971) devised T–M scales, of which some of the core concepts were attitudes to parental authority, gift-giving, and the role of women. Modernism is highly correlated with education and social class.

In some cases it is essential for the visitor to conform to rules, for example in matters of eating and drinking. In other cases the rules may be in conflict with his own values, the practice of his home organization, or the laws of his own country, as in the case of "bribery". There may be no straightforward solution to these problems, but it is at least necessary to recognize what the local rules are, and the ideas behind them, rather than simply condemning them as wrong.

Social relationships

The pattern of social relationships at work in the family, and with friends, takes a somewhat different form in different cultures, and different skills are needed to handle these relationships. Surveys by Triandis, Vassiliou and Nassiakou (1968) and other research workers have shown that relationships vary along the same dimensions in all cultures – in-group/out-group, status, intimacy, and hostility or competition.

FAMILY RELATIONSHIPS

In developing countries the family is more important than in developed countries. A wider range of relatives are actively related to; relationships are closer and greater demands are made. These include helping to pay for education, helping to get jobs, and helping when in trouble. Foa and Chemers (1967) point out that in traditional societies the family is the most important source of relationships, and many different role-relationships are distinguished, but relatively few outside the family. Throughout Africa and the Middle East the family takes a similar form — marriage is arranged as a contract between families, and money is paid for the bride, kinship is traced through the father and male relatives, and polygyny is accepted (Roberts, 1979). In China great respect is paid to older generations: parents are respected, large financial contributions are made to the family by unmarried children who have left home, regular visits are paid to the graves of ancestors. The family itself may take varied forms, such as having more than one wife, or a wife and concubines. The way in which different relations are grouped as similar varies: distinctions may be based primarily on age, generation, consanguinity or sex (Tzeng and Landis, 1979). Sex roles vary: in the Arab world women traditionally do not work or drive cars, but spend most of their time at home. The reverse operates in countries like Israel, China and Poland where women do nearly all the same jobs as men. Patterns of sexual behaviour vary — promiscuity may be normal, or virginity greatly prized; businessmen visiting parts of the East are sometimes embarrassed by being offered girls as part of the hospitality. Cultures vary from complete promiscuity before and after marriage to a complete taboo on sex outside marriage (Murdoch, 1949). Goody (1976) has shown that there is great control over premarital sexual behaviour in societies which have advanced agriculture, where marriage is linked with property (especially land) transactions so that it is necessary to control unsuitable sexual attachments. Americans, and to a lesser extent Europeans, mix work and family life, and receive business visitors into the home; Japanese and Arabs do not.

SUPERVISION OF GROUPS

In most of the world outside Europe and North America, there is greater social distance between ranks, more deference and obedience, and a generally more authoritarian social structure. Subordinates do not speak freely in front of more senior people, and less use is made of face-to-face discussion. Melikian (1959) found that Egyptian Arabs, whether Moslem or Christian, had higher scores on authoritarianism than Americans. While the democratic–persuasive type is most effective in the U.S.A. and Europe, this is not the case elsewhere. In India the authoritarian style has been found to be more effective; in China there was no difference and in Japan authoritarian-led groups did best with a difficult task (Mann, 1980). In Japan the teachers and superiors at work adopt an Oyabun–Koyun relationship, involving a paternalistic care for subordinates.

GROUPS

Ethnographic studies have shown that groups have more power over their members in a number of cultures – in Japan, China, Israel and Russia, for example. The individual is subordinated more to the group, and a high degree of conformity is expected. America and Europe are thought to be more individualistic, and social psychological experiments have shown relatively low levels of conformity in Germany and France. It has also been found that conformity pressures are stronger in the cultures where conformity is greatest. In Japan group decisions are traditionally carried out by a kind of acquiescence to the will of the group, without voting. In some cultures there is great stress on co-operation rather than competition in groups, e.g., in the Israeli kibbutz, Mexican villages and among Australian aboriginals (Mann, 1980).

CASTES AND CLASSES

In all cultures there are hierarchical divisions of status and horizontal divisions of inclusion and exclusion. The hierarchical divisions may take the form of social classes, which can be recognized by clothes, accent as in Britain, or other ways. There may be ethnic groups which have their places in the hierarchy, as in the U.S.A.; or there may be immutable castes, as in India. This creates special problems for visitors in India: European visitors are relatively rich and clean, and so appear to be of high caste, but also eat meat even with the left hand and drink alcohol like untouchables, so a special visitor caste, of *videshis*, has been created. However visitors to ashrams who adopt the costume of holy men do not fit this caste and cause great offence to the Indians (Wujastyk, 1980). The horizontal divisions between different tribes or classes are also of great importance. In Africa it may be necessary to make up work groups from members of the same tribe, and it would be disastrous to appoint a leader from another tribe. Similar clan divisions are of course found in Scotland, and also in China (Hsu, 1963). In-group versus out-group distinctions can take varied forms. Studies of helping behaviour have found that fellow-countrymen are usually given more help than visitors, but in Greece tourists are treated like family and friends (Triandis, Vassiliou and Nassiakou, 1968).

Motivation

Several forms of motivation have been found to differ on average between cultures. This means that typical members of another culture are pursuing different goals, and are gratified by different rewards. Sometimes the causes of these motivational differences can be found in other features of a culture. For example, societies which are constantly at war with their neighbours encourage aggressiveness in their young males (Zigler and Child, 1969).

ACHIEVEMENT MOTIVATION

McClelland (1961) found that cultures differed in the level of achievement motivation, as measured by the popularity of children's stories with achievement themes; the high need for achievement (n.Ach) countries had higher rates of economic growth, and this may be due in part to the motivational difference. The U.S.A. over the last century has been high in n.ach; underdeveloped countries have been lower. McClelland and Winter (1969) ran a training course for Indian managers, in which the latter role-played high n.Ach managers. The result was that they increased the size and turnover of their enterprises after attending the course. There is of course a wide range of individual differences within a culture, but it is worth realizing that in some areas individuals are likely to work hard to take risks in order to earn more money, improve their status, and to build up the enterprise in which they work. While in other areas people expect to be rewarded on the basis of the social position of their family or clan, not their own efforts.

ASSERTIVENESS

Assertiveness or dominance *v.* submissiveness, is one of the main dimensions along which social behaviour varies. In the U.S.A. social skills training has concentrated on assertiveness, presumably reflecting a widespread approval of and desire to acquire assertive behaviour. This interest in assertiveness is strong among American women, as part of the women's movement. It has also been suggested that the absence of universally accepted rules makes it necessary to stand up for your rights rather frequently.

Americans are perceived as assertive in other parts of the world. However there are some cultures, e.g. China and parts of Indonesia, where assertiveness is not valued, and submissiveness and the maintenance of pleasant social relations are valued more (Noesjirwan, 1978). In Britain candidates for social skills training are more interested in making friends. Furnham (1979) found that European white nurses in South Africa were the most assertive, followed by Africans and Indians.

EXTRAVERSION

Surveys using extraversion questionnaires show that Americans and Canadians are more extraverted than the British (e.g. Eysenck and Eysenck, 1969). What exactly this means in terms of social behaviour is rather unclear. It is commonly observed that Americans are good at the early stages of a relationship, where the British can be shy and awkward. In the U.S.A. the peer group plays an important part in the life of children and adolescents; and among adults great value is placed on informal relationships (Riesman, Glazer and Denney, 1955).

In the East great value is placed on maintaining good social relationships, so that assertiveness and disagreement are avoided, or at least confined to members of the same family, clan or group.

FACE

It is well known that in Japan, and to a lesser extent other parts of the Far East, maintaining face is of great importance. Special skills are required to make sure that others do not lose face. Foa, Mitchell and Lekhyananda (1969) found that students from the Far East who experienced failure in an experimental task withdrew from the source of the failure message. In negotiations it may be necessary to make token concessions before the other side can give way. Great care must be taken at meetings over disagreeing or criticizing, and competitive situations should be avoided.

VALUES

These are broader, more abstract goals, the general states of affairs which are regarded as desirable. Triandis, Malpass and Davidson (1972) studied twenty values by asking for the antecedents and consequences of eleven concepts. In parts of India they found that status and glory were valued most, whilst wealth was not valued (being associated with arrogance and fear of thieves), nor was courage or power. The Greeks valued punishment (which was associated with justice) and power. The Japanese valued serenity and aesthetic satisfaction, and disvalued ignorance, deviation and loneliness. Szalay and Maday (cited by Triandis, Malpass and Davidson, 1972) found that Americans rated *love* and *friendship* as their most important life concerns, *health* as 5th: Koreans ranked these values as 12th, 14th and 19th. Triandis (1971) found that "work" was regarded as a good thing in moderately difficult environments where economic development was rapid, but it was rated less favourably in easy or difficult environments.

Concepts and ideology

Certain aspects of life in another culture may be incomprehensible without an understanding of the underlying ideas. Some of these ideas are carried by language, and knowing a language deepens understanding of the culture. The words in a language reflect and provide labels for the cognitive categories used in the culture to divide up the world. The colour spectrum is divided up in different ways, and the colour words reflect this in different cultures (Berlin and Kay, 1969).

The same is true of every other aspect of the physical and social world, so that knowledge of the language provides knowledge of the culture. Translation of words may lead to changes of emotional association — the Australian word "Pom" doesn't only mean "British immigrant" but has negative and joking associations as well. Words in one language and culture may have complex meanings which are difficult to translate, as with the Israeli Chutzpah (= "outrageous cheek", such as exporting tulips to Holland), Russian *v.* Western concepts of "freedom" and "democracy", and the Japanese concept of the Oyabum—Koyum relationship.

There may be misunderstanding due to differences in thinking. Sharma (1971) notes how western observers have criticized Indian peasants for their passivity and general lack of the "Protestant ethic", despite having produced a great increase in productivity by adapting to the Green Revolution. African languages are often short of words for geometrical shapes, so that it is difficult to communicate about spatial problems. Some words or ideas may be taboo, e.g. discussion of family planning (Awa, 1979).

Some of the differences in rules which were discussed above can be explained in terms of the ideas behind them, as in the cases of "bribery" and "nepotism". Attitudes to business practices are greatly affected by ideas and ideology. Marxists will not discuss "profits"; Moslems used to regard "interest" as sinful. Surprisingly the stricter forms of Protestantism have been most compatible with capitalism and gave rise to the "Protestant ethic" (Argyle, 1972).

Training methods

Language learning

There are many cultures where visitors, especially short-term visitors, can get by quite well without learning the language. On the other hand this probably means that they are cut off from communicating with the majority of the native population, and that they do not come to understand fully those features of the culture which are conveyed by language. Language learning can be greatly assisted by the use of a language laboratory, and by textbooks like Leech and Svartlik's *A Communicative Grammar of English,* which provide detailed information on the everyday informal use of language.

Use of educational methods

Despite the use of more active methods of S.S.T. in other areas, for I.C.C. reading and lectures are currently the most widely used methods. The most sophisticated approach here has been the development of Culture Assimilators. Critical-incident surveys have been carried out on occasions when Americans have got into difficulty in Thailand, Greece, etc., and a standard set of difficult episodes has been written, for example:

One day a Thai administrator of middle academic rank kept two of his assistants about an hour from an appointment. The assistants, although very angry, did not show it while they waited. When the administrator walked in at last, he acted as if he were not late. He made no apology or explanation. After he was settled in his office, he called his assistants in and they all began working on the business for which the administrator had set the meeting. (Brislin and Pedersen (1976) pp. 90–1).

Several explanations were offered, of which the correct one is:

In Thailand, subordinates are required to be polite to their superiors, no matter what happens, nor what their rank may be. (*ibid*., p. 92)

and further information is added.

These episodes are put together in a tutor-text, which students work through by themselves (Fiedler *et al*., 1971).

There have been a number of follow-up studies of the use of culture assimilators, showing modest improvements in handling mixed cultural groups in laboratory settings, and in one case in a field setting. However not very much field assessment has been done, the effects of training have not been very striking, and the subjects used have all been of high motivation and intelligence (Brislin and Pedersen, 1976).

A similar method is the use of case studies. These are widely used for management training in international firms, the cases being based on typical managerial problems in the other culture. They play an important part in 2-week courses, using educational methods. It is common to include wives and children in such courses, with special materials for them too (DiStephano, 1979).

Educational methods can probably make a valuable contribution to cross-cultural training, since there is always a lot to learn about another culture. However, as with other skills, it is necessary to combine such intellectual learning with actual practice of the skills involved.

Role-playing

Several types of role-playing have been used for I.C.C., though it has not been the usual form of training. One approach is to train people in laboratory situations in the skills or modes of communication of a second culture, using videotape playback. Collett (1971) trained Englishmen in the non-verbal communication styles of Arabs, and found that those trained in this way were liked better by Arabs than were members of a control group.

The American Peace Corps has used simulation techniques to train their members. Trainees have been sent to work on an American Indian reservation, for example. Area simulation sites were constructed to train members for different locations e.g., one in Hawaii for Southeast Asia volunteers, complete with water buffaloes. However it is reported that these rather expensive procedures have not been very successful, and they have been replaced by training in the second culture itself (Brislin and Pedersen, 1976).

Interaction with members of the other culture

In the Intercultural Communication workshop trainees go through a number of exercises with members of the other culture, and use is made of role-playing and the study of critical incidents (Alther, 1975). This looks like a very powerful method, but no follow-up results are available. At Farnham Castle in Britain the training courses include meetings with members of the other culture, and with recently returned expatriates.

When people arrive in a new culture they are frequently helped both by native members of the culture, and by expatriates. Bochner, McLeod and Lin (1977) found that foreign students in Hawaii usually had friends of both kinds, who could help them in different ways.

Combined approaches

We have seen that each of the methods described has some merits, and it seems very likely that a combination of methods would be the most effective. This might include some language instruction, learning about the other culture, role-playing, and interaction with native members of the culture. Gudykunst, Hammer and Wiseman (1977) used a combination of several methods, though not including any language teaching, in a 3-day course, and found that this led to higher reported levels of satisfaction for Naval personnel posted to Japan.

Guthrie (1966) describes one of the training schemes used for the Peace Corps, for those going to the Philippines. The training included: (1) basic linguistics, so that trainees could pick up local dialects quickly; later this was replaced by teaching specific dialects; (2) lectures by experts on different aspects of the Philippines culture; (3) physical and survival training at the Puerto Rican jungle camp; as noted earlier this was later replaced by training in the culture itself.

Conclusions

A very large number of people go abroad to work in other cultures; some of them fail to complete their mission and others are ineffective, because of difficulties of inter-cultural communication.

Difficulties of social interaction and communication arise in several main areas: (1) language, including forms of polite usage; (2) non-verbal communication: uses of facial expression, gesture, proximity, touch etc.; (3) rules of social situations, e.g., for bribing, gifts and eating; (4) social relationships, within the family, at work, between members of different groups; (5) motivation, e.g., achievement motivation and for face-saving; (6) concepts and ideology, e.g., ideas derived from religion and politics.

Several kinds of training for I.C.C. have been found to be successful, especially in combination. These include language-learning, educational methods, role-playing and interaction with members of the other culture.

References

ALTHER, G. L. (1975) Human relations training and foreign students, *Readings in inter-cultural communication*, vol. 1 (Edited by HOOPES, D.). Intercultural Communications Network of the Regional Council for International Education, Pittsburgh.

ARGYLE, M. (1972) *The Social Psychology of Work*. Penguin Books, Harmondsworth.

ARGYLE, M. (1975) *Bodily Communication*. Methuen, London.

ARGYLE, M. and COOK, M. (1976) *Gaze and Mutual Gaze*. Cambridge University Press, Cambridge.

ARGYLE, M., SHIMODA, K. and LITTLE, B. (1978) Variance due to persons and situations in England and Japan. *British Journal of Social and Clinical Psychology*, 17, 335—7.

AWA, N. E. (1979) Ethnocentric bias in developmental research, *Handbook of Intercultural Communication* (Edited by ASANTE, M. K., NEWMARK, E. and BLAKE, C. A.). Sage, Beverly Hills.

BERLIN, B. and Kay, P. (1969) *Basic Color Terms*. University of California Press, Berkeley, Calif.

BOCHNER, S., MCLEOD, B. M. and LIN, A. (1977) Friendship patterns of overseas students: a functional model. *International Journal of Psychology*, 12, 277—94.

BREIN, M. and DAVID, K. H. (1971) Intercultural communication and the adjustment of the sojourner. *Psychological Bulletin*, 76, 215—30.

BRISLIN, R. W. and PEDERSEN, P. (1976) *Cross-cultural Orientation Programs*. Gardner Press, New York.

CHAN, J. (1979) *The facial expressions of Chinese and Americans*. Unpublished Ph.D. thesis, South Eastern University, Louisiana.

CHEMERS, M. M., FIEDLER, F. E., LEKHYANANDA, D., and STOLUROW, L. M. (1966) Some effects of cultural training on leadership in heterocultural task groups. *International Journal of Psychology*, 1, 301—14.

CLEVELAND, H., MANGONE, G. J. and ADAMS, J. G. (1960) *The Overseas Americans*. McGraw-Hill, New York.

COLLETT, P. (1971) On training Englishmen in the non-verbal behaviour of Arabs: an experiment in intercultural communication. *International Journal of Psychology*, 6, 209—15.

DAWSON, J., WHITNEY, R. E. and LAN, R. T. S. (1971) Scaling Chinese traditional—modern attitudes and the GSR measurement of "important" versus "unimportant" Chinese concepts. *Journal of Cross-Cultural Psychology*, 2, 1—27.

DISTEPHANO, J. J. (1979) Case methods in international management training, *Handbook of Intercultural Communication* (Edited by ASANTE, M. K., NEWMARK, E. and BLAKE, C. A.). Sage, Beverly Hills.

EKMAN, P., FRIESEN, W. V. and ELLSWORTH, P. (1972) *Emotion in the Human Face: Guidelines for Research and a Review of Findings*. Pergamon Press, New York.

ERICKSON, F. (1976) Talking down and giving reasons: hyper-explanation and listening behavior in inter-social situations. Paper presented at the Ontario Institute for the Study of Education Conference, Toronto.

EYSENCK, H. J. and EYSENCK, S. B. G. (1969) *Personality Structure and Measurement*. Routledge & Kegan Paul, London.

FIEDLER, F. E., MITCHELL, R. and TRIANDIS, H. C. (1971) The culture assimilator: an approach to cross-cultural training. *Journal of Applied Psychology*, 55, 95—102.

FOA, U. and CHEMERS, M. (1967) The significance of role behavior differentiation for cross-cultural interaction training. *International Journal of Psychology*, 2, 45—57.

FOA, U. G., MITCHELL, T. R. and LEKHYANANDA, D. (1969) Cultural differences in reaction to failure. *International Journal of Psychology*, 4, 21—6.

FURNHAM, A. (1979) Assertiveness in three cultures: multidimensionality and cultural differences. *Journal of Clinical Psychology*, 35, 522—7.

GILES, H. and POWESLAND, P. F. (1975) *Speech style and social evaluation*. Academic Press, London.

GOODY, E. N. (1978) Towards a theory of questions, *Questions and Politeness* (Edited by GOODY, E. N.). Cambridge University Press, Cambridge.

GOODY, J. (1976) *Production and Reproduction.* Cambridge University Press, Cambridge.

GRAHAM, J. A. and ARGYLE, M. (1975) A cross-cultural study of the communication of extra-verbal meaning by gestures. *International Journal of Psychology,* **10,** 57–67.

GUDYKUNST, W. B., HAMMER, M. R. and WISEMAN, R. L. (1977) An analysis of an integrated approach to cross-cultural training *International Journal of Intercultural Relations,* **1,** 99–110.

GULLAHORN, J. E. and GULLAHORN, J. T. (1966) American students abroad: professional versus personal development. *The Annals of the American Academy of Political and Social Science,* **368,** 43–59.

GUTHRIE, G. M. (1966) Cultural preparation for the Philippines, *Cultural Frontiers of the Peace Corps* (Edited by TEXTOR, R. B.). M.I.T. Press, Cambridge, Mass.

HAMMER, M. R., GUDYKUNST, W. B. and WISEMAN, R. L. (1978) Dimensions of intercultural effectiveness: an exploratory study. *International Journal of Intercultural Relations,* **2,** 382–93.

HEWES, G. (1957) The anthropology of posture. *Scientific American,* **196,** 123–32.

HSU, F. L. K. (1963) *Caste, Clan and Club.* Van Nostrand, Princeton, N.J.

INKELES, A. (1969) Making men modern: on the causes and consequences of individual change in six developing countries. *American Journal of Sociology,* **75,** 208–25.

KROUT, M. H. (1942) *Introduction to Social Psychology.* Harper & Row, New York.

LEECH, G. and SVARTLIK, J. (1975) *A Communicative Grammar of English.* Longman, London.

MANN, L. (1980) Cross cultural studies of small groups, *Handbook of Cross-cultural Psychology,* vol. 5 (Edited by TRIANDIS, H.). Allyn & Bacon, Boston.

MCCLELLAND, D. C. (1961) *The Achieving Society.* Van Nostrand, Princeton, N.J.

MCCLELLAND, D. C. and WINTER, D. G. (1969) *Motivating Economic Achievement.* Free Press, New York.

MELIKIAN, L. H. (1959) Authoritarianism and its correlation in the Egyptian culture and in the United States. *Journal of Social Issues,* **15** (3), 58–68.

MORRIS, D., COLLETT, P., MARSH, P. and O'SHAUGHNESSY, M. (1979) *Gestures: Their Origins and Distribution.* Cape, London.

MORSBACH, H. (1977) The psychological importance of ritualized gift exchange in modern Japan. *Annals of the New York Academy of Sciences,* **293,** 98–113.

MURDOCH, G. P. (1949) *Social Structure.* Macmillan, New York.

NOESJIRWAN, J. (1978) A rule-based analysis of cultural differences in social behaviour: Indonesia and Australia. *International Journal of Psychology,* **13,** 305–16.

OBERG, K. (1960) Cultural shock: adjustment to new cultural environments. *Practical Anthropology,* **7,** 177–82.

O'BRIEN, G. E. and PLOOIJ, D. (1977) Development of culture training manuals for medical workers with Pitjantjatjara Aboriginals. *Journal of Applied Psychology,* **62,** 499–505.

RIESMAN, D., GLAZER, N. and DENNEY, R. (1955) *The Lonely Crowd: A Study of the Changing American Character.* Doubleday, New York.

ROBERTS, G. O. (1979) Terramedian value systems and their significance, *Handbook of Intercultural Communication* (Edited by ASANTE, M. K., NEWMAN, E. and BLAKE, C. A.). Sage, Beverly Hills.

SAITZ, R. L. and CERVENKA, E. J. (1972) *Handbook of Gestures: Colombia and the United States.* Mouton, The Hague.

SEAFORD, H. W. (1975) Facial expression dialect: an example, *Organization of Behavior in Face-to-face Interaction* (Edited by KENDON, A., HARRIS, R. M. and KEY, M. R.). Mouton, The Hague.

SHARMA, H. (1971) Green revolution in India: A prelude to a red one? Unpublished paper (cited by AWA, 1979).

SHIMODA, K., ARGYLE, M. and RICCI BITTI, P. (1978) The intercultural recognition of emotional expressions by three national groups – English, Italian and Japanese. *European Journal of Social Psychology,* **8,** 169–79.

TAFT, R. (1977) Coping with unfamiliar cultures, *Studies in Cross-cultural Psychology,* vol. 1 (Edited by WARREN, N.) Academic Press, London.

TAYLOR, D. M. and SIMARD, L. M. (1975) Social interaction in a bilingual setting. *Canadian Psychological Review*, **16**, 240–54.

TRIANDIS, H. (1971) Work and leisure in cross-cultural perspective, *Theories of Cognitive Consistency: A Sourcebook* (Edited by ABELSON, R. P. *et al.*). Rand McNally, Chicago.

TRIANDIS, H. (1972) *The Analysis of Subjective Culture*. Wiley, New York.

TRIANDIS, H., MALPASS, R. S. and DAVIDSON, A. R. (1972) Cross-cultural psychology. *Biennial Review of Anthropology*, **24**, 1–84.

TRIANDIS, H. C., VASSILIOU, V. and NASSIAKOU, M. (1968) Three cross-cultural studies of subjective culture. *Journal of Personality and Social Psychology*, **8**, (Monograph Supplement), Part 2, pp. 1–42.

TZENG, O. C. S. and LANDIS, D. (1979) A multidimensional scaling methodology for cross-cultural research in communication, *Handbook of Intercultural Communication* (Edited by ASANTE, M. K., NEWMARK, E. and BLAKE, C. A.). Sage, Beverly Hills.

WATSON, O. M. (1970) *Proxemic Behavior: A Cross-cultural Study*. Mouton, The Hague.

WATSON, O. M. and GRAVES, T. D. (1966 Quantitative research in proxemic behavior. *American Anthropologist*, **68**, 971–85.

WUJASTYK, D. (1980) Causing a scandal in Poona. *The Times* (London), 24 April, p. 14.

ZIGLER, E. and CHILD, I. L. (1969) Socialization, *The Handbook of Social Psychology*, vol. 3 (Edited by LINDZEY, G. and ARONSON, E.). Addison–Wesley, Reading, Mass.

4

Meetings and misunderstandings

PETER COLLETT

WHEN CAPTAIN COOK arrived in the New Hebrides in 1771 he was greeted by a group of natives who came down to the beach and invited his crew ashore. They offered to haul the ship's boat through the surf. They then made signs for the boat to go round to a bay and finally directed the Englishmen round a rocky peninsula to a secure landing point. Cook tells us that when he came ashore he asked by signs for fresh water. The chief quickly dispatched one of his subjects to a hut and the man soon returned with a bamboo containing water. "I next asked, by the same means, for something to eat, and they as readily brought me a yam and some cocoa-nuts." Cook also reported that he was able to persuade the natives to lay down their weapons, that they informed him that they were cannibals and enquired whether he shared their taste for human flesh. All these transactions were effected by the use of pantomime. Although Cook is not explicit about the exact nature of the signs that he employed we can be sure, because his requests were satisfied, that the natives grasped his meanings.

The case of Captain Cook and the New Hebrideans was by no means an isolated incident. The narratives of foreign voyagers are full of accounts of pantomime communication between people who spoke different languages and who were able nevertheless to devise a *mano franca* for their immediate purposes. The first instance of gestural communication that we have on record is to be found in Xenophon's *The March up Country*, in which he relates how, during the retreat of the Ten Thousand Greeks across Asia Minor about 400 B.C., they reached Cheirosophos and there made signs to some Armenian boys as if they were deaf and dumb to show what they wanted.

When Columbus set sail from Lisbon in 1490 in search of a western route to the Indies, he took an Arabic-speaking baptized Jew with him as an interpreter, as he knew that Arab merchants traded in the realm of the Great Khan of Cathay. As his passage to the east was obstructed by the Americas, the presence of an Arabic speaker proved to be in vain, and he and his crew had to resort to manual communication when they arrived in the Bahamas. Other voyagers, such as Vasco da Gama, who followed in the search for a passage to the Indies, were similarly constrained by the absence of a common language with those whom they met on their way, and like Drake, Frobisher, Cortez, Pizarro, and the countless mariners and explorers who took part in the epic Voyages of Discovery, they were invariably reduced to using their hands and faces in order to make themselves understood.[1] *

The use of pantomime often serves the traveller well, but there are numerous cases which report failure of the medium, and no doubt there were even more which went unnoticed. Communications involving requests can easily be assessed simply by examining their consequences. Asking for water and receiving it, or making a sexual overture and being rebuffed (another case offered by the literature) is far less ambiguous than reference or naming, although even here one finds that travellers were able to construct rudimentary and reliable dictionaries of the local tongues simply by pointing at objects.

There are numerous reports of contact with indigenous populations which, unfortunately, need to be taken with a pinch of salt. So when, for example, Francis Drake writes that a local chief made himself a vassal of the Queen of England, merely by using signs, or when the Jesuit missionaries returned from America to tell how they had converted the locals by preaching the Gospel with hand signs, we have no alternative but to assume that a process of legitimation rather then manual communication was at work.

By using the hands, eyes and face, travellers have been able to make their intentions and desires understood to people who inhabit an otherwise totally alien world. True, there are cases where they have been unable to comprehend each other, and although these may be more then we wish to concede, the fact remains that widely diverse and hitherto unrelated peoples have been able to communicate without the advantage of speech. The hands are often reckoned to be the deaf man's friend, but in the absence of a shared language they are also a reliable interpreter. One might imagine, with the advent of the standard dictionary and the acculturation of most of the world's population, that the hands would have reached a point of premature retirement from their long occupation in the service of understanding. But this is not so, and those who watched the final instalment of Attenborough's television programme, *Life on Earth,* will have appreciated that manual and facial signing are still the only vehicle available to the anthropologist who encounters a new people. If you saw the programme you will have witnessed a remarkable meeting between an Australian official and a group of New Guineans who had never met Westerners before. What was striking about the encounter was its timelessness. The official, being ignorant of the natives' language, is forced to greet them non-verbally. He utters some words and they reciprocate in kind, but both parties seem perfectly aware that what they are saying is far less important than what they are doing. At one point the official indicates that he wants the natives to go back to their

*Superscript numbers refer to Notes at end of chapter.

village and collect other members of their community. They disappear into the forest and emerge soon afterwards with their fellows.[2]

We find in this unassuming incident a tiny cameo of what has been happening for centuries. However, in this instance the official is a representative of a powerful modern state. But for all that this gives him he may as well live in another New Guinean village. Because he does not speak the language of his hosts he is forced to make strange noises, contort his face and wave his arms about in order to make himself understood to a group of individuals who inhabit a world that his own ancestors did more than 4000 years ago.

Nothing illustrates the psychic unity of mankind and its innate capacity for intersubjectivity more dramatically than the mutual comprehension that the body affords. The hands, as we have seen, occupy a central role in the process of constructing mutual intelligibility between total strangers, but even though this is often so, it is not always the case that hand movements are understood by members of different communities. In fact there are innumerable instances where they give rise to serious misunderstandings. In order to see why some signs underline and others undermine understanding it will be necessary to introduce a few distinctions.

Broadly speaking there are three categories of expressive hand movements. The first, certainly in terms of the phylogenesis of gesture, is what we might call the *mimic signals*. Here the gesturer attempts to mimic the object or activity being referred to. He may scratch the ground in order to refer to a bull, run a finger across his throat to signal death, or clench a fist to indicate his anger. Mimic gestures bear an iconic relationship to their meanings, but *symbolic gestures,* or what Efron (1941) called *emblems*, bear an arbitrary relationship to their meanings. Emblems have the character of items in language, in that they possess no obvious connection between the action that is performed and the meaning that is intended. Just as one common meaning can be manifested in quite distinct vocal articulations in different languages, so too that same meaning can be represented in quite distinct motor articulations in different repertoires of emblems. The third and final category of gestures is what Efron called *batons*, those manual movements that orchestrate or beat time to the spoken word. While mimic gestures and emblems can be used independently or in concert with speech, it is in the general nature of batons that they can only be deployed as a means of assisting and emphasizing speech.

Although the evidence is not as explicit as we might have wished, it seems fair to assume that most of the manual signs employed by ancient mariners and explorers were of the mimic kind. When the Spaniard Don Diego de Prado landed near Orangerie Bay in present-day Papua, he showed the natives that he wished to drink by "putting the hand in the mouth" and that he wanted fire "by blowing with the mouth". The Arctic explorer, Frobisher tells us that as a group of Eskimos were about to leave him they pointed at the sun and raised three fingers to show when they would return. The fact that Don Diego received water and a fire brand, and the fact that Frobisher's Eskimos returned three days later testifies to the power of mimic gestures. Because mimic gestures bear an obvious, although not a necessary relationship to what is being signified, they are more widely employed and more widely understood. This is not to suggest that all mimic gestures have the same shape, for even the simple act of miming drinking can be, and in fact is, performed variously throughout the world. For example, within Europe we find that the gesture which mimes glass-holding is used in the north, while the gesture in which the thumb mimics the neck of a bottle is employed in the south. But the important point about mimic gestures is that their morphology is constrained by the activity or object that they are designed to copy or represent, and for this reason, even if they differ, they are more likely to be understood by people who use somewhat different gestures.

Emblems on the other hand have become detached from the process that gave them birth. While mimic gestures possess a direct relationship to their meaning, the relationship between the meaning and the morphology of an emblem is at one removed. Take the simple case of the vertical "horns" sign, which is used throughout the Mediterranean as a manual imputation of cuckoldry. By extending the first and last finger from a clenched fist one suggests, in effect, that someone is being cheated by his wife. Now the imagery of this gesture relies on its connection with the horns of an animal, although which animal we are not quite sure. The gesture refers to a pair of horns and *through this* to the characteristic of cuckoldry associated with a particular horned animal. The point about emblems is that, like words, they do not carry their etymologies around on their backs, and that is why their origins are extremely difficult to determine. Not only does this thwart the student of manual signals and confound his speculations but, more importantly, it means that the meaning of an emblem cannot automatically be recovered by inspecting its shape. Within a cross-cultural context we find therefore that although they are capable of variation, mimic gestures are more readily understood, even by those to whom they are totally alien. Emblems, on the other hand, are notoriously difficult to understand, and they can give rise to serious misunderstandings when people from different societies meet. The difference between mimic gestures and emblems can be understood in terms of the underlying structure of their semantics. Mimic gestures possess a simple association of reference, while emblems have an arbitrary link grafted on to a simple association. This distinction, incidentally, finds its linguistic parallel in the difference between onomatopoeic and arbitrary vocalizations.

The emblems found in one society are, for the most part, not shared with those in other societies. This general rule, which derives from the arbitrariness of the semantic relations in emblems, has two interesting exceptions. The first is the obvious case produced by diffusion, where one society borrows a sign and its associated meaning from another and accepts it as its own. The second case occurs where two societies happen on the same gesture but use it in the service of quite different meanings. There are several interesting cases of this second type within Europe.

Throughout most of western Europe, not to mention the Americas, a raised thumb is used as a signal of approval or approbation. But there are countries, most notably Greece, where this self-same gesture is employed as an insult. Among the Greeks it is often associated with the expression, "Katsa pano" or "sit on this!". And even when it is performed silently its meaning is perfectly understood. For the Greeks it contains none of the positive connotations that surround its use in our society, but instead it is used as a vulgar taunt. Another insulting gesture employed by the Greeks is the *Moutza*. This sign is peculiar to the Greeks and consists in splaying the fingers and thumb of the hand and pushing it towards one's adversary. It can also be done with both hands, and a comic version of the gesture is sometimes performed by presenting the soles of both feet as well, thereby producing a four-fold insult and a highly precarious state of affairs for the gesturer. The Moutza is an ancient sign, the origin of which can be found in the old Byzantine practice of parading chained criminals through the town while the local populace collected dirt and refuse from the streets and thrust it into their faces. This practice is now happily extinct, but having shed its origins, the gesture still lives on as a highly emotive insult. The peculiar shape of the Moutza renders it liable to misunderstanding. For most foreigners it appears to be a fairly innocuous, if not neutral sign, and the fact that it offers no obvious clues to its distasteful nature means that it can readily be mistaken as intending a meaning that would otherwise be associated with five digits. This did in fact happen a few years ago when Nottingham Forest football club played a team in Athens. The sports correspondent for the *Observer* reported that young Greek fans approached the English players and indicated what they expected the likely score to be — five nil! Had he been aware of this gesture he would have realized that it was intended as a taunt and not some adolescent prognostication. A Greek reporter in England might of course make a similar mistake. The most common manual insult used by the English involves thrusting the hand upwards with the palm facing backwards and the first and second fingers splayed to form a "V". One can readily imagine a Greek reporter filing a story back to Athens saying that the English fans expected their team to win by a margin of two goals! It is all too easy to pour scorn on our two reporters, but in the absence of information to the contrary they would have no option but to assume that the gestures they witnessed conveyed the same meanings as those with which they were personally acquainted — unless of course there was some contextual indication to the contrary. But let us return to the question of context and its role in the interpretation of gestures in a moment.

We have shown, very briefly, that two societies can employ the self-same gesture in the service of totally different communicative ends, in other words that we can have a shared gesture with unshared meanings. This general case may be formally represented as follows, where the gesture, G, has meaning M in one

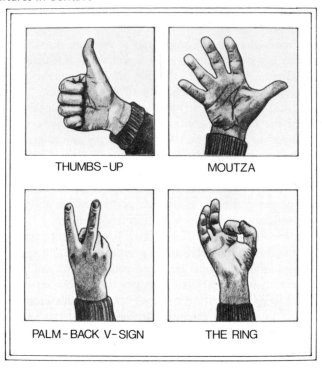

THUMBS-UP   MOUTZA

PALM-BACK V-SIGN   THE RING

FIG. 3. Emblematic gestures.

society and meaning M^1 in the other, and where M is not the same as M^1.

$$\text{Society 1:} \quad G \rightarrow M$$
$$\text{Society 2:} \quad G \rightarrow M^1$$
$$M \neq M^1$$

The question now arises as to what will happen when a member of one society uses such a gesture in the presence of members of the other society. We are inclined to assume that the members of each society will draw their usual conclusions; that those, for example, who use the gesture as an insult will interpret it as such whoever performs it. But as it happens the obvious outcome is only one among many. Let us consider the full range of possible outcomes, and attempt, where possible, to explore the circumstances under which each will occur.

When we have a state of affairs in which two societies attach different meanings to the same gesture, then its use by a member of one society in the presence of members of the other may lead to misunderstanding. Misunderstandings have a simple property of mismatch between intended and inferred meanings, and they will tend to occur when there are no reasonable grounds for the recipient to

FIG. 4. Winston Churchill with a group of Greeks in 1949. The Greek in the centre is producing a palm-back V-sign rather than the Churchillian palm-front gesture, and he is therefore unknowingly insulting Churchill. All things being equal a Greek is unlikely to produce a palm-front V-sign because this gesture serves as an abbreviated form of the Moutza, which is the national manual insult of the Greeks. (Reproduced by kind permission of Popperfoto)

draw an alternative conclusion. When our English reporter was treated to a flurry of Moutzas, he took the outstretched digits to signify a predicted score because there was in effect no other inference he needed to draw within that setting. Structurally, we may for the moment represent that process of encoding and decoding as shown in Block A. This diagram captures the essentials of the case of

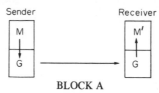

BLOCK A

the Greek fans and the English reporter, and at first glance it appears to offer a reasonable representation of how a misunderstanding could arise when a shared gesture with unshared meanings is employed interculturally. But the diagram ignores two important aspects of the case, namely the respective affective values of the encoded and decoded meanings, and the inferred value of the action sequence within which the gesture is embedded. As a rule we could say that when the gesture in question has a positive or neutral value for the receiver he will be most likely to settle for his initial inference, but that when the gesture is embedded within a sequence which he imputes with a negative value he will be more likely to review his initial impression. On the other hand, when the gesture has a negative value for the receiver he will be more likely to give the sender the benefit of the doubt and merely to put it down to his ignorance of local custom, unless of course it is located in what he takes to be a negative sequence, in which case he is more likely to take it at face value. The interpretation of other people's gestural intentions is by no means a mechanical affair, and the fact that the foreigner inadvertently insults the local is not always taken as grounds for objection. In fact the foreigner is usually given some kind of dispensation on account of his assumed ignorance. Georg Simmel (1950) had some interesting things to say about the special status of the stranger in society. He made the point that conventions governing the indigenous population are often relaxed, if not waived, where the foreigner is concerned. However he neglected to point out that although the locals may be prepared to make allowances for the foreigner's ignorance, they may nevertheless hold quite fixed ideas and prejudices about such ignorance. In other words a Frenchman travelling through England could quite easily get away with ordering two drinks with a palm-back V-sign, but he might still receive the scorn that comes from being uninformed about English customs.

Apart from those instances where shared gestures with unshared meanings lead to unintended misunderstanding, and those where mitigating factors are brought into play, there is another class of outcome which needs to be considered. This involves the perceptual distortion of gesture, and is best illustrated by the case of the ring sign in France.

The ring sign is performed by bringing the tips of the thumb and the index finger together so that they form a circle. For most of us this gesture signifies that everything is in order. We often associate it with the expression "O.K.", and have done so to a point where it has become known as "The O.K. gesture". Now the meaning that we attach to the ring is the same as that applied to it by most Frenchmen who live in the north and by some who live in the south of France. For the remainder the ring means zero or worthless. What we have here are two meanings which draw their symbolism from different morphological features of the same sign – the O.K. meaning, relying on the precision grip of the thumb and first finger, and the zero meaning, drawing on the circular shape which is formed by bringing these digits together. We would have an extremely simple story if all Frenchmen knew and employed the gesture for both meanings or if those who used it for one were at least aware of the competing meaning. But this, it has been discovered, is not always so. A large selection of the population employs the gesture for one meaning while remaining totally ignorant of its alternative meaning (see Morris *et al.*, 1979).

This peculiar state of affairs can be explained by reference to several defining features of the ring gesture in France. Firstly, it occupies second place to the thumbs up gesture as a means of conveying approval, and for this reason its Gallic ambiguity is less likely to attract the attention of those who use it. Secondly, it is characteristically employed in conjunction with speech and therefore liable to be overlooked as a mere adjunct to the spoken word. Thirdly, it has the morphology of what is otherwise a perfectly good baton gesture, which means that it can readily be mistaken as a means of emphasizing speech rather than vice-versa. These three features of the ring sign – its non-salience, its temporal contiguity with speech and its similarity to a baton – provide the necessary conditions whereby it can be mistaken for a simple baton. We have, in other words, a case of *emblem-blindness*, one in which the emblem is, as it were, perceptually transformed into a baton, or batonized, and therefore not noticed as being a distinct unit with a meaning other than the one which the receiver uses personally. It appears that Frenchmen who use the zero meaning see users of the O.K. meaning as employing an emphatic device just as those who use the O.K. meaning see users of the zero meaning as doing likewise. In this illustration we find a ready case of a shared gesture with unshared meaning, but one which, but virtue of its properties, cannot give rise to misunderstandings nor, for that matter, to a process whereby receivers look for mitigating factors to explain senders' actions. Diagrammatically this may be represented as shown in Block B.

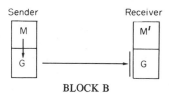

BLOCK B

Throughout our discussion we have been concerned with cases where misunderstanding and attempts at mitigation arise because societies attach different meanings to the same gesture. There is however a special class of case where these same outcomes can occur with similar but unshared gestures and unshared meanings. These derive from what we might call a process of *perceptual approximation*. If we were to devise a metric for the description of any one gesture we would probably find that its various instantiations show a strongly peaked distribution or distributions around a point or points that could be regarded as the most representative form of forms of the gesture. But while most gestures possess a typical tempo and amplitude; that is, while we are quite fussy about how we produce our gestures, we are less exact in our identification of them. We are usually more ready to accept someone else's performance of a gesture as being of a certain type than we would be in our performance of that gesture, and as a consequence a quite different gesture performed by a member of another group may be construed as one in our own repertoire to which it bears the closest resemblance or approximation. Among the Italians for example, a flick of the ear lobe will denote homosexuality, while for the Portuguese a clasp of the ear lobe is used as a sign of approval. The Italians do not possess an ear-clasp nor do the Portuguese have an ear-flick gesture, but when one of these nationals performs his own gesture in the presence of the other there is a strong likelihood that under certain circumstances it will be perceived as having the morphology of his own gesture. The relationship between the gestures and the meanings in the two societies can be represented as follows:

$$
\begin{aligned}
\text{Society 1:} &\quad G \rightarrow M \\
\text{Society 2:} &\quad G^1 \rightarrow M^1 \\
\text{where} &\quad G \simeq G^1 \\
\text{and} &\quad M \neq M^1
\end{aligned}
$$

and the process of misunderstanding that can develop can be indicated as shown in Block C. The process of perceptual approximation can arise because the

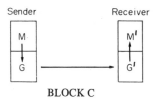

BLOCK C

latitude of acceptance for decoding gestures is greater than the corresponding latitude of acceptance in their production. This process is further aggravated by the absence of gestures which compete for a related sector of the gestural space. Quite simply, individuals in a society which has both an ear-flick and an ear-clasp would possess more precise criteria for the identification of each, and they would therefore make fewer perceptual mistakes than either the Italians or the Portuguese.

In Morris' (1957) important paper on "typical intensity" he makes the point that every signal has a distribution about a central tendency which is the typical intensity of that signal. For example, in our society there are probably two typical intensities for hand-clapping — a relatively fast clap which is used to applaud, and a relatively slow clap which is used to convey a sense of boredom or impatience. Were we to graph instances of these two signals against an axis of clapping tempo we should probably find that their distributions do not overlap and that their typical intensities are therefore quite distinct. Morris' observations can be developed further. The notion of typical intensity relates to the modal pattern in the distribution of instances of a signal as it is produced by individuals who share a code, but not to the modal pattern in the distribution of instances that these same individuals would perceive as that signal. In other words, typical intensity refers to the manner in which a signal is *produced*, not to the manner in which actions are *recognized* as instances of that signal. Now it seems very likely that the typical intensity of a signal's production distribution is much the same as the typical intensity of its recognition distribution, but that the dispersion of the recognition distribution will be greater than the dispersion of its production distribution — in other words, that the members of a community will be more strict in how they produce a signal than in what they admit as instantiations of that signal. Of course it could be suggested that because most of the cases where a signal is produced also involve cases of its being recognized by others, there will be a close correspondence between the production and recognition distributions of that signal. However it is worth noting that this may not necessarily be the case for the simple reason that actions which are not intended as a particular signal (and which therefore fall outside its production distribution) may nevertheless be construed as instances of that signal (see Figure 5).

The central tendency of both the production distribution and the recognition distribution of a signal is likely to be greater when there is another signal in the

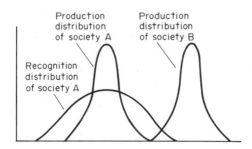

FIG. 5. Schematic representation of production and recognition distributions.

vicinity. In other words, a society which has an applause handclap but no impatience handclap will be able to entertain a more widely dispersed applause handclap distribution than a society which has both types of handclapping. When different societies come into contact several things can happen. We have already noted that when societies have a shared signal with a shared meaning they will, where this signal is concerned, be more likely to understand each other, but that when they have a shared signal with unshared meanings they are more likely to misunderstand each other. But even when two societies do not actually share a signal, their members may nevertheless misunderstand each other. This may happen because the signal which falls within the production distribution of one society falls within the recognition distribution, but not the production distribution, of another society. It is therefore not necessary for societies to have colonized the same tract of motor territory for them to misunderstand each other. It is merely enough that they regard the actions produced by other people as being similar to those produced by themselves.

A rather interesting example of the way in which the same motor territory can be segmented according to several quite different principles is provided by the case of head movements for affirmation and negation. There are, as far as we can tell, three distinct codes for "yes" and "no" in Europe. The first, which we might call the "nod—shake code", involves a movement of the head up and down in the sagittal plane for "yes", and a movement from side to side in the transverse plane for "no". This code is used throughout most of Europe, from the United Kingdom and Portugal on the west to Russia on the east, and Italy and Yugoslavia on the south. In the nod—shake code the nod is initiated with either an upward or a downward movement, while the shake is initiated with either a move to the left or a move to the right.

The next code is the "dip—toss code", where a downward movement of the head in the sagittal plane is used to signal "yes", and an upward movement of the head in the same place is used to signal "no". This code is used in Greece, Turkey and, together with the nod—shake code, in southern Italy and Sicily. In this code the affirmative gesture begins with a downward movement and the gesture of negation begins with an upward movement. Seldom does one find the dip or the toss being repeated. When either is repeated to convey emphasis then it is usually separated by a short period of stasis between the gestural units. In this respect the dip—toss code is quite unlike the nod—shake code, where the repertoire can readily accommodate repetition without stasis between successive units because the gestural units occupy different planes.

The third code is the "roll—toss code", which consists of a roll of the head across the shoulders in the frontal plane for "yes", and an upward movement of the head in the sagittal plane for "no". This code is used in Bulgaria and parts of Yugoslavia. The roll can be initiated with either a movement to the left or a movement to the right, while the toss can only be initiated with an upward movement (see Figure 6).

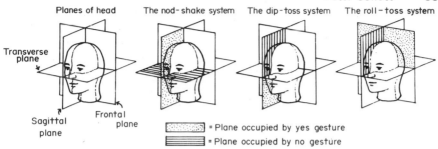

FIG. 6. Systems of affirmation and negation.

The first thing we notice about these three codes is that they have selected different tracts of the motor territory available to the head in which to express affirmation and negation. The nod—shake code has colonized upward and downward movements in the sagittal plane for "yes", and left and right movements in the transverse plane for "no"; the dip—toss code has taken over downward movements in the sagittal plane for "yes" and upward movements in the same plane for "no"; the roll—toss code has adopted left and right movements in the frontal plane for "yes" and upward movements in the sagittal plane for "no". The second point to notice is that certain gestures do not make a distinction with respect to initial direction of movement, while others do. In other words it does not matter whether one begins a head-shake with a movement to the left or a movement to the right, for in both cases the resultant gesture will be understood as meaning "no". However initial direction of movement makes a crucial difference in the dip—toss code, because both items in the code occupy the same plane and are primarily distinguished by initial direction of movement. The fact that some gestures are unconcerned about initial direction of movement, while others rely on it to define their meaning, is rather reminiscent of what happens in language, where different allophones can represent the same phone. For example in the case of English the /l/ sound in words like *leave* and *meal* is phonetically different but not phonemically different. In other words, because they can be distinguished by the linguist, but are rarely distinguished by the average speaker—hearer, they may be regarded as allophones of the same phone. The same kind of thing happens with head movements for "yes" and "no", so that while the trained observer may concern himself with whether a head-shake begins with a move to the left or a move to the right, the average user of the gesture does not. That is, shakes which begin with a movement to the left and those which begin with a move to the right are allokinemes of the same kineme. They may be kinetically or morphologically distinct, but they are kinemically or semantically identical.

The third thing to notice is that what are quite distinct kinemes for one society may simply be allokinemes of the same kineme for another. This is found in the case of movements in the sagittal plane in the nod—shake and dip—toss systems. In the former, upward and downward movements are merely allokinemes of the same kineme, in other words variants of the same gesture, whereas in the latter these movements are distinct kinemes, in other words different gestures. Notice that where gestures for affirmation and negation are concerned, this only happens in the sagittal plane and not in the transverse or frontal planes. This is undoubtedly due to the fact that while we are bilaterally symmetrical about the sagittal plane (our left side looks like our right side), we are asymmetrical about the transverse plane (our top half is unlike our bottom half) and asymmetrical about the frontal plane (our front half is unlike our back half). This means that while the sagittal plane can accommodate different gestures or kinemes, the other two planes cannot do so without placing unnecessary demands on people who use and need to make sense of the gestures.

When members of societies which use codes that overlap come together there is often a serious problem of confusion. The most commonly reported case of misunderstanding arises between users of the nod—shake code and the dip—toss code, specifically in relation to upward movements of the head. In the nod—shake system the gesture of affirmation can be initiated with either an upward or a downward movement, and it may or may not contain emphatic repetition. In the dip—toss code, on the other hand, the toss is almost invariably executed with an upward movement and without repetition. However an important feature of the toss is that it is often accompanied by raised eyebrows, closed or half-closed eyes and/or a click of the tongue. The full compound gesture includes all of these components, while abbreviated forms of the gesture contain one or more of these components. One abbreviated form of the toss consists of a slight raise of the head without raised brows, closed eyes or the click. Morphologically this is remarkably similar to a truncated nod, and that is why so many users of the nod—shake code experience difficulty when confronted with a gesture of negation which looks exactly like a variant of their own gesture of affirmation.[3] This is less of a problem for the nod—shake user in a dip—toss society where the code is used consistently. In these circumstances he will usually be able to learn, although not without some difficulty, that an upward movement only means "no". However if some of his hosts decide to be kind by using his code then his problems are likely to be compounded by the fact that he will be unable to ascertain whether a toss is intended as meaning "yes" or "no". This of course is always the problem for the foreigner who finds himself in a society which attaches a different meaning from his own society to a particular sign, and where the foreigner or a member of the host society accommodates to what he takes to be the needs of the other person.[4]

One final point that should not go unmentioned is that while gestural differences can be a source of misunderstanding between members of different societies, they can also afford an important opportunity for cryptic communication between members of the same society. We are told, for example, that the St

FIG. 7. Captive crewmen of the USS *Pueblo*, an American spy ship captured by the North Koreans. Three of the crewmen are producing the insulting middle-finger gesture (known to the Romans as *digitus impudicus*) to show their contempt for their captors. (Reproduced by kind permission of Associated Press)

Valentine's massacre, during which the inhabitants of Palermo slaughtered the occupying French garrison, was arranged entirely through the gestural argot of the streets. It is no coincidence that several secret societies have grafted their sign of mutual identification on the handshake – the place where it is least likely to be recognized by others. A particularly fascinating case of cryptic signalling occurred when the American spy ship, the *Pueblo*, was captured by the North Koreans in 1968. The captain and his crew were duly persuaded to confess their misdemeanours and their crimes against the People's Republic. Afterwards, to show that they were in good health, the North Koreans photographed the crew and sent the picture to Washington. But the photograph gave the lie to the embarrassing announcement that the crew had been forced to make. There, written large in a language that Americans would understand, sat several members of the crew with their middle fingers extended to show their contempt for their captors and therefore the worthlessness of their confessions.

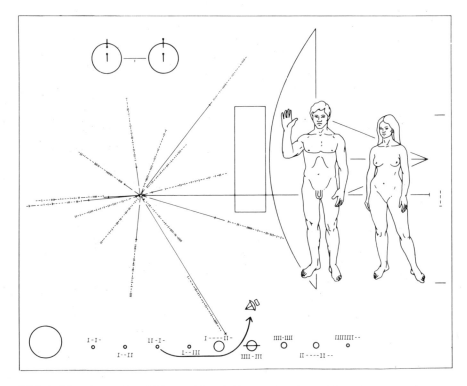

FIG. 8. The plaque aboard Pioneer 10 and 11, showing the position of the Earth and the creatures who built the spacecraft. The man has his hand raised in a gesture of salutation. (Reproduced from *The Dragons of Eden* by Carl Sagan. Reprinted by permission of the author and the author's agents, Scott Meredith Literacy Agency, Inc., New York and Hodder & Stoughton Limited.)

The hands have played a major role in contacts between different peoples. Through the use of pantomimic signs those who would otherwise have been deaf and dumb to each other's desires have been able to reach a mutual understanding, enter into commerce and ultimately learn each other's language. Too often, however, we have assumed that what is common to most men is common to all, and it is only with some reluctance that we have come to accept that such seemingly natural gestures as shaking the head for negation, beckoning with an upward movement, pointing with the index finger or greeting with an outstretched palm are not universal acts. When Pioneer 10 was launched from Cape Kennedy on 1 December 1970 it bore a metal plaque which, if examined by some alien intelligence in the future, would indicate the location of Earth. It also had an illustration of a man and a woman, he with his hand raised and his fingers spread in the act of greeting. We can only hope that the aliens who eventually intercept the spacecraft are not of Greek descent and that they do not take this gesture amiss.

Notes

1. Many of the examples of contact with other societies during the Age of Discovery are taken from Hewes' interesting paper on the subject (Hewes, 1974).
2. This event is briefly described in Attenborough's book, *Life on Earth* (1979).
3. Jakobson (1972) reports that when Russian soldiers visited Bulgaria in 1877–8 during the war with Turkey they were struck by the diametrical opposition between their own gestures for "yes" and "no" and those used by the Bulgarians. This only makes sense in view of Jakobson's suggestion that the Bulgarian code consists of a lateral shake in the transverse plane for "yes" (i.e. like the shake in the nod–shake code) and an upward toss for "no". However there is now some evidence that Jakobson is mistaken in respect of the Bulgarian gesture for "yes", and that it involves a roll or head-rock in the frontal plane rather than a shake in the transverse plane (see Collett, 1981). These movements are notoriously prone to perceptual distortion, and it seems that what Jakobson and the Russian soldiers took to be a head-shake was in fact a head-roll. In view of our earlier discussion of typical intensity, we would now say that the Russian soldiers construed the roll as a shake because the production distribution of the Bulgarian roll fell within the recognition distribution of the Russian shake.
4. When this does happen the result is not unlike the well-intentioned muddle that takes place in O. Henry's essay, "The Gift of the Magi". A young couple decide to give each other a present at Christmas, but neither has any money, so he sells his gold watch to buy her a brush and comb, while she cuts and sells her beautiful hair to buy him a watch-chain.

References

ATTENBOROUGH, D. (1979) *Life on Earth.* Collins, London.
EFRON, D. (1941) *Gesture and Environment.* King's Crown Press, New York. (Republished in 1972 as *Gesture, Race and Culture.* Mouton, The Hague.
COLLETT, P. (1981) Principles of contrast (unpublished).
COLLETT, P. and CHILTON, J. Laterality in negation: Are Jakobson and Vavra right? *Semiotica.* In press.
HEWES, G. (1974) Gesture language in culture contact. *Sign Language Studies,* 4, 1–34.
JAKOBSON, R. (1972) Motor signs for 'yes' and 'no'. *Language in Society,* 1, 91–6.

MORRIS, D. (1959) "Typical intensity" and its relation to the problem of ritualization. *Behaviour*, 11, 1–12.

MORRIS, D., COLLETT, P., MARSH, P. and O'SHAUGHNESSY, M. (1979) *Gestures: their Origins and Distribution*. Jonathan Cape, London.

SIMMEL, G. (1950) *The Sociology of Georg Simmel* (trans. K. Woolf). Free Press, Glencoe, Ill.

5

Language as the bridge

VERNER C. BICKLEY

What greatly attracts me to the Buddha
is the civilized concern which he shows
for the temperate use of language.

For him a right way of speaking is one
of the strands in the eightfold path leading
to enlightenment and the end of suffering.

To attain this right way all lies,
all bitter and double-tongued words,
all idle babbling, must be avoided.

So equally must harsh abusive speech,
arrogant usage heeding only itself,
and crude expression tending to corrupt.

Style also is important, and bombastic
inflated language is condemned no less
than gentility and plausible fine words.

Above all the Buddha values restraint
with words, knowing that silence is often
more expressive than the finished poem.

Language of the Buddha — Raymond Tong

Introduction

LANGUAGE is a form of human activity which makes it possible for human
beings to think of past, present and future situations and make plans relating to
them. As a mode of thought, it is not simply an instrument which conveys and
receives messages. It does, however, enable the individual to communicate with
and stimulate responses from persons in his and other speech communities. The
messages which are passed between individuals do not always lead to better

understanding. Both cultural and linguistic barriers exist which may sour relations. The fact that everyday things are done differently in different cultures often leads to misunderstanding and even within an apparently homogeneous language community, varieties of the same language may be culturally divisive.

In some societies linguistic rivalry may be associated with ideas of status and class. For example, the use of the wrong variety of language in a particular situation may create obstacles to social and financial advancement or barriers can be set up through the differences revealed in the use of different linguistic "codes". Geertz (1963) included differences over language issues among the foci around which "primordial discontent" tends to crystallize, and considered that several of these foci are usually involved concurrently, sometimes at cross-purposes with one another. Regional conflicts, for example, might stem from differences in language and culture, whilst religion and custom can form a basis for national disunity.

Language differences can exacerbate tensions between individuals in the same language community, or in different language communities within a single country, or they can create an inter-cultural problem which affects individuals from different countries.

Languages and varieties of languages can, however, provide a "bridge to understanding" when they are used to *mediate* between persons from the same or from different communities. The languages (or language varieties) themselves may function in a mediating way, or the individuals participating in a speech event may employ particular languages or varieties of languages for mediating purposes, as indicated in Table 5.

The use of language to strengthen cohesion in common language communities has been documented by writers such as Marshall (1968) who has described how talking is an aid to peaceful social relations among the Kung Bushmen of south-

TABLE 5   *Use of languages and language varieties for purposes of mediation*

INDIVIDUALS	Languages and varieties of languages and forms of "linguistic etiquette" used by individuals for mediating purposes in their own cultures and language communities (choices may be habituated as well as subjectively motivated).
	Languages and varieties of languages used by individuals for mediating purposes in situations involving persons from cultures and language communities other than their own. Knowledge of aspects of the "other" culture, as well as the person's own culture, is important.
	Languages and varieties of languages used by individuals for mediating purposes in situations involving persons from countries other than their own.
GOVERNMENTS	Languages and varieties of languages selected by governments for mediating purposes *intra*nationally.
	Languages and varieties of languages selected by governments for mediating purposes *inter*nationally.

west Africa, and Phillips (1965) who has listed a variety of behaviours in Thai culture for managing or minimizing unpleasantness when social avoidance is not possible.

Some studies have been made (e.g. by Ervin-Tripp, 1968) of the social relations between different language communities and of the function of language in cultural mediation (Bochner, 1981). What follows in the first part of the chapter is a description of ways in which language and language varieties are used by individuals, some of whom may have inter-cultural roles to play as mediators. In the second part of the chapter some examples are given of languages which are selected by governments to mediate between different cultures of a particular society and between societies.

Languages chosen by individuals for mediating purposes

Bilingualism, multilingualism and mediation

It is possible for members of a particular cultural group to belong to several language communities, one of which may be common to all of the groups. For example, the increasing number of people in *Indonesia* who use a form or forms of Bahasa Indonesia (Indonesian language — the national language and the official language), constitute a common language community. Each person in this community, however, will have his own idiolect — his own characteristic usage, which may, of course, change in the course of his life and which may interfere with mutual understanding. He may also belong to two, or more than two, communities, ranging in our example from the Javanese and Sundanese language communities in Java, the most densely populated island and area in the country, to the Christian Batak speech community of Sumatra.

Membership of more than one language community involves degrees of bilingualism and multilingualism which will vary according to the use of the languages concerned. Thus, in many societies, the need to make use of two or more languages is the result of geographical, historical or political causes. In some countries, for example, the language of two predominant linguistic groups may have national status and the members of such groups may be required to learn both languages.

Thus, in the Cape, Transvaal and Orange Free State provinces of *South Africa*, English and Afrikaans are compulsory for all children. In the Natal province, English is the medium of instruction and Afrikaans is taught as a second language. Proficiency in both languages is a condition of appointment to the civil service and to posts in the school system.

In *Canada* bilingualism, as defined by the Royal Commission on Bilingualism and Biculturalism (1967), applies only to the nation's two official languages, English and French. There are, therefore, many persons considered unilingual in terms of the two official languages, but who are actually bilingual. Generally these are Canadians of ethnic origins other than French or British, born in Canada or abroad, and who first learned the language of their own group — for example, German, Ukrainian, or Italian. They have subsequently acquired, for mediating purposes between themselves and members of the British and French groups, one of Canada's official languages, most often English.

Language varieties determined according to their users

Although the Census of Canada listed so many different ethnic origins and "first languages" within the Canadian population that it was impossible for the Commission to study the contribution of each group separately, most schools, in practice, provide instruction in English and/or French. The situation is different in *Singapore* which has a bilingual policy of providing parity of treatment to four official languages: Malay, Tamil, Chinese and English. All four languages are available up to the secondary level, so that in each language-medium school there is always a second official language taught and used in instruction. However, the major language (or medium) may not be the "first language" of the students. The second offical language used in instruction is often a "third language" and there is also a variety of contacts with other languages.

In the English-medium schools, for example, English is used as a medium for the study of a wide range of subjects geared to the School Certificate examination. The students studying these subjects and the teachers teaching them move in different language communities and use varieties of languages inside these communities. Thus a student of Chinese ethnic background who uses Hokkien at home may be taught history by a teacher of Indian ethnic background who speaks Tamil in his home. Both student and teacher, therefore, leave different language communities in the home for another language community in the school which they join for educational purposes. The Hokkien student, however, might speak a variety of Chinese which would be unintelligible to a Chinese student living in the same street or studying in the same class as himself, whilst the Indian teacher, although distinguished by his own characteristic usages of Tamil, would probably be employing a variety of it that would be intelligible to other users of the language in the environment of his home or his school. In other words the student, although still belonging to the Chinese language community, may speak a variety of Chinese which could be classified as a language or a *dialect* not necessarily mutually intelligible with other varieties of Chinese. The teacher, on the other hand, may speak a variety of Tamil which although it could still be classified as a *dialect,* would have sufficient features similar enough to other varieties to make it intelligible to users of these varieties.

The English language (which has developed its own Singaporean characteristics) serves in such a situation, not only as an educational medium, but also as a language which mediates between two persons and possibly two cultures: the Indian and the Chinese.

English in Singapore, as we shall see later, is regarded as an international language which is highly functional to economic progress. There is also increasing evidence (e.g. Chiew, 1972; Murray, 1971; Tan and Chew, 1970) that it is developing into a *lingua franca* which mediates between different ethnic groups, at least among the middle- and upper-class segments of the population, and that it is supporting the emergence of a "Singapore identity".

In the Chinese-medium schools of Singapore, the Pekingese form of Mandarin has been designated as the major language of instruction. Students and teachers in these schools are usually Chinese by ethnic origin but may use different dialects of Mandarin or different Chinese languages in their homes. Thus a student who uses Hokkien at home may be taught geography by a Chinese teacher who speaks Hakka in his own home but teaches through the medium of the Kwangsi form of Mandarin. The kind of Mandarin taught will, of course, depend on the teacher's own idiolect and on whether or not he learnt the Mandarin in the People's Republic of China, Taiwan, Hong Kong or other areas where the language is current. In this case, teacher and student, although from the same language community and of the same racial background, use different and mutually unintelligible varieties of the language at home but make use of a third variety of the language which, like English in the English-medium schools, may serve a mediating purpose as well as an educational purpose. The mediation here, however, is not between persons from two cultures, rather it is between persons whose ancestors came from one society, but whose "first languages" are mutually unintelligible.

Language varieties determined by social functions

The above examples show that varieties of language can be determined according to their users. These varieties are determined by the regions of their origin or by social factors. Varieties are, however, also determined by the way each member of a language community employs language for different social purposes. *Medium* distinguishes the different forms of language used for speech and writing. The extent of differentiation between these two forms varies among different speech communities and, in some cases, has historical causes. In the case of classical Chinese, for example, writing and speech were widely separated so that the written language was not affected by dialectal changes and even in its most colloquial form differed from the spoken language. The written language was the carrier of the ancient Confucian culture and the skilful calligraphy necessary to express this culture was regarded as an art equivalent to the art of painting in the West.

Convergence of the spoken and written forms of language took place as the result of the work of the "May 4 Movement" in 1920. The Cantonese, Fukienese, Swatow and Amoy communities, each with their own dialects, had to become acquainted with a form of Mandarin which was simpler than the classical medium it replaced, but which was to serve a similar purpose in that it made accessible the content of the classical system; in other words it served as a link between a number of different ethnic and linguistic groups. Here the medium is the mediator.

The differentiation between speech and writing, and the divergency between them characteristic of the classical system in *China*, arose from the particular function of language in a society which was the product of an ancient civilization. The written form was selected as the form most suited to express the Confucian culture and to carry it into home and school. In other words, a choice of resources was made. This choice is also exercised within the written and spoken media themselves, when different types of language are selected for different communicative purposes, as in religious, scientific and legal language; or when the style of discourse is determined by the relations between the participants, the setting and the topic. The differences between the kinds of language thus selected have been called differences of *register* and this represents the second variety along the scale of varieties which are distinguished by social function.

The choice of register is wide for the individual in his own language. It can become wider still and more complex when he operates in a second language or in a foreign language. Thus an Indonesian university teacher of Chinese ethnic background, who is an expert in the field of economics, would probably deliver his lectures through the medium of English. The choice of language in this situation may be influenced by the lack of suitable reading matter in Indonesian relevant to the subject. It may also be consequent upon the teacher's own educational background if he has followed a programme of higher study in an English-speaking country.

The variety of English spoken is not, however, determined by these factors alone. The register will be affected by the interaction of other variables such as the listeners' experiences of the English language, the setting, the sociological attributes of the students (their age, sex, etc.) and their ability to follow the lecturer's idiolect, marked, as it may be, by characteristics of his Chinese language and the dialect of that language as he has learned it in Indonesia; and also by the fact that he may have learned his own English through the medium of Dutch.

In this example the choice of language determined the variety of language used and the range of registers within that variety. The original choice may be dependent upon a number of factors including, in this case, a shortage of suitable texts in the official language and the speaker's educational background. It may also depend upon the speaker's attitude towards the language selected and the attitudes taken up by other people inside and outside his language community, and on whether or not the language selected is required to mediate between persons from different ethnic backgrounds. A typical class at the University of Indonesia, for example, would include persons from a variety of linguistic and cultural backgrounds. In most cases, Bahasa Indonesia (Indonesian language) would serve as the mediating language, although English might sometimes be called upon to fill such a role.

Code-switching and mediation

As we have seen, a mediating role may be assumed by an individual who is able to employ more than one language or dialect and is thus able to "switch codes". Bailey (1969) describes how in the Kond hill country of *India*, persons known as "Digaloos", who were invariably "Untouchables", were employed as middle-men and as mediators between the Konds and the Oriya-speaking persons from the Orissa plains around the Kond hills, who were hired by the East India Company to make trading contacts with the hill people. As bilinguals able to converse with both the Kui-speaking Konds and the Oriya-speaking Orissa peoples, the Digaloos were able to bring both groups together and at the same time to derive a satisfactory profit from the arrangement.

Gosling (1964) has noted that the Hokkiens from Amoy were probably the earliest immigrants in the *Malayan Peninsula* and many intermarried with Batak and Balinese slaves to found a race of "Babas", retaining for a time Chinese dress and customs, but ultimately assimilating so that their language was superseded by Malay. An exception was the Baba community of Trengganu whose members differed from many of the Babas of Malacca and the other Straits Settlements in that they retained the use of the Hokkien language as their first language. However, they also spoke perfect Trengganu Malay, and frequently used it in conversation among themselves, even though Hokkien was their principal language. Important for external contacts, Malay was used as the mediating language with other Chinese dialect groups, including recent Hokkien-speaking immigrants. Gosling describes here a situation in which a so-called "metropolitan" or "model" language (Malay) is used for mediation.

Varieties of language, such as *linguae francae* (or contact languages), which have sprung from metropolitan languages, are used to establish rapport between groups of people who do not have a common language. *Pidgins* are examples of *linguae francae* used for such purposes. Some pidgins were used for centuries as mediating trade languages, for example, Black Portuguese, Black French and Black English as used on the west coast of Africa, and Swahili on the eastern coastline of the continent. These hybrid languages, based usually on metropolitan languages, but differing as to pronunciation, vocabulary and syntax, become *creoles* when they are acquired by the children of pidgin speakers as first (native) languages. Creoles may be used in addition to the parent languages to enable two groups to make culture contact. They may, however, eventually displace one of the parent languages and, in consequence, lose something of their value as languages of mediation.

A language used on a large scale for purposes of international communication may be described as a true *lingua franca*. With approximately 500 million users on four continents a strong claim may be made for English as such a language although, as Quirk and Kachru (1980) point out, there are no intrinsic linguistic characteristics which entitle English to this status. The users of English differ in the uses they make of it and the ways in which they use it, so that a *distance* is being created between native varieties and non-native varieties which is leading on the one hand to the 'nativization' of English[1]* while, on the other hand, English has had an effect on a number of major indigenous languages in the Pacific, Asia and Africa.

Despite the apparent fragility of English in a country such as India, following the achievement of political independence the language began to gain ground after it was adopted as a link (and therefore a *mediating*) language for national and international communication. Kachru (1978) notes that English has become a part of the culture of South Asia and argues that the language has been *South Asianized* and that it has had a marked effect not only on South Asian languages but also on South Asian literatures. South Asian English literature is a manifestation of what has been called the literature of cross-cultural contact, described by Amirthanayagam (1979) as the artistic expression of the harmonies and discords created by the process of cross-cultural interaction. A study of literature from this new perspective under way at the East—West Center in Hawaii is expected to provide valuable insights into the literatures of different countries and to elucidate aspects of the nature of contemporary literary creativity. Such a study, according to Amirthanayagam, offers a way of understanding the responses of one culture to other cultures, since contact literature embodies the actual and continuing connections among cultures.

Translation, translators and mediation

Languages and language varieties, as has been indicated, are determined according to their users and according to the different social functions which require their participation. They may be regarded, therefore, as individually differentiated forms of behaviour determined specifically by communicative situations.

Newmark (1976) has shown how such different communicative situations may affect the work of the translator. His scheme (Fig. 9), adapted from Frege (1952), is illustrated diagrammatically by an instrument consisting of three levels (XYZ), which may be compared to the tubes of a jointed telescope. He uses this to observe a text which exhibits the three functions of language (ABC) in varying degrees. He may have to

> deflect his instrument, which may be focused mainly at A for a poem, or B for a technical report, or C for an advertisement, but sometimes rests between A and B for a description of nature in the poem, or between B and

* Superscript numbers refer to Notes at end of chapters.

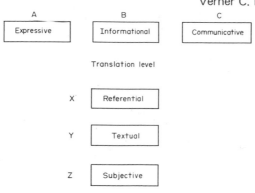

FIG. 9   Text function

C for the final recommendations of a report, as no text and few sentences are undiluted A or B or C. Even names like "Johnny" or "Petrushka" may be C as well as B. Whilst the translator always works from X, he continuously checks Y against X. Level Z, the partly conscious and partly unconscious element corresponding to the text writer's A, is always present, but the translator has to reduce its influence to a minimum, until he is left with what appears to him to be an almost gratuitous choice between equally valid units of language, which may be lexical or grammatical; this then becomes a question of stylistics, and his version on this level of *quot homines, tot sententiae* (so many men, so many opinions) may be as good for the others (Newmark, 1976, p. 16).

Newmark's scheme draws attention to the difficulties involved in *interlingual translation* — the interpretation of the verbal signs of one language by the verbal signs of another.

Nida (1976) describes three different ways (philological, linguistic and sociolinguistic) in which the principles and procedures of translation have been formulated. Philological theories of translation have been concerned with so-called literary texts; linguistic theories are based on a comparison of the linguistic structures of source and receptor texts rather than on a comparison of literary genres and stylistic features; and sociolinguistic theories relate translation to communication theory.

It is this latter type of translation that involves the translator (and the interpreter), as mediator between cultures. As mediator, the translator is concerned with the individuals involved in the translation relationship, the original writer (or speaker) and what is written or said, the reader(s) of, or the listener(s) to the original text, and the reader(s) of or listener(s) to the translation. The task is extraordinarily difficult. Goethe (1826) remarked that translation was impossible, essential and important. Richards (1953) has called it "probably the most complex type of event yet produced in the evolution of the cosmos".

Bickley (1975) has noted that translation problems provide persuasive evidence that it is difficult to express for one speech community experiences that are rooted in another. He observes that, to some extent because of differences between ethnographical and psychological approaches to the issue, a debate still continues as to whether or not the difficulties occur because language differences predispose cognitive processes to operate in differing ways, or because of differences in the social structures of such communities.

The links between language and culture and thought which have concerned scholars for many years, raise difficulties for the translator since the "real linguistic fact" (Malinowski, 1935) is the full utterance within its "context of situation", and a translation can never therefore be just a substitution of word for word, but must involve the translation of whole contexts. Misunderstandings caused by inadequate translation run the gamut from laughable to most serious. The *Honolulu Advertiser* newspaper of 13 May 1974, reported that two words and someone who translated them incorrectly from Italian to English were blamed for sensational — but erroneous — statements that Capuchin monks were abandoning their traditional vows of celibacy. According to the superintendent of the Capuchin College in Washington, 29.6 per cent of the monks said that they wanted to have "intimo rapporto" (closer friendship) with women. International wire services translated the Italian phrase as "sexual relations".

A grave example of misunderstanding caused by the ambiguity of a Japanese word is the meaning given by different individuals to the word *mokusatsu* — the word used when Japan responded to the Potsdam Declaration. According to Kazuo Kawai (1950), who during the war years was editor of the *Nippon Times,* rough translations of *mokusatsu* are "to be silent", "to withhold comment" or "to ignore". Kawai suggests that "to withhold comment" probably came closest to the true meaning, implying that while something was being held back, there was information that would be forthcoming. Kawai contends that this meaning was what the Japanese government wished to convey. However, Tokyo's newspapers and the Domei Press Agency reported that the government held the Potsdam Declaration in contempt, and that the Suzuki government had rejected it. The Pacific War Research Society in their *Japan's Longest Day* (1968) noted that literally *moku* means "to be silent" and *satsu* means "to kill". They point out that in the *Kenkyusha Dictionary* the word is defined as "take no notice of; treat with silent contempt; ignore by keeping silent". It also means "remain in a wise and masterly inactivity". It is their view that it is this latter definition that Suzuki had in mind. At a news conference a day after the government announcement had appeared in the press, Suzuki called the Potsdam Declaration a "thing of no great value", and used the term *mokusatsu.* According to the foreign minister that was not the intention of the cabinet. Nevertheless, the damage had been done.[2]

Nida (1964) describes one form of translation (intersemiotic) as the trans-
ference of a message from one kind of symbolic system to another. For example,
in semaphore, the meaning of a flag is rendered as a verbal message. *Intersemiotic
translation* is, of course, necessary across languages and their cultures since not
all language is verbal, and communication includes gestures, facial expressions
and posture, and features of non-verbal phonology such as loudness, tempo and
pitch. Ekman, Friesen and Ellsworth (1972) have postulated that persons of
different cultures exhibit the same facial expressions when they experience such
emotions as anger, disgust, fear, happiness, sadness and surprise. Brislin (1976)
notes that when people speak the same language they know what facial signals
go with what words, and so can interpret the *interaction* between these two
signals. But when a communicator interacts with a person who speaks a different
language, the other person might be able to study the communicator's facial
cues but will *not* be able to associate these cues with exact words and sentences.
Hence more mistakes of attribution of intent will be made in such a situation,
unless there is a good interpreter who can understand and communicate the
entire meaning contained in the message. As Boucher (1979) has pointed out,
not only does the accuracy of translation affect the comparability of studies
across cultures, it also affects the comparability across researchers within the
same culture. He reports that, in a study in progress at the East—West Center,
anger, rage and fury were all translated into the single term *marah* by bilingual
Malays. These same translators gave the single term anger for three distinct but
similar words, such as *marah, naik darah* and *panas hati.*

Good interpreters in such cases would need to know both languages well and
to recognize that a problem exists. They would then be equipped to act as links
between persons from two cultures and thus be able to serve as mediators.

The law, lawyers and mediation

Intralingual translation is defined by Nida (1964) as rewording something
within the same language. As such it is of great concern to lawyers and those
interested in legal processes. The law, with its verbal apparatus of "rights",
"duties", and "wrongs", is a particular application of language as a means of
social control. The problem is that, like the cultures of which they are a part,
languages are dynamic and therefore raise problems for the lawyer as mediator
in his own culture or society (which may contain a number of cultures), or when
he plays the mediating role inter-culturally, on the international scene. Glanville
Williams (1945) has remarked on the ambiguities of words, used referentially,
which give trouble to lawyers not only in manipulating their own technical
language but also in the construction of non-legal language in documents. Many
words change their meaning in the course of time, some becoming restricted,
some widened, and some transferred by metaphor, the original meaning either
remaining or disappearing.

In the English language, for example, "asylum", originally any refuge, now means in particular a refuge for those mentally diseased, but the old meaning has not quite disappeared, for example, "political asylum". "Accident", etymologically, can mean anything that happens, and this meaning is preserved in the judicial determination that murder is an "accident" within the Workmen's Compensation Acts in Britain. The word can, however, also mean damage not caused intentionally, or damage not caused by fault. "Committee" originally meant one individual to whom something was committed, the stress being on the last syllable. Both this meaning and this pronunciation have survived in some contexts, for example, in British Lunacy Law; but generally nowadays a committee is not one person but a body of persons, and in this meaning the stress is shifted to the middle syllable.

In addition to their referential functions, words also have emotive functions which express affective or volitional attitudes or arouse such attitudes in others. As such they produce further headaches for the lawyer, when used either intraculturally or interculturally, since the term "emotive" covers "love, joy, hope, wonder, desire, reverence, obedience, amusement, sympathy, social, moral and religious feeling, rage, fear, grief, horror, disgust and every other affective—volitional state" (Williams, 1945, p. 887).

The commonest type of emotive statement is the value-judgement, a statement of approval or disapproval, usually in the form of a generalization. Value-judgements need delicate handling by the mediating lawyer when he is involved in intercultural disputes since "rights", "duties", even "justice" itself, have different meanings in different cultures.

Experts and immigrants as mediators

Persons mediating between cultures do so in a variety of social roles. Taft (1981) lists thirteen such roles.[3] One other — the role of *expert* — will be added to the list and discussed here.

Experts and counterparts

Development assistance may involve the appointment to a host country of a foreign expert who may be a citizen of the country which is providing the assistance, or a citizen of a "developed" or "developing" country supported by an international organization. Typically, the expert works with a "counterpart", a national of the country in which the project is being carried out. The expert may be an administrator, an adviser to a counterpart who is in an executive, decision-making position, or he may have been recruited to assist with institution-building through, for example, the training of personnel.

In a manual prepared by the World Federation for Mental Health, edited by Margaret Mead and published by UNESCO in 1953, the expert is identified as a person who is immediately concerned, at any level, with purposive technological change, and is sent to bring the benefit of his experience to countries applying for technical assistance.

The manual was intended to be a guide to the kind of thinking and the kind of activity which might be of value in facilitating the technological change itself and in preserving the cultural integrity of those among whom the changes were to be introduced. It acknowledged that each culture was unique, that each particular situation within which a change was occurring or was to be made was unique, that it was not possible to lay down prescriptions for what was to be done in any particular case, and that there must always be specific co-operation with members of the particular community in which a demonstration was to be made or a new practice tried out.

The problem of language was recognized as a serious one. Exact meanings had to be explored; questions of adapting old words to new ideas, as opposed to coining new words, had to be weighed; and choices had to be made among rival dialects and local languages. There was no possible prescription except the insistence upon taking into account the culture and the situation and the individuals involved.

The manual recommended that working groups planning the introduction of technical change should consist of members of more than two cultures. Such groups should include the members of the culture in which the change was being introduced, members of the culture whose developed professional skills and resources were being drawn upon, and members of a third culture, who could maintain a certain objectivity and prevent the consuming group and the resource group from being deadlocked or developing an isolated bit of behaviour in which conflicts between, for example, Indonesian and American value systems might become frozen.

What applied to the involvement of members of different cultures and different levels of organization applied equally to the inclusion of different professions; having more than two professions and including one with less involvement would provide steadiness of teamwork.

Such measures were a protection against the intrusion of bias, and a certain guarantee that the programmes developed and the steps taken could both embody and be to a degree unhampered by the vested interests, and old and new, conscious and unconscious, prejudices of all those concerned.

> It will be recognized that this recommendation is again based on the principle that culture is mediated through persons, and that a culture, or a profession, or a level of administration, or a point of view cannot be represented by a charter, a diagram, or a printed description, but only by living human beings who themselves embody the position which is to be taken into account (Mead, 1953, p. 308).

The manual contains some perceptive short studies of aspects of technical change.

It recognized, as has been indicated, the importance of participation by representatives of the host culture (the counterparts) and envisaged teams which
would also include representatives of third cultures. Experts, counterparts and
third culture representatives would all serve as mediators.

As one means of development assistance, however, the expert—counterpart
model has not been free of criticism. In 1968, for example, Tagumpay-Castillo
listed a number of problems connected with American research in developing
countries; and in 1973 Hall and Dieffenbach reported a Nepalese complaint
about experts' salaries and living standards. Inquiries into the success or failure
of the relationships between members of the cross-national, cross-cultural teams
recommended by UNESCO have focused mainly on the separate problems of
experts and counterparts. The Bureau of Applied Social Research at Columbia
University, however, in collaboration with five other research centres in Paris,
Washington, Bogota, Lagos and Kathmandu, examined the *relations between*
experts and counterparts involved in development projects in Colombia, Nigeria
and Nepal in agriculture, geology, health, higher education and technician
training.

Reporting this study in 1979, Glaser presented its conclusions in proposi-
tional form under the headings Systemic Traits of the Host Society, Systemic
Traits of the Host Government, Character of the Work, Character of the Donor,
Personal Characteristics of Expert and Counterpart, and Organization of the
Team. Although the survey was conducted in only three countries and the results
were not, therefore, definitive, the preliminary findings indicated that expert—
counterpart relationships (the mediating relationship) were affected by nineteen
factors ranging from the cultual distance between the donor and the host country,
to the presence or absence of language barriers between expert and counterpart,
or between the expert and host nationals.

On the latter point, Glaser concludes that many experts work well in their
first new foreign language. However, if the expert is unable to communicate with
the counterpart and hosts in the local language, and requires instead that they
speak his language, then (particularly in administrative agencies):

(1) Contacts at work between expert and counterparts are limited. The expert
    hesitates to go through the intervening barrier of secretaries and clerks, or
    often cannot get through.
(2) There are less personalized relations, fewer off-the-job contacts, because
    wives cannot communicate.
(3) Each knows less about the other's work schedule, achievements, opinions,
    motivations, and future plans.
(4) There is a greater use of bilingual intermediaries.

Inability to speak the local language weakens the prestige and effectiveness of
the expert if it is one of the "international languages", e.g. English, French,

Spanish; and if the expert must work closely with technicians or ordinary citizens.

Glaser's generalizations indicate that relationships between experts and counterparts are primarily determined by cultural differences and/or by cross-cultural sensitivity. For example, the host country' s level of economic develop-ment affects the character of such relationships since, the more technically advanced the country, the more does cultural conditioning increase the demand for experts who have occupied high status positions in their own countries.

In the first part of this chapter we have examined some of the ways in which languages are used by individuals for mediating purposes. Participants in a speech event from the same language community may use their common language for mediation. Marshall (1968) and Phillips (1965) have given examples of how this is done in an African language community and in Thai society. Geertz (1960), in a much-quoted example, has noted that in Javanese society the participants in a speech event will use "linguistic etiquette" to protect their "inward feelings from external disturbances" (that is they use language in order to *mediate* with each other). Wolf (1956), in a study of aspects of group relations in Mexico, has described the linguistic activities of persons who mediate, and so serve as "cultural brokers", between community-oriented groups and nation-oriented groups operating primarily through national institutions. These mediators must serve some of the interests of groups operating on both the community and the national level, and they must also cope with the conflicts raised by the collision of these interests.

Persons from the same country may come from different language com-munities. The chances of their dialogue being mutually satisfactory may be increased if each is able to make use of a third language, which may be a national language such as Bahasa Indonesia, or an international language such as English which has acquired certain national characteristics as has English in India. But knowledge of a third language alone is not enough. The speakers are more likely to be able to mediate successfully with each other if they also have some know-ledge of each other's culture. So, in Indonesia, in the case of a discussion between, say, a Batak speaker from Sumatra and a Javanese speaker from Java, it would be advantageous if both understood the rules of discourse in each other's com-munities, although it would probably not be necessary to adhere to these rules in the third "mediating" language, which could be Bahasa Indonesia.

Stylized speech patterns in Javanese, include, as Geertz (1960), has pointed out:

> not only qualitative characteristics of the speakers — age, sex, kinship relation, occupation, health, education, religious commitment, family background — but also more general factors: for instance, the social setting (one would be likely to use a higher level to the same individual at a wedding than in the street); the content of the conversation (in general one uses lower levels when

speaking of commercial matters, higher ones in speaking of religious or aesthetic matters); the history of social interaction between the speakers (one will tend to speak rather high, if one speaks at all, with someone with whom one has quarrelled); the presence of a third person (one tends to speak higher to the same individual if others are listening). All these play a role, to say nothing of individual idiosyncratic attitudes (p. 258).

If the participants are unable to speak to each other in a third language, then it is possible that the mediating services of a third speaker may be necessary. The mediator in such a case, and also in the case of a situation involving persons from different nations as well as different speech communities, must be familiar not only with the languages of the other two participants, but should also have some knowledge of each other's culture. These differences between situations involving persons from the same culture and the same language community, persons from different language communities in the same country, and persons from different countries and different language communities are summarized in Table 6.

TABLE 6   *Uses of languages by individuals for purposes of mediation*

Same culture and language community and same country	Both participants in speech event use their common language and observe linguistic and cultural "etiquette" for purposes of mediation.
Different language communities and cultures. Same country and different countries.	Participants in dyadic situation must use third language if neither understands language of the other. Knowledge of each other's culture increases chances of successful mediation. Third language may be other language of their country or an "international" language.
	When persons *A* and *C* from two different language communities (and, possibly, *countries*) do not have a third language, then third person (*B*) may serve as mediator and should preferably know languages and aspects of cultures of *A* and *C*.

Language used to mediate between societies and cultures

This second section of the chapter notes examples of languages which are selected deliberately by governments for use intra-culturally. Such "language planning"[4] may be conducted for political, economic and social reasons and concomitantly for purposes of mediating between different cultural groups[5] as in, for example, West Malaysia, Singapore, Indonesia, the Philippines and the United States.

In the case of a relatively "unilingual" country such as Japan, "language planning" may still proceed as, for example, the decision to adopt English as a school subject in a majority of Japanese schools to introduce Japanese students to a language of international communication: or the decision to provide considerable financial and administrative support for the teaching of Japanese in other countries, particularly in Asia.

When individual languages are compared, it is possible to distinguish them along scales in a typological classification. Stewart (1968) divided languages along one axis according to type and along a second axis according to function. The differentiation into types is made in terms of four attributes of which the first is *standardization* (whether or not there exists for the language a codified set of grammatical and lexical norms which are formally accepted and learned by the language's users); the second is *autonomy* (whether or not the linguistic system is "unique and independent" and autonomous in terms of any other linguistic system with which it is not historically related); the third is *historicity* (whether or not the language is the result of a process of development through use over time); and the fourth is *vitality* (whether or not the language has an existing, unisolated community of native speakers).

Stewart notes that in the typology *standardization* is used to indicate *formal* standardization. Few of the world's languages have been codified in this way. However, many languages have been *informally* standardized "when there is a certain amount of normalization of language behavior in the direction of some linguistic usage with high social prestige " (p. 534).

The four attributes can be combined in various ways to produce (in Stewart's typology) seven language types, ranging from standard to pidgin. These are *standard*, combining all four attributes: examples are English, French and German which are official languages of modern Europe; *classical,* combining the first, second and third, for example, classical or literary Arabic; *artificial,* marked by the first and second but not by the third and fourth, for example, Esperanto and Voläpuk; *vernacular,* combining the second, third and fourth, but not the first attribute, for example, most tribal languages of Africa; *dialect,* combining the third and fourth attributes but not the first and second, for example, Schwyzer-tütsch in Switzerland; *creole,* possessing only the fourth attribute; and *pidgin* possessing none of the four attributes.[6]

Examples of the first, second, fourth, fifth and seventh (standard, classical, vernacular, dialect and pidgin) are to be found in West Malaysia, Singapore, and Indonesia. In West Malaysia and Singapore, various Chinese languages (particularly Mandarin and Hokkien), Malay, Tamil and English can be classified as standard; high Tamil, Arabic and ("Raja") Malay and *Lingua de Christao*[7] as dialects; and English as pidgin. Wong (1980) has pointed out that most English-speaking Malaysians are in command of two varieties of Malaysian English — one a wider speech form virtually indistinguishable from forms of educated British, American, or New Zealand English, and the other a local "dialect" used mainly in speech and limited to conversation on everyday matters with familiars who are also Malaysians. The "wider speech form" departs from other varieties of educated English at the level of vocabulary by including loan words derived from other contact languages and from local circumstances; at the level of pronunciation, particularly in the matter of word stress; and to a very limited extent at the level of syntax. The local "dialect" is a much "barer" and more simplified variety of English. It is not, however, a pidgin, although a form of pidgin English is used also in certain situations. In Indonesia, Javanese, Sundanese, English, Dutch and Bahasa Indonesia can be classified as standard languages; while Madurese, various Chinese languages and languages such as Balinese, Batak, and Minangkebau can be styled vernacular when they are spoken by persons originating from the regions in which speech communities of these particular languages are grouped.

In all three areas, a form of Malay is used in households and other limited situations. In West Malaysia and Singapore it will have absorbed elements from different Chinese and Indian languages and of the English lexis. In Indonesia it may have some of the lexical and phonological characteristics of other Indonesian languages and dialects and of Dutch (e.g. Kantur — meaning office).

Functional classification

Languages may also be compared as to *function*. Different languages can have differing functions as media of communication within a state and each may perform several roles. The functional categories suggested by Stewart (1968) are:

(1) *Official* — the use of a language as the legally appropriate one for all political and cultural representative purposes on a nationwide basis.
(2) *Provincial* — the use of a language provincially or regionally.
(3) *Wider communication* — the use of a language, other than an official or a provincial one, across language boundaries within a nation.
(4) *International* — the use of a language as a major medium of communication which is international in scope, e.g. for diplomatic relations, foreign trade, etc.
(5) *Capital* — the use of a language as the primary medium of communication in the vicinity of the national capital.
(6) *Group* — the use of a language primarily by the members of a single ethnic or cultural group, or sub-group.
(7) *Educational* — the use of a language, other than an official or provincial one, as a medium of instruction, either regionally or nationally.
(8) *School subject* — the language which is commonly taught (other than one which already has an official or provincial function) as a subject in secondary and/or higher education.
(9) *Literary* — the use of a language primarily for literary or scholarly activities.
(10) *Religious* — the use of a language primarily in connection with the practice of a religion.

To Stewart's categories should be added *National,* since national languages are distinguished in some countries from official languages. In Singapore, for example,

Mandarin Chinese, Malay, Tamil and English are official languages but Malay has also been given the status of a national language.

These categories can be cross-classified with language types. Thus, in West Malaysia, Malay is a standard language according to type which also functions as a language of wider communication, an international language, a school subject and, to some extent, a literary language. In Singapore, English is an official language and, in common with Mandarin, Malay and Tamil, a standard language. In Indonesia, English is a standard language, an international language and a school subject.

English as a mediating language in Indonesia, West Malaysia,
Singapore, the Philippines and the United States

INDONESIA

In the former Netherlands East Indies the language of learning and the most important key to "Western" culture was Dutch. It was the medium of instruction at the secondary level and despite a number of Indonesian intellectuals, influenced by nationalism,[8] pressing for the development of Malay as the national language, its speakers, whether Dutch or Indonesian, enjoyed considerable social prestige. The revolutionary course steered by the nationalists following the Second World War, however, hardened their attitude towards Dutch. Ultimately a complete ban was placed on the use of the language after the confiscation of Dutch estates and other property in 1957 and the severance of diplomatic relations between Holland and Indonesia in 1960. It was not until recently that the ban has been lifted and diplomatic relations restored.

The curricula of the secondary schools in the Netherlands East Indies included a number of non-Indonesian languages and these were taught as foreign languages. Among them was English, an important subject in the secondary schools of Holland, and an essential choice for the syllabus in the Indies, because it was widely used in neighbouring countries. English was employed as a *lingua franca,* a mediating language, between Dutch and other members of the business community and it was a world language, a common language for the conduct of international affairs. One consequence of the pre-war Dutch educational system, which restricted higher education to a limited number of the indigenous peoples, was that Indonesia was encouraged to turn to other Western powers for assistance after independence had been achieved. The volume of aid received from English-speaking countries after the Second World War stimulated the spread of the English language and increased its usefulness as a means of access to scientific and technical information. Dutch education policy was therefore one of the several factors responsible for the supersession of Dutch and the elevation of English into the position of first foreign language, a position which it still holds officially in the present education system.

The English language is now the first foreign language taught in schools in Indonesia. It is used as a mediating language between Indonesian officials and bureaucrats and foreign diplomats and representatives of the foreign business community, although Bahasa Indonesia is also used for such purposes.

WEST MALAYSIA AND SINGAPORE

The education imparted by the English-medium schools of pre-Second World War Malaya and Singapore, although often said to be "literary" in nature, was also vocational in that it provided adequate training for various categories of clerical and administrative employment, and parents were influenced by career opportunities it offered to their children. This pressure to learn the English language increased as the economy of the two areas expanded through the success of the Malayan rubber and tin industries, and the transformation of Singapore from a small fishing village to a large entrepôt port.

It was the colonial government's post-war policy in both Malaya and Singapore to steadily increase opportunities for all ethnic groups to learn English in English-medium schools, to develop training courses for teachers of English in Chinese-medium schools, and to introduce English as a compulsory subject in all Malay, Chinese and Indian schools. This policy did much to establish the language as a unifying, mediational force and offset the pre-war tendency of the English-medium schools to create an elite. Encouragement of a language which had international status, and which could lead to qualifications in technical and professional disciplines, put many of the new skills within reach of the inhabitants and smoothed the path to independence by providing a core of trained personnel able to assume responsibilities previously exercised by expatriate officials.

In Singapore, English still plays a major role in the schools as a medium of instruction and also as a "second" language. It is the language of administration and of international trade. Kuo (1976), using data based on a Communicability Index, confirms that Malay and English should be considered the *linguae francae,* or mediating languages, of Singapore, although Hokkien is used as a *lingua franca* among the various Chinese language and dialect groups. Kuo's analysis shows that there is a dual linguistic system in Singapore. Malay, especially its pidginized variant, "Bazaar Malay", is used among people of different ethnic backgrounds in the market-place and other traditional sectors of society. English is the common language among the more modern groups, and for the more official or more formal functions. This pattern is paralleled by another dual system in the Chinese community, whereby Hokkien is used in the traditional sector in inter-language and dialect group communication, and Mandarin for the more formal and official functions. Malay and Hokkien, therefore, are more often used in situations that are more traditional, whereas English and Mandarin are used for more formal mediational situations.

In West Malaysia, as has already been observed, English no longer has the status of an official language. It is, however, the major "second" language of the Malaysian educational system and it is used mediationally between different cultural and linguistic groups.

In both West Malaysia and Singapore, stable local varieties of English are achieving status. Wong (1980) has given a partial description of two varieties of Malaysian English. Descriptions of contemporary varieties of Singaporean English are to be found in Tongue (1974) and Crewe (1977).

THE PHILIPPINES

The present linguistic policy of the Philippines arose out of the nationalist movement and out of the education policy of the United States, the colonial power in the country before the Second World War. It was believed that English, as the language of commerce, culture and science, could work as a political catalyst to bind the Filipinos into one nation, the report of the United States Philippines Commission of 1905[9] stating: "If we can give the Filipino husbandman a knowledge of the English language, and even the most elemental acquaintance with English writings, we will free him from that degraded dependence upon the men of influence of his own race." The Commission recommended that Spanish and English be the two official languages of the government, and in the first general elections held in 1907 the vote was given to all male adults able to read and write in Spanish, English or Tagal (Tagalog). The adoption of English as one of the official languages led to its being made a medium of instruction in the schools. This innovation did not go uncriticized. The Secretary of Public Instruction, Dr George Bacobo, said: "No foreign language can be the genuine vehicle of our inmost thoughts, our intimate feelings. No foreign language can be the expression of our national soul."[10]

Bacobo's sentiments were echoed by a number of thoughtful Filipinos who supported the idea of developing a national language that would be of autochthonous origin. As Yabes (1967) notes, no less a person than an American Vice-Governor advocated the use of the vernaculars as media of instruction because he believed that the language into which a child was born was the best for the first 4 or 5 years of schooling.

The adoption of one of the native languages of the Philippines as the basis for the development of a national language was agreed by the delegates to the Constitutional Assembly, which met in 1934 to write a constitution for a Philippine Commonwealth which would serve preparatory to the establishment of an independent Philippines Republic. The Constitution established in 1935 named English and Spanish as official languages but proclaimed: " . . . The National Assembly shall take steps toward the development and adoption of a common national language based on one of the existing native languages. Until otherwise provided by law, English and Spanish shall continue as official languages."

In 1940 an executive order made Pilipino, based on Tagalog, a required subject in the public schools. Pilipino was advocated as a mediating language, such a language being needed to help strengthen national unity since none of the other languages of the Philippines Islands was spoken nationally. The question of whether Pilipino was appropriate for the purpose was raised at the 1971 Constitutional Convention, as Juco (1977) has reported:

> In the first place, the Tagalog dialect was not the vernacular of most of the delegates; in the second place, the issue had loomed largely in the political campaigns of prospective Constitutional Convention delegates, particularly those in the southern Philippines, where the campaign promises to bat for a differently based national language, and sometimes to bat for ascendancy of the local or regional vernacular . . . (p. 10).

Could a language be found which could function as a national language and so become a language of mediation between different linguistic and cultural groups? The 1973 Constitution attempted to resolve the question by stating that the Constitution itself should be promulgated both in English and in Pilipino, that English and Pilipino should be the official languages but that steps should be taken towards the development and formal adoption of a common national language to be known as Filipino.

The situation today is that English and Pilipino are recognized as official languages. Both languages are authorized as media of instruction from the third grade while in the first and second grades the medium of instruction is one of the eight official "vernaculars".[11] During these two years English and Pilipino may be taught as subjects. In 1973 the National Board of Education expressed its support for the policy of "developing a bilingual nation able to communicate in Pilipino as well as in English" and also stated that "steps shall be taken toward the development of Pilipino until it shall have attained such a stage of development as to warrant its formal adoption as the common national language to be known as 'Filipino' " (Juco, 1977, p. 12).

Barring other constitutional changes in the Philippines, the mediating language is therefore to be *planned* and there is, as Juco (1977) has observed:

> . . . the possibility of "Pilipino" (with a "P") continuing to be used and developed and, by an eclectic process, being infused with more extensive words and idioms to the extent that it will, over the years, evolve into a language that can be called "Filipino" (with an "F") that can then be formally adopted — the major objection at the [Constitutional] Convention being that it was Tagalog-based, but not inferring that it could not evolve into "Filipino" (with an "F") if it were more generously based (p. 13).

THE UNITED STATES

In 1833 in England, John Arthur Roebuck, in a speech made to a Parliament newly expanded following the enfranchisement of the middle classes by the 1832 Reform Bill, remarked that France, Prussia and Saxony had introduced systems of popular education. He then put forward a motion asking the House to legislate that "to this end the aid and care of the State are absolutely needed".

Two years before Roebuck's speech, missionaries in the Kingdom of Hawaii founded schools intended to perform functions different from those common in Hawaiian culture. In 1831 they established a school, "Lahainaluna", for the training of teachers. In 1896, 2 years after the establishment of the Hawaiian Republic,[12] was founded the institution later to become the first Territorial Normal School and in 1921 a Mr Benjamin Wist was appointed Principal. Wist was dedicated to the idea of Americanizing the diverse ethnic groups of the Islands. In his Ph.D. dissertation on "American Foundations of Public Education in Hawaii", submitted to Yale University, he wrote:

> Due to the American influences upon the political, social and economic development of Hawaii, the public school system became American; but likewise, by virtue of its American character, public education in Hawaii helped materially in the development of the American ideology (p. 354).

According to Minogue (1971), the development of secondary education was advanced as a political argument for achieving statehood, while also seen as a means of Americanizing diverse ethnic groups and as a way of achieving equality of educational opportunity.

Today, according to a statement adopted officially by the Board of Directors of the American Association of Colleges for Teacher Education,[13] multicultural education recognizes cultural diversity as a fact of life in American society. This cultural diversity is a valuable resource that should be preserved and extended. Education for cultural pluralism should, the statement affirms, include the encouragement of multiculturalism, multilingualism and multidialectism.

In 1967, Title VII, the Bilingual Education Program, was introduced as an amendment to the Elementary and Secondary Education Act of 1965. Bilingual education was stated by the United States Office of Education to mean the use of two languages, one of which is English, as media of instruction. The programme has been referred to as being ". . . in support of dual-language schooling in terms that permit both the ethnocentrists and the cultual pluralists to see what they want to see" (Gaarder, 1970, p. 163). It has also been described as an anti-poverty measure, "directed really towards functional non-English speaking monolinguals" (Roeming, 1970, p. 372).

No matter how the terms of the Act are interpreted, it seems likely that children in the United States will now have the opportunity to receive formal education in their own language,[14] in addition to English, which will mediate between them and their ethnic heritage. Gaarder (1970) draws attention to the importance of strengthening bilingual education programmes and to the need for assistance from trained investigators who will need to address such questions as: How can project directors ascertain quickly and fairly the degree of scholarly competence of persons who might be employed as teachers or aides in the non-English medium? How can the extent to which non-English mother-tongue children possess and control that tongue be measured?

Attempts to answer questions of this kind were made in the "first seventy-six bilingual education projects" (see Gaarder, 1970), and in such projects as, for example, the Ilokano[15] Bilingual/Bicultural Educational Planning project sponsored by the Culture Learning Institute of the East—West Center in 1975.[16]

The project research team found that there was little support for a transitional programme for immigrant children which would provide subject-matter instruction in Ilokano while the learners were adjusting to life in the United States. They did, however, discover that there was considerable interest in receiving assistance from the schools in maintaining both fluency in the Ilokano language and an understanding of Filipino cultures.

Both Ilokano and English were seen to be mediating languages in the Hawaii situation. Ilokano mediates between persons of Philippine ethnic origin and their culture, whilst English mediates between such persons and other cultures in Hawaii's multicultural society.

Conclusion

In this chapter we have examined some of the ways in which languages and varieties of language are used for purposes of mediation, that is, to create "bridges to understanding" for individuals from the same cultures or from different cultures. We have observed that variations within languages and varieties of languages can serve different social contexts and can have different mediating functions, and we have given examples of bilingual and multilingual situations in which mediating roles are assumed by individuals, and of languages that have been selected deliberately by governments as languages of mediation.

Communicative acts are related to aspects of social reality which are determined by cultural norms. Further study is needed of the mediating function of certain speech acts, as those acts are both extrinsically and intrinsically determined.

Notes

1. For example, in West African English, *chewing-sponge* or *chewing stick* ("twig used for cleaning teeth"). See Kachru (1980) for other examples.
2. I am indebted to Mr Norman Geschwind of the East—West Center Culture Learning Institute for drawing my attention to Mr Kawai's article, and to the publication of the Pacific War Research Society.
3. Interpreter, tourist guide, industrial relations conciliator, marriage counsellor, ombudsman, student counsellor, native welfare officer, representative of ethnic communities on a government board, factory foreman, representative of workers on a management committee, manager of touring sportsmen or entertainers, business agent for a foreign company, intelligence agent.

4. Information about the field of "Language Planning" is given in the *Language Planning Newsletter,* published four times a year by the Culture Learning Institute of the East—West Center, Hawaii. A *Directory of Language Planning Organizations* and a *List of References for Students of Language Planning* have been published by the Institute.

5. For example, Bangladesh. The National Education Commission's Report of 1975 asks "that the importance of the mediatory role of English as an international language be realized by the society".

6. Note, however, that recent studies of pidgins and creoles have emphasized the need to describe these varieties as they are actually *used* by their speakers. Mühlhäusler (1974), for example, has concluded that pidgins are languages that are different in degree and not in kind from languages that have, or have had, native speakers. In a discussion of the roles of both linguistic and extralinguistic factors in defining pidgins, he gives definitions of the four linguistic criteria that he believes must be combined to yield a pidgin; namely, *simplification, impoverishment, unintelligibility* and *stability.* Extralinguistic parameters of pidginization (and creolization) are: (a) nature of contact, (b) duration of contact, (c) illiteracy and second language learning, (d) cultural differences between groups, (e) prestige of target language, (f) prestige of pidgins and creoles, (g) numbers of speakers, (h) sex of speakers, (i) official language policy, (j) race relations, (k) group solidarity and (l) isolation versus contact with regard to the target language.

7. In 1641 the Portuguese colonialists in Malacca were attacked by the Dutch who eventually occupied the town. Despite the hostility of the Dutch, the Portuguese and Eurasian survivors continued to practise their Catholic faith in secret and preserved themselves as a distinct group, with their own customs and language derived from sixteenth-century Portuguese.

8. In 1942 the Japanese military forces occupying the Indies banned Dutch and encouraged the learning of Japanese. They also authorized the Malay language as the official medium until Japanese became widely known. In 1945 the leaders of the Indonesian Republic declared Malay to be the official national language.

9. Published, Washington, D.C., 1906.

10. Quoted by J. R. Hayden (1942) *The Philippines, A Study in National Development,* Macmillan, New York, p. 592.

11. In Tagalog-speaking areas, Pilipino can be used as a language of instruction from Grade I.

12. Hawaii was annexed in 1898 and the Republic then became a territory of the United States.

13. In "No one model American", *Journal of Education,* **24** (4) (Winter 1973), 264:5.

14. That there has been a declining interest in the United States in foreign language teaching is indicated by the establishment in 1978 of the President's Commission on Foreign Language and International Studies. A survey of attitudes toward foreign language study carried out under the auspices of the Commission found that of the 40 per cent who claimed familiarity with at least one foreign language, only 30 per cent had studied a foreign language in school, and of those, only 8 per cent had studied a foreign language for 4 or more years. Over 75 per cent of the respondents could not speak, read or write any language but English. (See Bulletin 2, President's Commission on Foreign Language and International Studies, August, 1979.)

15. Ilokano is one of the eight major regional languages of the Philippines.

16. *Report of the Ilokano Bilingual, Bicultural Planning Conference* East—West Culture Learning Institute, Honolulu, Hawaii, 1975.

References

AMIRTHANAYAGAM, J. G. (1979) *Contact Literature in Cross-national Perspectives.* Honolulu, Hawaii (East—West Center Program Catalogue), p. 23.

BAILEY, F. G. (1969) *Stratagems and Spoils.* Oxford University Press, Oxford.

BICKLEY, V. C. (1975) Culture, cognition and the curriculum. *East–West Center Culture and Language Learning Newsletter,* 4 (1), 1–11.

BOCHNER, S. (Editor) (1981) *The Mediating Person.* Schenkman, Boston.

BOUCHER, J. (1979) Culture and emotion, *Perspectives on Cross-cultural Psychology.* (Edited by MARSELLA, A., THARPE, R. and CIBOROWSKI, T.). Academic Press, New York.

BRISLIN, R. (1976) Introduction, *Translation: Applications and Research* (Edited by BRISLIN, R.). Gardner, New York.

CANADA (1967) *Report of the Royal Commission on Bilingualism and Biculturalism.* Queen's Printer, Ottawa.

CHIEW, S. K. (1972) Singapore national identity. Unpublished master's thesis, University of Singapore.

CREWE, W. (Editor) (1977) *The English language in Singapore.* Eastern Universities Press, Singapore.

EKMAN, P., FRIESEN, W. F. and ELLSWORTH, P. (1972) *Emotion in the Human Face: Guidelines for Research and an Integration of Findings.* Pergamon, New York.

ERVIN-TRIPP, S. (1968) Interaction of language, topic and listener, *Readings in the Sociology of Language* (Edited by FISHMAN, J.). Mouton, Paris.

FREGE, G. (1952) Sense and reference, *Translations from the Philosophical Writings of Gottlieb Frege* (Edited by GEACH, P. and BLACK, M.). Blackwell, Oxford.

GAARDER, A. B. (1970) The first seventy-six bilingual education projects, *Report of the Twenty-first Annual Round Table Meeting on Linguistics and Language Studies* (Edited by ALATIS, J.). Georgetown University Press, Washington, D.C.

GEERTZ, C. (1960) *The religion of Java.* Free Press of Glencoe, New York.

GEERTZ, C. (1963) *Old Societies and New States.* Free Press of Glencoe, New York.

GLASER, W. A. (1979) Experts and counterparts in technical assistance, *Bonds without bondage: Explorations in transcultural interactions* (Edited by KUMAR, K.). The University Press of Hawaii, Honolulu.

GOETHE, J. W. (1826) *Samtliche Werke. Volume 39, 1826.* Munich: Propylaen Edition, 1909. (Letter to Thomas Carlyle.)

GOSLING, L. A. P. (1964) Migration and assimilation of rural Chinese in Trengganu, *Malayan and Indonesian Studies* (Edited by BASTIN, J. and ROOLVINK, R.). Oxford University Press, Oxford.

HALL, D. E. and DIEFFENBACH, A. E. (1973) Compensation of foreign advisers in developing countries. In *Focus: Technical Cooperation,* a supplement to the *International Development Review,* 15 (3), 3–6.

JUCO, J. M. (1977) Bilingual education under the new constitution, *The Filipino Bilingual* (Edited by PASCASIO, E.). Ateneo de Manila University Press, Manila.

KACHRU, B. (1978) English in South Asia, *Advances in the Study of Societal Multilingualism* (Edited by FISHMAN, J.). Mouton, The Hague.

KACHRU, B. (1980) The pragmatics of non-native varieties of English, *English for Cross-cultural Communication* (Edited by SMITH, L.). Macmillan, London.

KAWAI, K. (1950) Mokusatsu, Japan's response to the Potsdam declaration. *Pacific Historical Review,* 19, 409–14.

KUO, E. C. (1976) *A Sociolinguistic Profile of Singapore.* University of Singapore Press, Singapore.

MALINOWSKI, B. (1935) *Coral Gardens and Their Magic.* Allen & Unwin, London.

MARSHALL, L. (1968) Sharing, talking and giving: relief of social tensions among Kung Bushmen, *Readings in the Sociology of Language* (Edited by FISHMAN, J.). Mouton, Paris.

MEAD, M. (1953) *Cultural Patterns and Technical Change.* UNESCO, Paris.

MINOGUE, W. J. D. (1971) *Hawaiian and New Zealand Teacher Education.* New Zealand Educational Institute, Wellington.

MÜHLHÄUSLER, P. (1974) *Pidginization and Simplification of Language.* Department of Linguistics, Research School of Pacific Studies, The Australian National University, Canberra.

MURRAY, D. (1971) Multilanguage education and bilingualism: the formation of social brokers in Singapore. Unpublished doctoral dissertation, Stanford University.

NEWMARK, P. (1976) The theory and craft of translation. *Language Teaching and Linguistic Abstracts,* 9 (1), 5–26.

NIDA, E. A. (1964) *Towards a Science of Translating.* Brill, Leiden.

NIDA, E. A. (1976) A framework for the analysis and evaluation of theories of translation, *Translation: Applications and Research* (Edited by BRISLIN, R.). Gardner, New York.

PACIFIC WAR RESEARCH SOCIETY (1968) *Japan's Longest Day.* Kodansha International, Tokyo.

PHILLIPS, H. P. (1965) *Thai Peasant Personality.* University of California Press, Berkeley, Calif.

QUIRK, R. and KACHRU, B. (1980) Introduction, *English for Cross-cultural Communication* (Edited by SMITH, L.). Macmillan, London.

RICHARDS, I. A. (1953) Toward a theory of translating. *Studies in Chinese Thought* (American Anthropological Association), **55**, Memoir 75. University of Chicago Press, Chicago.

ROEMING, R. F. (1970) Bilingualism and the national interest, *Report of the Twenty-first Annual Round Table Meeting on Linguistics and Language Studies* (Edited by ALATIS, J.). Georgetown University Press, Washington, D.C.

STEWART, A. W. (1968) A sociolinguistic typology for describing national multilingualism, *Readings in the Sociology of Language* (Edited by FISHMAN, J.). Mouton, Paris.

TAFT, R. (1981) The personality of the mediating person, *The Mediating Person* (Edited by BOCHNER, S.). Schenkman, Boston.

TAGUMPAY-CASTILLO, G. (1968) A view from Southeast Asia. *American Research on Southeast Asian Development: Asian and American Views* (Edited by S.E.A.D.A.G.). The Asia Society, New York.

TAN, R. and CHEW, S. F. (1970) An analysis of the attitudes of pupils in Chinese medium, English medium and integrated schools on selected variables. Unpublished paper, University of Singapore.

TONG, R. (1975) Language of the Buddha. *English Language Teaching,* 30 (1), 3.

TONGUE, R. (1974) *The English of Singapore and Malaysia.* Eastern Universities Press, Singapore.

WILLIAMS, G. (1945) Language and the law. *Law Quarterly Review,* 61 (2), 180; 61 (5), 887–8.

WOLF, E. R. (1956) Aspects of group relations in a complex society: Mexico. *American Anthropologist,* 58 (6), 1065–78.

WONG, I. (1980) English in Malaysia, *English for Cross-cultural Communication* (Edited by SMITH, L.). Macmillan, London.

YABES, L. Y. (1967) Developing a national language for the Philippines, *The Modernization of Languages in Asia* (Edited by ALISJAHBANA, S. T.). Malaysian Society of Asian Studies, Kuala Lumpur.

6

Cross-cultural interaction, social attribution and inter-group relations[1]*

JOS JASPARS AND MILES HEWSTONE[2]

Now let me tell you about an experiment that was made in the Kingdom of Kerman. It so happens that the people of this kingdom are good, even-tempered, meek and peaceable and miss no chance of doing one another a service. For this reason, the king once observed to the sages assembled in his presence: "Gentlemen, here is something that puzzles me, because I cannot account for it. How is it that in the kingdoms of Persia, which are such near neighbours of ours, there are folk so unruly and contentious that they are forever killing one another, whereas among us, who are all but one with them, there is hardly an instance of provocation or brawling?" The sages answered that this was due to a difference of soil. So the king thereupon sent to Persia, and in particular to Isfahan aforementioned, whose inhabitants outdid the rest in every sort of villainy. There, on the advice of his sages he had seven ships loaded with earth brought to his own kingdom. This earth he ordered to be spread out like pitch over the floors of certain rooms and then covered with carpets, so that those who entered should not be dirtied by the soft surface. Then a banquet was served in these rooms, at which the guests had no sooner partaken of food than one began to round on another with opprobrious words and actions that soon led to blows. So the king agreed that the cause did indeed lie in the soil.

The Travels of Marco Polo

Introduction

ALTHOUGH it is an ancient and widely held belief that interaction between individuals belonging to different cultures and different groups will reduce ethnic prejudice and inter-group tension and improve relations between the groups, recent social psychological research has shown that this is only true

*Superscript numbers refer to Notes at end of chapter.

when certain conditions are satisfied (Amir, 1969, 1976; Triandis and Vassiliou, 1967).

Amir, who has summarized most of the research on social contact in ethnic relations, concludes that some of the favourable conditions which tend to reduce prejudice are:

(a) When there is equal status contact between members of various ethnic groups.
(b) When the contact is between members of a majority group and higher status members of a minority group.
(c) When an "authority" and/or the social climate are in favor of and promote the intergroup contact.
(d) When the contact is of an intimate rather than a casual nature.
(e) When the ethnic intergroup contact is pleasant or rewarding.
(f) When the members of both groups in the particular contact situation interact in functionally important activities or develop common goals or superordinate goals that are higher ranking in importance than the individual goals of each of the groups (Amir, 1969, p. 338).

In addition Amir concludes from his review that some of the conditions which strengthen prejudice are:

(a) When the contact situation produces competition between groups.
(b) When the contact is unpleasant, involuntary, tensionladen.
(c) When the prestige or status of one group is lowered as a result of the contact situation.
(d) When members of a group or the groups as a whole are in a state of frustration.
(e) When the groups in contact have moral or ethnic standards which are objectionable to each other.
(f) In the case of contact between a majority and a minority group, when the members of the minority group are of lower status or are lower in any relevant characteristics than the members of the majority group (Amir, 1969, p. 339).

Although this is a fair summary of the findings reported in the literature, it is clear that these conclusions offer very little in the way of *explanation*. Such results may be of some practical value, but they do not provide us with any theoretical insight into the processes involved in inter-group relations, which would allow us to generalize in a more coherent fashion to other situations.

There are, of course, a great number of "theories" about ethnocentrism, prejudice, inter-group relations and social or ethnic stereotypes, but most of these theories are comparable to Amir's summary in the sense that they consist of singular propositions relating a variety of social or psychological variables to characteristics of inter-group relations. The most complete collection in this respect is probably LeVine and Campbell's (1972) catalogue of ethnocentrism hypotheses.

In recent years these classical theories have been criticized because they view a person's social identity as an epiphenomenon of inter-group relations (Billig, 1976; Tajfel and Turner, 1979). In addition they evaluate the pursuit of a positive ethnic or social identity negatively, because it involves ethnocentric attitudes and negative out-group stereotypes (Taylor and Simard, 1977). To stress these points Tajfel and his colleagues (Billig, 1973; Tajfel, 1970; Tajfel and Billig, 1974; Tajfel et al., 1971; Turner, 1978) have demonstrated in a number of so-called "minimal group" experiments that even a superficial categorization of individuals into groups, without any realistic conflict or competition, is sufficient to produce in-group—out-group bias in the allocation of rewards, or penalties (see Hewstone, Fincham and Jaspars, 1981). On the basis of these studies Tajfel (1978) argues that such a social categorization has consequences for a person's self-definition in terms of the social category or group to which he or she belongs and hence will lead to a search for positive social identity through social comparison with relevant out-groups. According to Tajfel's (1974, 1978) theory individuals strive for psychological distinctiveness along positively valued dimensions, for example by re-evaluating previously negative characteristics, so that they contribute towards a positive social identity. The example *par excellence* of this strategy is the adoption by Black consciousness movements of the slogan "Black is beautiful".

It is important to compare this functional theory of inter-group relations with LeVine and Campbell's (1972) learning theory approach to the "grain of truth" notion of stereotypes. LeVine and Campbell argue that stereotyping can be understood in terms of Hull's (Hull, 1952; Spence, 1956) learning theory where response strength is a multiplicative function of stimulus intensity (v) and intra-psychic determinants — drive (D), incentive value (K) and habitualization (H) (see also Campbell, 1967). Applying this model to stereotypes LeVine and Campbell consider the stereotypes or images which persons or groups have of each other as perceptions which reflect both the character of the group being described and the character of the group doing the describing. The upshot of this principle, according to LeVine and Campbell, is that "the greater the real differences between groups on any particular custom, appearance, item of material culture, the more likely that culture trait is to appear in the stereotyped imagery each group has of the other" (1972, p. 167). Apart from the fact that this may be a hypothesis which is very difficult to test when no information is available about the real differences, it is a prediction which is at odds with the suggestion made by Tajfel, that groups select or re-evaluate those characteristics which contribute most to their positive social identity (see Van Knippenberg and Wilke, 1979). The crucial difference appears to be that LeVine and Campbell assume *latent* agreement in the reciprocal stereotypes of groups which, however, may manifest differences in stereotyping when the evaluative components (D, K, H) are taken into account. In the case of two groups (the English and Americans) we are confronted with the following situation (see LeVine and Campbell, 1972, p. 172):

		Description of Group A	Group B
Description by	Group A	a+ reserved	c− intrusive
		b+ respect privacy	d− forward, pushing
	Group B	a− snobbish	c+ friendly
		b− cold, unfriendly	d+ outgoing, open.

Such a view assumes that there is, for example, a *real* difference between the English and Americans with regard to degree of introversion or extraversion. However, introversion (which according to both the English and the Americans is characteristic of English people) is evaluated differently by the two groups. Whereas the English rate it positively and interpret it in terms of reserve and respect for privacy, the Americans rate it negatively, labelling it as snobbishness, coldness or unfriendliness. Similar reasoning would account for the differences in descriptions of the Americans by the English and Americans.

This analysis raises at least two questions. In the first place one might ask how the English or Americans know about such real differences? Research concerning introversion—extraversion in English and Americans (Eysenck and Eysenck, 1969; Riesman, Glaser and Denny, 1955) is probably not known to a representative sample of the English or Americans who would have direct knowledge of such studies. It is much more probable that any knowledge of real differences people have is in the form of social representations (Moscovici, 1961; Moscovici and Farr, in press) which are shared by members of both groups, serve as justifications and explanations of their own and other people's behaviour (Deschamps, 1973–74; Doise, 1978), and have a common (social) origin and as such constitute a (social) reality *sui generis.*

This leads us to pose our second question, which is whether there has to be, originally, any real difference at all between the attributes of members of one's own or other groups. If the English and Americans come out equally on one of Eysenck's personality questionnaires both groups might regard themselves as, say, friendly and the other group as intrusive. It would all depend, Tajfel would argue, to what extent such interpretations or re-evaluations contribute to the positive social identity of the group members. Let us take an example from a recent study by van Knippenberg (1978). Van Knippenberg found that students from Dutch polytechnics and universities differed in their perception and evaluation of themselves and members of the other group. University students were seen by polytechnic students as scoring higher on a combined *scientific* and *status* dimension than the polytechnic students themselves. One might argue that such a difference has a basis in reality, given that the university students get a more scientific training and receive a higher income and social position later in life. The judgements of the university students were similar to those of the polytechnic students, but less extreme. However, both polytechnic students and university students regarded themselves as more *practical* and more *human* than members of the other group. If there is a real difference in this respect between both groups this would be hard to explain in terms of LeVine and Campbell's theory. Apparently group members can create for themselves a positive social identity irrespective of any real differences.

What seems to be important is to realize where the real differences are which may lead to stereotyping or negative inter-group relations. In an experiment such as the one mentioned above, or in the already mentioned inter-group experiments, such differences as can be perceived exist at the level of *behaviour* in an interaction situation or, as in the minimal group experiments and the experiment of van Knippenberg, in the (social) categorization of individuals into two or more groups. Differences in attitudes are not perceived as such because they are latent dispositions which are attributed to people on the basis of their behaviour, or their belonging to certain social categories. Which attributions are made depends on a number of variables which have been discussed by LeVine and Campbell (1972), Amir (1969) or Triandis and Vassiliou (1967), but it is essential to see that we are in fact dealing with an *attribution* process. At least in principle, the process of attributing certain traits to individuals in cross-cultural contact or inter-group situations might be regarded as a special way of explaining one's own or other people's behaviour and actions by attributing the causes of that behaviour to certain traits.

Interpreting stereotyping as a causal attribution process in an inter-group context immediately raises questions which have to do with the rather individualistic approach of attribution theory as developed by Heider (1944, 1958), Jones and Davis (1965) and Kelley (1967, 1973). As we have pointed out elsewhere (Hewstone and Jaspars, in press (a)) the social dimensions of attribution processes have been seriously neglected in several ways. In the first place traditional explanations in attribution theory assume that an observer regards the other person or him/herself as an isolated individual without taking into account the fact that he or she is a member of a social group. Secondly, it should be realized that attributions are probably not arrived at in isolation by the observer who, according to Kelley (1967), carries out some sort of intuitive analysis of variance. Rather, attributions are generated through social interaction with other individuals who do or do not share the individual's initial perceptions and inferences (Hewstone and Jaspars, in press (b)). Thirdly, we want to emphasize that attributions are not made for their own sake but are usually called for in a particular social context. For example, it may make quite a difference whether foreign students try to explain the behaviour of their hosts to themselves while in the host country, or to their hosts, or to friends and family in their own country after they have returned home.

The study of the relationship between cross-cultural interaction and stereotyping as an expression of inter-group relations could benefit from considering the assignment of stereotypes as the outcome of an attribution process which may have important social functions in creating a positive social identity for the in-group members. It is the attribution process in this social context which we regard as a missing link in the study of inter-group relations and which is the focus of this chapter. However, before we can discuss such an application of attribution theory we will briefly outline the basic tenets of the various theories which have been presented under this heading.

Attribution theory in social psychology

It is not our intention, nor would it be possible, to give here a complete exposition of attribution theory as it has developed in social psychology over the last 10—15 years. We merely want to highlight those issues in attribution theory which are of direct relevance to the study of cross-cultural interaction and inter-group relations. For a more complete discussion we refer to the (original) publications of Heider, Kelley, and Jones and Davis (Heider, 1944, 1958; Jones, 1979; Jones and Davis, 1965; Kelley, 1967, 1973; Kelley and Michela, 1980).

According to Kelley, attribution theory "is a theory about how people make causal explanations, about how they answer questions beginning with 'why'" (Kelley, 1973, p. 107). He goes on to point out that the theory developed in social psychology as a means of dealing with questions which are concerned with the causes of observed behaviour, as seen by the man in the street. Such causes can, broadly speaking, either be sought in a characteristic of the person or in the environment. The theory deals both with the question of self-perception and with the perception of the behaviour of others. The crucial question for attribution theory, as far as the perception of others is concerned, is to specify how an observer arrives at a causal understanding of observed behaviour. Which information does the observer use? Kelley (1973) outlines two different cases depending upon the amount of information available to the attributor. In the first case the attributor has information from multiple observations, thus permitting him or her to observe and respond to the *covariation* of an observed effect and its possible cause. In the second case the attributor has information from only a single observation which makes it necessary for him or her to take account of the *configuration* of factors that are plausible causes for the observed effect.

Following suggestions made earlier by Heider (1958, p. 297) and Duncker (1945, p. 64) Kelley argues that it is convenient to conceptualize the process of causal attribution of observed behaviour (in the case of covariation) as a common-sense replica of analysis of variance. In this model the factors are *persons, entities* and *time/modalities*. Each factor contributes a particular kind of information: from persons we derive *consensus* information, from entities we derive *distinctiveness* information, from times/modalities we derive *consistency* information. The covariation principle suggests that the effect is seen as caused by the factor with which it covaries and experiments conducted by McArthur (1972) and others (see Kelley and Michela, 1980) confirm that consistency, consensus and distinctiveness do indeed affect the attribution of causality in the way predicted by Kelley, although not all factors are of equal importance.

The discussion of Kelley's three informational criteria (consensus, consistency and distinctiveness) leads to a more general question, concerning "psychological epistemology", i.e. the veridicality of our beliefs and judgements of the world. A person can, according to Kelley, know that his or her perceptions, judgements and evaluations of the world are true to the extent that he/she can confidently make an entity attribution. Of particular importance for the study of stereotypes is Kelley's liberal interpretation of the process of causal attribution when he writes that:

> the ascription of an attribute to an entity amounts to a particular causal explanation of effects associated with that entity — reactions or responses to it, judgments and evaluations of it, etc. So all judgments of the type 'Property x characterizes Entity y' are viewed as causal attributions (Kelley, 1973, p. 107).

This is certainly a somewhat questionable and elastic use of the notion of causal explanation since it is by no means evident that any attribute ascribed to an entity is always seen by the man in the street as actually producing the effects associated with that entity. For instance, an attribute may be seen as nothing more than a shorthand expression for the observed actions of a person. It may well be that the ascription of an attribute to an entity may have the function of a causal attribution, but it seems reasonable to make a distinction between such implicit attributions and attributions which are explicitly based on inferences from observed behaviour. We should also be aware that we are talking about the explanation of behaviour and not about the explanation of the direct or indirect effects of individual or collective behaviour; however, these effects may influence the process of inferring the causes of the behaviour which produces the effects. In fact the theory of Heider (1958), expressed in his naive analysis of action, and the Correspondent Inference theory of Jones and Davis (1965) take the relations between action and outcome into account.

Thus far we have referred to Kelley's model for multiple observations, and his taxonomy of relevant information, but on what principles does the observer operate when only single observations are available? Kelley has suggested two principles or causal schemata which observers may use to arrive at causal attributions in this latter case. The first principle is known as the discounting principle and states that the role of a given cause in producing a given effect is discounted if other plausible causes are present. The second principle is called the augmentation principle and refers to the familiar idea that when there are known to be constraints, costs, sacrifices or risks involved in taking an action the action is attributed more to the actor than it would be otherwise. The discounting principle and the augmentation principle are examples of what Kelley calls a multiple sufficient cause schema and a compensatory cause schema. A more complete discussion of these and other schemata need not detain the present argument (see Kelley, 1972). It is, however, important to point out here that Kelley holds that the layman has a repertoire of such schemata available for trying to interpret social reality. He goes on to emphasize the importance of considering the interplay of these schemata and new information which rests on covariation of "cause" and "effect". It appears that existing causal preconceptions are much more powerful determinants of causal attributions than are observed covariations. Furthermore, simple, main effects schemata are preferred over more complex ones.

Emerging from this brief outline of attribution theory there are three main points which appear relevant to the study of cross-cultural interactions:

(1) The suggestion that when multiple observations are available an observer will attribute the cause of the observed behaviour to either something in the person or to the situation on the basis of the covariation of the behaviour across actors, entities and times (occasions).

(2) An observer will experience his or her judgement as true to the extent that consensus, distinctiveness and consistency information provide for an entity attribution.

(3) In addition to basing attributions upon observed covariation of the factors mentioned, an observer will be influenced in his or her judgement by causal schemata such as the discounting principle, the augmentation principle, and so on.

Although there is a great deal of similarity between Kelley's theory of causal attribution, Heider's naive-analysis-of-action model and Jones's correspondent inference theory, there are a number of relevant differences which are important for the study of attribution processes in cross-cultural interaction. Heider's theory is, in essence, equal to Kelley's theory because one can argue that Kelley merely elaborates Heider's suggestions that causal analysis is "in a way analogous to experimental methods" (Heider, 1958, p. 297). However, Heider originally discussed phenomenal causality as an example of unit formation. Actor and act, act and outcome, cause and effect were seen as examples of dynamic *Gestalt* formation or kinematic integration (Michotte, 1946). In this view it seems less important for causal attribution that covariation across persons, entities and times occurs. Rather, Heider argues, *Gestalt* factors like proximity, contiguity and *Prägnanz* (good form) will determine whether a causal attribution is made to the person or to the situation. On the basis of these *Gestalt* principles Heider also shows that in general a person attribution is much more likely than a situation attribution. But person attribution does not only occur because it more often makes a good *Gestalt*. Heider quotes with approval Fauconnet's rhetorical question: "Is a first and personal cause anything else but a cause conceived in such a way, that it can be held responsible, that it can furnish something fixed and constant to which sanction can be applied" (Heider, 1944, p. 361). The fact that a person is seen as a first or "local" cause beyond which we do not retrace the chain of causal inferences implies that (the effects of) the behaviour can much more easily and justifiably be annulled by "destroying" the absolute origin of the effects. This motivational basis of causal attribution processes has even wider implications in the case of inter-group behaviour. If the choice in causal attribution is between a person and a situation attribution, "person" and "situation" are constituted, in the case of inter-group relations, by members of in- and out-groups. Attributing the cause of certain events to an out-group or (one of) its members and blaming them as scapegoats then "exonerates the members of the ingroup from any blame for their conditions and prevents a lowering of the selfesteem of the ingroup members" (Heider, 1944, p. 369).

In his *Psychology of Interpersonal Relations* (Heider, 1958), Heider adds to this *Gestalt* analysis of personal causality the criterion of equifinality. Personal causality is then equated with intentionality for which the fact that different acts may lead to the same outcome (equifinality) is a clear indication. Thus in addition to the criteria which Kelley has formulated for causal attribution we now have Heider's *Gestalt* principles and the notion of equifinality as another set of possible independent variables which may influence causal attribution. Research by Michotte (1946) and more recent research (Kelley and Michela, 1980) have shown that these factors do indeed have an influence on causal attributions.

Finally, before we can turn to the question of ethnic stereotyping and inter-group relations, we have to consider several criteria put forward by Jones and Davis (1965) and Jones (1979) for inferring dispositions from acts. In their theory of correspondent inferences Jones and Davis have suggested that the fewer distinctive reasons an actor has for an action, and the less these reasons are widely shared in the culture, the more informative is that action about the identifying dispositions of the actor. More specifically, Jones and Davis argue that the disposition or the intention governing an action is indicated by those of its consequences not common to the alternative actions and the fewer such non-common effects, the less ambiguous is the attribution of the intention or the disposition (*the non-common effects* principle). The second factor which affects causal attribution, according to Jones and Davis, is the observer's beliefs about what other actors would do in the same situation (*social desirability*). If few persons would have acted as the actor does, the action is seen as revealing a person's intentions and dispositions. Thus in Western culture it may mean little that a man holds open a door for a woman; if the same man slammed the door in the woman's face, we might learn more about his true intentions and dispositions. Thirdly, Jones and Davis suggest that the observer makes a personal attribution if the action affects the actor personally (*hedonic relevance*). Thus if our Western man holds the door for a woman whom we know he is "interested" in, we might make a person attribution. Research based on correspondent inference theory has by and large confirmed that these factors do indeed affect causal attribution to persons.

Having considered some of the relevant basic principles of attribution theory we are now ready to consider the implications of an attributional approach to cross-cultural interaction, ethnic stereotyping and the study of inter-group relations in general.

Attribution theory, cross-cultural interaction and inter-group relations

Basic distinctions

Before embarking on this ambitious synthesis a few basic distinctions are necessary. First of all it is important to distinguish between situations in which in-group members or individuals belonging to one culture are indeed in inter-action with members of the out-group or other culture and situations where no direct contact exists. In the first case it seems natural to proceed from Kelley's *covariation* model of attribution; in the second case Kelley's *configurational* approach makes more sense. This is not to say that one should not pay attention to the causal schemata which people bring into cross-cultural interaction. Such schemata may in effect be extremely important, but from a theoretical point of view it makes sense to develop the pure case where people interact with members of other groups about whom they do not have any clear preconceptions and consider in the second instance how attributions based on observed covariation are affected by pre-existing causal notions.

In the second place we should take into account the nature of cause and effect in particular attributions. Attribution theory as formulated by Kelley, Heider and Jones has been applied mainly to the explanation of observed behaviour in terms of more or less permanent latent dispositions of persons and situations. It is concerned with the inference of an unobservable cause from observable behaviour. In certain cases we are, however, not interested in the explanation of the behaviour as such, but in the explanation of the effect or outcomes of behaviour or even in the (social) conditions which are characteristic of a group of individuals. It makes quite a difference whether we want to understand why someone makes certain political statements, why an accident happens or why someone is un-employed.

The attribution process becomes more complex when we are dealing with the explanation of social conditions which are used to characterize an individual. A state of affairs which we describe as unemployment is clearly not to be taken as behaviour (although it does refer to or imply a particular behaviour), nor is it to be seen necessarily as the outcome of the behaviour of the person who may be characterized by it. When a person or a group of people is unemployed, someone or something either directly or indirectly is seen as the cause, but such a cause is often only an intermediate cause which may be traced back to another first or ultimate cause (Fincham and Jaspars, 1980). In the case of unemployment we can give the state, a Conservative policy or the poor management of an employer as the cause of unemployment, but policies or management decisions can be seen as caused by practices and attitudes of workers. A social condition can thus be explained by indirectly attributing the cause of this condition to personal dispositions (attitudes of workers) or more directly to external social factors such as a government policy or a management decision (for studies on social conditions see Hewstone and Jaspars, in press (a)).

One final consideration should be mentioned before we discuss the application of attribution theory to inter-group relations and cross-cultural interaction. In many inter-group relations studies subjects are asked to judge themselves and members of particular out-groups on a number of personality attributes. From an attributional perspective such a procedure short-circuits, so to speak, the attribution process by not presenting subjects with the particular acts committed by individual members of the out-group or in-group. If such stereotype ratings are to be interpreted as the result of attributional processes, which is how Kelley interprets them (Kelley, 1973), we will have to consider such judgements as implicit attributions which are inherent in stereotypes. Such implicit attributions may, however, turn out to be quite different from explicit attributions based on observed behaviour or events. Sometimes studies confuse such attributions with simple descriptions of actual behaviour which may reflect misconceptions.

Covariation and attribution in cross-cultural interaction, or on how to shake hands with a foreigner

In his hilarious handbook for beginners and advanced pupils on *How to be an Alien,* George Mikes (1966) describes the complexities of what is seemingly the simplest form of cross-cultural interaction: when to shake hands with an Englishman. Starting from this simple example it is easy to see how attributions based on observed covariation may deviate from the general predictions of Kelley (1973). The easiest way to illustrate this point is to consider Kelley's "covariation cube" with the added distinction that at least one of the persons in the cube belongs to a group or culture different from that of the other persons in the cube (Fig. 10). If we consider the attributor as belonging to the same group as the actor(s) s(he) observes, Kelley's analysis of variance predicts that an entity attribution will be made when all persons observed show the behaviour (consensus) all the time (consistency) with respect to the same entity (distinctiveness). A handshake is therefore interpreted as a consistent social custom which is elicited by the behaviour of another person or the social occasion (circumstance). However, if we now consider the situation where the people who meet belong to different cultural groups, which differ with respect to this particular custom, we see that the behaviour also covaries with the social categories describing the differences between the groups. Since the same social occasion does not elicit the response in one group, but does so consistently and uniformly with members of the other social group a person attribution or an attribution to something in persons belonging to the same group is much more likely. In other words when an

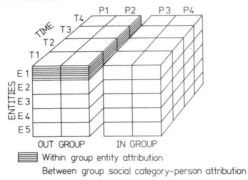

FIG. 10   The analysis of variance framework for making causal inferences in inter-group situations (after Kelley 1973)

Englishman does not extend his hand to greet a Polish visitor to Britain who is used to this custom, the latter may attribute the former's response as a sign of some personal quality of English people, such as unfriendliness.

Stereotyping an out-group member in this way can thus be explained as person attribution which is confounded with social category attribution. This is a prediction which follows directly from Kelley's analysis of variance model in which the person is nested within a social category distinction.

We should notice, however, that cross-cultural covariation also leads to person attribution. "We shake hands because we're friendly, they don't because they are unfriendly." If the context is not cross-cultural it seems perfectly natural to expect a situational explanation of the kind which explains such greeting behaviour as prescribed by social custom. This conclusion suggests immediately an interesting interpretation, which can be derived from Jones's correspondent inference theory. Jones and Davis (1965) and Jones (1979) have suggested that the attribution of a personal disposition is more likely to occur when behaviour is out of role, i.e. does not conform to custom or normative expectations. In the case of greeting behaviour it is easy to see that not performing the required or expected behaviour will be explained in terms of the other person's attitudes or intentions. If such behaviour occurs in someone belonging to a different social or cultural category the person attribution is associated with belonging to that different category.

Heider's *Gestalt* approach to the naive analysis of action strengthens even more the case for person attribution in cross-cultural interaction since it suggests that the person and his or her acts form a stronger *Gestalt* than the act and situational factors which also determine it. This will certainly be the case when the process of social categorization is enhanced by highly salient characteristics of group membership in cross-cultural interaction. In Heider's terminology such a situation will increase the *"Prägnanz"* of personal characteristics when searching for an explanation of manifested behaviour.

Summarizing thus far our extension of attribution theory to cross-cultural interaction we argue that:

(1) Behaviour of members of other groups perceived as out-of-role and un-expected from the perspective of one's own group is more likely to lead to person attribution.

(2) Since social categorization in terms of cultural differences is probably very salient in such situations, the person attribution will be associated with the perceived difference in culture.

(3) The same behaviour which gives rise to person attribution cross-culturally may lead to a situational attribution within a particular group or culture because social categorization does not covary with the behaviour, but is constant.[3]

Until now we have only considered cross-cultural interaction which brings to the fore differences in behaviour between members belonging to different cultural groups. What if such differences do not exist or the only difference which exists concerns the fact that individuals belong to different groups?

The prediction which follows from our cloven covariation cube (see Fig. 10) is obvious and in line with the explanations which have been offered for the actor—observer differences in attribution at the individual level. Cross-cultural interaction could lead to in-group—out-group differentiation in attribution based on cognitive factors as suggested by Jones and Nisbett (1972). It seems reasonable to argue that an observer in cross-cultural interaction has more information about the behaviour of the members of his or her culture or group than about persons belonging to another culture or group. Paraphrasing Kelley and Michela (1980) one might say that the observer may know nothing more about the actor, who belongs to a different group or culture, than his or her behaviour in a limited range of situations, but the observer knows of the behaviour of in-group members in many situations and is aware of its cross-situational variability. At the individual level this hypothesis has been tested directly for the actor—observer diffe-rence (Lay et al., 1974; Lenauer, Sameth and Shaver, 1976; Nisbett et al., 1973; for a review see Monson, in press). The social extension of the actor—observer difference in attribution to in-group—out-group differences suggests immediately that perceived cross-situational variability of behaviour could directly be tested at the group level. The further suggestions made by Nisbett et al. (1973, study 3) that there is a gradient of dispositional attribution which relates inversely to the total amount of information available about other persons, can also be directly extended to the group level when we are considering differences in dispositional attribution with respect to more than one out-group.

It has also been suggested that the actor—observer difference may be explained cognitively by a difference in visual perspective, in that the actor attends to his or her task while the observer attends to the actor's behaviour. Attempts to manipulate the perspective of the observer, e.g. by showing the actor a videotape replay of his or her behaviour, have shown that this leads indeed to less situational attribution (e.g. Eisen, 1979; Storms, 1973). An analogous change in perspective is possible in cross-cultural interaction when we compare newcomers' judgements of their own group with the judgements of people who have already spent some time in the other culture. One would expect those who have already spent some time in the new culture to have developed a different perspective, to look upon the newcomers as out-group members and to make more dispositional attributions than the newcomers themselves will do.[4]

Apart from the cognitive explanation we have suggested for in-group—out-group differences in attribution we should also consider, just as in the case of actor—observer differences, whether motivational factors might be involved in this social attribution process. A plausible common-sense hypothesis which has been tested in several actor—observer studies is that an actor is egocentrically concerned with receiving credit for actions which have positive consequences and avoiding blame for actions which lead to negative outcomes. If such an egocentric motivation were to play a role, we could expect internal actor attribution and external observer attribution in the case of positive behaviour and the reverse in the case of negative behaviour. Results of various studies (see Kelley and Michela, 1980; Monson, in press) are, however, contradictory in the sense that the effect has only been found in some studies and not in others.

One reason why the results of these studies are not so clear-cut is perhaps that there are processes at work which operate, in part, at cross-purposes. There is in the first place Nisbett's (Jones and Nisbett, 1972) cognitive theory which predicts an actor—observer main effect. The egocentric theory predicts an interaction effect of the actor—observer difference and outcome valence. But there is also the correspondent inference theory developed by Jones and Davis which predicts that there is a greater likelihood of dispositional attribution when the effects are highly desirable for the actor. In fact, Jones and Davis generate rather confusing predictions in this respect, since they also argue that out-of-role (e.g. socially undesirable) behaviour leads to dispositional attribution. For simplicity, our predictions deal just with their first prediction.

Systematically we therefore have the complex expectations, shown in Table 7, for actor—observer differences in attribution. If we assume that the three processes just described are of equal strength in their effect on attribution we have to predict an interaction effect of the actor—observer difference and outcome valence in the sense that one's own negative behaviour will be different from all other conditions in that it will lead to more situational attribution. One could in general not expect a difference between self and other attribution for positive behaviour or an effect of outcome valence for attributions made by an observer. However, if under particular circumstances the effects of the three processes are of unequal strength any of these theories could be confirmed. It is therefore not easy to say which conditions would favour one or the other of the theories mentioned. It has been suggested by Snyder, Stephan and Rosenfield (1976)

TABLE 7   *Actor-observer differences
in attribution based on Nisbett's cognitive
theory (C), Snyder's egocentrism model
(E) and Jones and Davis's hedonic
relevance hypothesis (H)*

		Outcome	
		Positive	Negative
Actor	C	Situational	Situational
	D	Dispositional	Situational
	H	Dispositional	Situational
Observer	C	Dispositional	Dispositional
	D	Dispositional	Situational
	H	Situational	Dispositional

that a competitive situation would favour an egocentric attribution, because the tendency to attribute own gain to a personal disposition will be strengthened by the tendency to make a dispositional attribution for the other's loss. In general one might expect the egocentric hypothesis to become more important when the observer is affected in one way or another by the behaviour of the actor. The desirability hypothesis might apply especially when the difference between actor and observer vanishes because they share a common viewpoint. If outcomes refer to acts which are *socially* desirable one might argue that both actor and observer will agree in this respect and infer that in general people want to do good things and only do bad things intentionally.

The last considerations bring us back to the original question which we set out to answer in this section: will the same behaviour be attributed differently if it is shown by an in-group or an out-group member? The answer to this question can now be qualified. We do expect dispositional attribution of behaviour by out-group members and situational attribution of behaviour by in-group members, especially when there are only intrinsic outcomes. However, when behaviour is clearly perceived as positive or negative we expect that positive behaviour of in-group members and negative behaviour of out-group members will be dispositionally attributed, whereas negative behaviour of in-group members and positive behaviour of out-group members will be situationally attributed. In addition to this we expect that, irrespective of in-group—out-group membership, socially desirable behaviour will be more strongly attributed to person dispositions. We would expect the same attributional processes to take place when positive or negative social conditions are attributed with in-group—out-group categorization.

Social attribution and culturally determined causal schemata

In the previous sections we have only looked at the possible transformations of attribution theory when actual interaction takes place between persons belonging to different social and cultural groups, or categories. In many cases we seem to be willing to make inferences about other people's behaviour on the basis of indirect information. The classical studies on stereotypes refer very often to national or cultural groups who have never, or only rarely, been in contact with each other (e.g. Katz and Braly, 1933). Clear stereotypes certainly appear to exist in such circumstances, but the genesis of these stereotypes must be considered as different from stereotypes which might emerge through cross-cultural interaction. It seems even more likely that the latter kind of stereotypes, and the attributional processes they imply, are more basic in the sense that no-one ever enters into cross-cultural interaction without any preconceptions about the other culture. For this reason LeVine and Campbell (1972) consider stereotypes between autonomous, independent groups as distinct from stereo-types held by ethnic groups which are integrated within a single political and economic order. LeVine and Campbell argue that in the first situation, when little or no actual opportunity for mutual observation exists, the groups are more ambiguous stimuli for each other and allow more autistic perception, "These fantasies may represent the wishes or fears of the in-group and may serve the group's need for solidarity, dominance or self-esteem or its members' individual motives" (LeVine and Campbell, 1972, p. 165).

It is precisely at this point that Kelley's ideas about causal schemata and Tajfel's theory of inter-group relations appear to complement each other. If there is, as Tajfel (1978) argues, a need for positive social identity which a person can achieve through social comparison based on social categorization, there are at least two ways in which a positive social identity can contribute to, for example, a high self-esteem via configurational attribution processes, as suggested by Kelley. The first case is represented by situations in which we are concerned with the common-sense explanation of social events which can be cast in an attributional schema analogous to the internal—external distinction made by Kelley in his configuration model. At the level of explanations for individual behaviour or interpersonal events the internal—external distinction is equated with the differentiation in personal and (social) situational causes. When consider-ing the internal—external distinction at the group level the out-group becomes the situational and the in-group the "personal" cause. Once we accept this interpretation of attribution theory at the inter-group level Kelley's discounting principle can easily explain the scapegoat phenomenon to which Heider has already referred in attributional terms. It follows from the discounting principle that attributing the cause of certain events to an out-group excludes in-group attribution, and hence may exonerate the in-group from any blame for their social conditions and thus prevent a lowering of the self-esteem of in-group members. An extension of the discounting principle to positive social events would follow in the same way. A victory by one's own group over another is probably more often interpreted as the result of own strength than as weakness in the adversary.

However, other causal schemata are probably called upon in other circumstances. External events probably require a multiple necessary cause schema, but it would be interesting to see whether such a schema is less likely to be invoked at the group level than at the individual or inter-personal level. Thus far we have made a distinction between in-group and out-group which is analogous to the person—situation distinction in attribution theory. However, the parallel can also be drawn in another way. One might equally well ask whether behaviour of in-group members or events directly or indirectly "caused" by in-group members are interpreted in a different way from similar actions or events related to out-group members. The predictions one could offer here are similar to the ones which were discussed for the covariation model. Assuming that one is more familiar with situational factors which can potentially explain behaviour and social events of in-group members a discounting principle is more likely to operate for out-group behaviour, whereas a multiple necessary cause schema can be called upon to explain in-group behaviour.

In the previous example we only discussed the common-sense explanations of one and the same social event or social act which could either be attributed to the in-group or out-group, or to personal or situational causes. In many situations we are confronted with a perceived or reported difference between in-group and out-group which calls for an explanation. We have already discussed this problem for the situation in which one is actually able to observe covariation of "cause" and "effect". However, if the (reported) observation is confined to one instance, a configurational explanation has to be sought. In this case we have to realize that, just as in the situation of selective cross-cultural interaction, the information which is available to the individual may have been selectively acquired or transmitted. In this case selectivity takes on a different form. We would like to put forward the hypothesis that where information is transmitted via news media a bias in the form of extreme instances takes place (for evidence of this bias see Husband, 1977). If news media are biased towards reporting extreme events, the consequence of this is that the likelihood of reporting positive (or negative) instances associated with one or the other group is very high. Given such reported instances, people will, according to Tversky and Kahneman (1974), ignore the base rate of such instances, forget that such extreme instances are very rare and infer that there are large differences between in-group and out-group which call for an explanation. The inferred association of such differences with particular out-groups can be understood also as a non-common effect according to Jones and Davis's correspondent inference theory which leads to person rather than situational attribution.

The veridicality of social stereotypes: an attributional illusion

Attribution research has paid hardly any attention to the phenomenon of attribution validity, although Kelley (1973, p. 111) regards this as one of the most important uses to which the analysis of variance conception of the attribution process can be put. As we pointed out earlier, Kelley argues that an individual can know that his or her judgements are correct or true when an entity attribution can be made, that is:

> If (a) my response is associated *distinctively* with the stimulus, (b) my response is similar to those made by other persons to the same stimulus (there is *consensus*), and (c) my response is *consistent* over time on successive exposures to the stimulus and as I interact with it by means of different sensory and perceptual modalities (Kelley, 1973, p. 112).

Extending Kelley's test for attributional validity to the level of inter-group relations, we arrive immediately at the conclusion that stereotypes of out-group members must be valid or true, since the response to out-group members is distinct, consistent and in agreement with the response of other in-group members. The flaw in this argument is, of course, that consensus[5] is confined to in-group members. This implies that as long as the comparison of judgements or attributions is limited to one's own group there is, according to attribution theory, no way in which an individual can distinguish between illusion and reality, or between objective and social reality. This may be one of the reasons why it is so difficult to influence social stereotypes. For the analysis of inter-group relations this is an extremely important conclusion because it implies that the veridical nature of stereotypes provides us with an explanation of our own responses, which locates the cause of our response in the out-group member and thereby justifies it. LeVine and Campbell (1972) refer to the phenomenon of the in-grouper who perceives the different characteristics of the out-group causing his hostility. Sartre, a long time ago, exposed the fallacious nature of this justification in his analysis of anti-semitism by applying the same reasoning to matters of taste in general; this leads to the conclusion that "Il doit y avoir quelque chose dans la tomate, puisque j'ai horreur d'en manger" (There must be something wrong with tomatoes if I dislike them) (Sartre, 1954, p. 11).

Accuracy and decomposition of stereotypes

We want to add one final observation to the attributional analysis of inter-group relations and stereotypes. We pointed out in the previous section that the restriction of consensus to the in-group leads to an inference of the veridicality of stereotypes. This means, of course, that the illusion of veridicality should not arise if observers belong both to in-group and to out-group, since discrepancies will emerge between attributions and perceptions of in-group and out-group members. The fact that auto- and heterostereotypes (Triandis and Vassiliou, 1967) and in-group and out-group attributions are different raises the question of the "accuracy" of heterostereotypes with respect to autostereotypes. Since the difference . between heterostereotypes and autostereotypes is a complex measure it could be decomposed along the same lines as suggested by Cronbach (1955) for the analysis of inter-personal perception. If both in-group and out-group members are asked to judge themselves and each other on a number of trait scales (or are asked to explain a particular act or event in situational or dispositional terms) one can in general express the inaccuracy of the judgement or attribution as:

$$DO_i^2 = \frac{1}{kN} \underset{o}{\Sigma} \underset{t}{\Sigma} (Y_{oti} - X_{ot})^2$$

X_{ot} indicates the autostereotype of out-group (member) o on trait t.

Y_{oti} indicates the heterostereotype of out-group (member) o on trait t by in-group member i.

Where i indicates a judgement made *by* an in-group member;

t is the trait on which the judgement is made;

o indicates the judgement *of* an out-group or in-group member;

k is the number of traits *on* which o are judged;

N is the number of out-group members;

D^2 is the overall inaccuracy or discrepancy of auto- and heterostereotype or attribution.

In addition to the accuracy analysis Cronbach has also suggested that one can analyse the discrepancy between the self-description of the observer and his or her description of other persons. Applied to the inter-group situation this means that we can analyse the assumed similarity between autostereotype and heterostereotype. This is an interesting question because it suggests to some extent a test of LeVine and Campbell's hypothesis that heterostereotypes are a function of "projective" factors within the observer and real characteristics of groups, the "kernel of truth". Cronbach has suggested a similar projective interpretation for the assumed similarity of others in interpersonal judgements (Cronbach, 1955, p. 181). If we apply the same notion to group stereotypes we can investigate the projective nature of heterostereotypes by comparing these with the autostereotypes of the in-group. The overall discrepancy can be analysed in the same way as we have suggested for the comparison of the heterostereotype with the autostereotype of the out-group (see Cronbach, 1955). The interesting implication of the projective hypothesis suggested by LeVine and Campbell is that the heterostereotype of the out-group can be interpreted as a function of the autostereotype of the out-group and the autostereotype of the in-group.[6]

Apart from this suggestion one might attempt to predict which component of the discrepancy between the heterostereotype and either one of the autostereotypes contributes most to the overall difference. Since most theories of ethnocentrism, prejudice and inter-group relations (see LeVine and Campbell, 1972) predict that heterostereotypes are more negative than autostereotypes, irrespective of the content of the stereotype, one would have to expect that the elevation component is the major contributor to the discrepancy between autostereotypes and heterostereotypes. We should, however, differentiate our prediction for the comparison of the in-group with the out-group stereotype. There are in fact three different predictions which follow from the general notion:

(1) The autostereotype of the in-group is more positive than the heterostereo-type of the out-group. (We are better than they are.)
(2) The heterostereotype of the out-group is more negative than the autostereo-type of the out-group. (They are worse than they think.)
(3) The autostereotype of the in-group is more positive than the heterostereo-type of the in-group. (We are better than they think we are.)

The two Cronbach analyses deal with the first and the second ethnocentrism hypotheses, i.e. accuracy refers to prediction 2, assumed similarity to prediction 1. The third prediction follows logically from a consideration of the basic data set as represented in Table 8. Whereas prediction 1 compares AS_i with HS_{oi} and

TABLE 8   *Three basic forms of inter-group evaluations*

	Evaluation of	
Evaluation by	In-group	Out-group
In-group	ASi	$HSo.i$
Out-group	$HSi.o$	ASo

ASi = autostereotype of in-group
$HSi.o$ = heterostereotype of in-group by out-group
ASo = autostereotype of out-group
$HSo.i$ = heterostereotype of out-group by in-group

prediction 2 HS_{oi} with AS_o, prediction 3 compares AS_i with HS_{io}. The de-composition of the discrepancy implied by the third prediction does not, how-ever, introduce a new analysis because it is formally similar to Cronbach's assumed similarity analysis. The only difference is that one is now looking at the other side of the coin, i.e. the similarity assumed by the out-group with respect to the in-group.

The important point in this "unfolding" of the general notion of inter-group evaluation is that it is by no means clear which one of these predictions follows from various theories and which one is confirmed by empirical data. As we have shown elsewhere (Warnaen and Jaspars, in press) one cannot understand inter-group evaluations without considering the structural or cultural relations which exist between the social or ethnic groups concerned.

If these structural–cultural relations imply differences in status or power within a particular society, it is to be expected that inter-group evaluations, such as the evaluation component of stereotypes, will reflect the power structure and interfere with the general tendency to have a negative attitude towards out-groups. This would mean that the evaluation or the evaluative components of autostereotypes of various groups are unequal and (hence) $HS_{oi} \neq HS_{io}$. The consequence of unequal positions for the inter-group evaluations can easily be seen if one takes into account the fact that the evaluations made are probably comparative judgements as suggested by Festinger for interpersonal relations (Festinger, 1954) and by Tajfel (1978) and Turner (1975) for inter-group relations. We suggest that the process of social comparison which Festinger proposed for self-evaluation can be extended to the evaluations of others both at the individual and at the group level. Just as in Festinger's theory we assume that an individual for the purpose of self-evaluation will compare the self or own-group with other individuals or other groups which are superior to the self or own-group in the interpersonal or social structure. We add, however, to the Festinger–Tajfel–Turner theory the notion that the evaluation of others or other groups will make use of the same comparison levels as the one used for self-evaluations. Regarding evalua-tion as a function of the ratio of perceived actual level to comparison level we set the following values for the conditions represented in Table 9. Referring to

TABLE 9   *A social comparison model for inter-group evaluation*

	Evaluation of	
Evaluation by	HS Group	LS Group
HS Group	$\dfrac{H}{H + \delta}$ (2)	$\dfrac{H}{H + \delta}$ (4)
LS Group	$\dfrac{H}{L + \delta}$ (1)	$\dfrac{H}{L + \delta}$ (3)

HS = High status
LS = Low status

our original three predictions we can now see that for a high-status group judging itself and a low-status group, or being judged by a low-status group, leads to a confirmation of prediction 1, and prediction 2, but not to a confirmation of prediction 3. If we take the case of the low-status group we find, however, exactly the reverse. Predictions 1 and 2 are not confirmed, whereas prediction 3 is.

One of the interesting points of the analysis just offered is that it has direct implications for the results to be expected with respect to some of the other components of stereotypes. The component which is labelled differential eleva-tion by Cronbach refers at the group level to the discrepancy between the heterostereotype of a particular out-group and the autostereotype of that out-group. So far we have only considered in our analysis the case of one out-group and for that reason the elevation and differential elevation components are confounded. However, if we were to extend the matrix in Table 9 to more than one out-group and generalize our model to the situation of multiple inter-group relations we would be able to create separate predictions for elevation and differential elevation. We will not discuss this extension here in detail, but it is probably intuitively clear that the predictions made before about the elevation component in the case of two groups remain the same for multiple group comparisons. The differential elevation component introduces a new element into the analysis. Briefly stated, the model presented here does imply the significant contribution of a differential elevation component, because it can readily be seen that the larger the perceived "real" differences become, the more strongly the prediction should be confirmed.

Similar arguments can be presented for the other components of stereotypes. The component which is labelled stereotype accuracy by Cronbach can be interpreted at the inter-group level as social judgements concerned with the "generalized" out-group. In this component it is the context of the stereotype which becomes important. LeVine and Campbell (1972) have mentioned several instances of such generalized out-group stereotypes, such as the differences seen between urban and rural groups, majority and minority groups, northerners and southerners, higher and lower social class, etc. The suggestion here is that each inter-group judgement contains at least to some extent this generalized component. It will be interesting to see how important this component is. Functional theories of prejudice, like the theory of the authoritarian personality (Adorno et al., 1950), imply a great deal of generality of this kind in judgements of minority groups, but the theory has never been tested along the lines suggested here. It is, however, not unlikely that many stereotypes also contain quite a few specific content elements which can probably only be understood if one is familiar with the particular social relations between such groups as these have developed historically. It would be hard to understand, for example, the nature of anti-semitism in Europe without taking into account the historical dimension of the relationship between Jews and Christians.

So far this analysis has focused on the decomposition of stereotypes as the end-point of inter-group attribution processes. It should be obvious by now that the same analysis can be applied to the attribution process itself by focusing on the dispositional or situational nature of the attributions made for in-groups and out-groups. Given a particular act or event, presented as either associated with an in-group or an out-group (member) we may find, as suggested before, differences in attributions to the person or the situation depending upon the nature of the outcome.

The decomposition of attribution is, however, not very revealing if we confine ourselves simply to crude person or situation attributions, which moreover might be negatively connected, thus leaving us only with one "trait" to analyse. If we were to study inter-group attributions in a more refined manner by considering a variety of personal and situational factors, the decomposition of such multiple attributions might give us a better understanding of inter-group relations.

Empirical studies

There are unfortunately very few studies which have dealt with inter-group relations from an attributional point of view or with attribution at the inter-group level. As such this chapter must stand as a largely programmatic contribution to the development of attribution theory and the study of inter-group relations, and should be considered as complementary to a related analysis which we have offered elsewhere (Hewstone and Jaspars, in press (a)). In this other paper we have considered in more detail several empirical studies and for that reason we will not discuss at great length any of these studies here. We would like to present, however, some of the published results which are directly relevant to the ideas discussed in the previous sections of this chapter.

We have in fact only discovered three studies (Mann and Taylor, 1974; Stephan, 1977; Taylor and Jaggi, 1974) which deal directly with the issue of inter-group attributions in a cross-cultural context. In the study by Taylor and Jaggi, Hindu Ss were asked to attribute the behaviour of in-group (Hindu) and out-group (Muslim) members performing socially desirable or undesirable acts to internal or external causes for the behaviour. The results are presented in such a way in Table 10 that a direct comparison with the three predictions made in a

TABLE 10   *Percentage of internal attributions made of socially desirable and undesirable acts performed by in-group and out-group members*

	Outcome		
	Positive	Negative	
In-group	58.25	2.25	30.25
Out-group	12.5	32.25	22.37
	35.37	17.25	

After Taylor and Jaggi, 1974.

previous section is possible (see pages 139—141). Obviously, all the attribution effects which were mentioned in our earlier discussion appear to be presented in the Taylor and Jaggi study. Positive outcomes appear to receive more personal attributions than negative outcomes do, but out-group attributions are less personal than in-group attributions. These main effects are, however, almost completely overshadowed by the interaction effect which follows from the ego-centric hypothesis. Predicting the cell means from a design matrix with two main effect variables (in-group—out-group G, positive—negative outcome O) and one interaction variable GO, we find that:

$$A_p = 0.19\,G + 0.42\,O + 0.88\,GO$$

where A_p = mean attribution to person for the various conditions;
$\quad\; G\;$ = in-group—out-group variable;
$\quad\; O\;$ = outcome variable;
$\quad\; GO$ = interaction variable of G and O.

The variance attributable to the in-group difference ($0.19^2 = 0.04$) is negligible and hence the generalization of Nisbett's Actor—Observer hypothesis to in-group—out-group attribution without taking the outcome into account does not seem warranted for this type of behaviour (being generous, cheating, helping, ignoring, praising, scolding, sheltering). In fact there is a tendency in the direction opposite to that one would expect on the basis of actor—observer differences. The social desirability hypothesis appears to be confirmed slightly ($0.42^2 = 0.18$) but overall the egocentric hypothesis is by far the winner, explaining $0.88^2 = 0.77$ per cent of the variance in means.

It is a pity that Taylor and Jaggi did not collect attributions of Muslim subjects because such additional data would have allowed us to analyse the data along the lines suggested in the previous section. Such data have, however, been collected in the two other studies mentioned above. Mann and Taylor (1974) asked 100 English-Canadian students and sixty-four French-Canadian students to indicate the degree to which five positive and five negative acts performed either by English or Canadian persons were caused by an equal number of relatively stable traits.[7]

The results of this study — which are unfortunately not reported in detail — are somewhat disappointing, presumably because of the choice of the traits which appeared to correspond clearly to prevailing stereotypes and may therefore not have allowed for any clear differentiation. The overall pattern of significant trait attributions shows that French- and English-Canadian Ss agree in making more dispositional attributions for positive acts of French- than of English-Canadian actors, whereas the reverse is true for negative acts, as can be seen in Table 11.

However, to present the results in this way is somewhat misleading because Table 11 does not show the nature of the traits involved. Mann and Taylor have

TABLE 11   *Trait attributions for English- and French-Canadian actors*
by English and French Ss of positive and negative acts

	English-Canadian actors		French-Canadian actors	
	Positive	Negative	Positive	Negative
English-Canadian Ss	11	12	18	4
French-Canadian Ss	10	12	16	6

After Mann and Taylor, 1974.
Note: Cell values indicate the number of significant effects reported by Mann and Taylor.

chosen behaviours which "reflected" such internal traits as friendly/unfriendly, successful/unsuccessful, tolerant/intolerant, brave/cowardly, considerate/inconsiderate and sociable/non-sociable.[8] In terms of content the results of Table 11 simply mean that both English- and French-Canadians see themselves and each other as successful and brave, whereas the English-Canadians are seen by everyone as inconsiderate and non-sociable and the French-Canadians as sociable and considerate. It is the latter difference which explains the positive trait attributions of the French-Canadians. If other (more positive English) traits had been chosen the results might have come out in the opposite direction. Because there is hardly any difference between autostereotypes and heterostereotypes of English- and French-Canadians it is of course impossible to undertake a decomposition of the discrepancy between the two.

The final study which will be discussed here presents us with more interesting results. Stephan (1977) conducted an experiment using Black, Chicano and Anglo students from the fifth and sixth grade of segregated and integrated schools in a south-western city of the U.S.A. They were asked (among other things) to choose between an internal and an external attribution for three positive and three negative behaviours of a person who was characterized as belonging to one of the three ethnic groups mentioned.

The results reported by Stephan can be summarized again in a table which is directly comparable with Table 7 presented earlier. As can be seen in Table 12 there is again, just as in the Taylor and Jaggi and the Mann and Taylor studies, a strong effect of the nature of the act. Positive behaviour is attributed more to personal causes than is negative behaviour. Compared with this effect the egocentrism effect is very weak although it is significant for the Anglos. No clear in-group—out-group effect, as predicted on the basis of Nisbett's actor—observer difference, appears to occur.

We may also consider the results obtained by Stephan from the point of view of the inter-group evaluations which take into account the larger social system of which the groups are part. We should realize that the Anglos are, in Stephan's words, "the high power majority group" and the Chicanos and the Blacks the

TABLE 12   *Percentage of dispositional attributions for positive and negative behaviours of in-group and out-group actors*

	Behaviour	
	Positive	Negative
In-group	81.2	45.3
Out-group	77.5	46.5

After Stephan, 1977.
Note: Results of the three different ethnic groups are averaged.

minority groups. To simplify the discussion we consider only the difference between dispositional attributions for positive and negative acts, treating this measure as an index of the extent to which positive behaviour is interpreted as the outcome of personal rather than situational factors. Thus the results can be presented as in Table 13. The results of Chicanos and Blacks confirm the expecta-

TABLE 13   *Differences between dispositional attributions for positive and negative acts of Anglos, Chicanos and Blacks*

	Anglos	Chicanos	Blacks
Anglos	0.38	0.39	0.40
Chicanos	0.32	0.41	0.32
Blacks	0.20	0.23	0.33

After Stephan, 1977.
Note: 0.38 = 0.86 −0.48.

tion that positive behaviour of in-group members is attributed more to personal factors than is positive behaviour of out-group members. The attributions of the Anglos, however, make sense only if one assumes that the subjects make use of a discounting principle and take into account the differences in social conditions of Anglos, Chicanos and Blacks. Attribution to personal causes for positive behaviour of Blacks is stronger because their social situation is apparently seen as insufficient to explain the behaviour, whereas this is not the case to the same extent for Anglos and Chicanos. The Anglos, aware of the "inferior" social position of the Blacks, discount this as a possible cause of the behaviour.

The results show once more how difficult it is to understand attributions between groups without allowing for the larger social structure of which the groups are a part. On the other hand we find at the same time that knowledge of causal schemata is essential for the explanation of the inter-group attributions. The data presented by Stephan force us to extend the three factor theory presented in Table 7, with an additional component which becomes relevant where in-group and out-group do not have equivalent positions in society.

Summary and conclusions

In this chapter we have attempted to draw together research on ethnic stereotypes, inter-group relations and attribution theory. Research on social contact and inter-group relations has led to many contradictory results, as was shown by Amir (1969), and some understanding of the effects of social contact on ethnic prejudice has been obtained by specifying the conditions under which cross-cultural contact leads to either positive or negative effects on inter-group relations. However, these conditions have not been put into a systematic framework which might lead to a more satisfactory explanation of inter-group relations as affected by cross-cultural interaction. We believe that attribution theory offers such a systematic framework, which may make the contradictory results obtained in the past more intelligible. Attribution theory applied to inter-group relations, moreover, leads to new and interesting hypotheses about the effects of cross-cultural contact.

The major contribution of this chapter, as we see it, is the emphasis we have put upon the fact that ethnic stereotypes or, in general, evaluative judgements of in- and out-group members should be seen as the outcome of an attribution process and not simply as distorted perceptions. Such a view makes clear why such personal evaluations occur in the first place. We have argued that in an inter-group situation behaviour which would normally lead to situational (entity) attribution, will lead to person attribution because of the added covariation with the observable social categorization. Such an effect, we have argued, will increase in strength because the interaction which takes place between individuals belonging to different ethnic groups is very often highly selective in nature.

It also follows from an attributional point of view that different attributions will be made for in- and out-group members when observers are confronted with exactly the same behaviour by an in-group or an out-group member. We have pointed out, however, that a simple actor—observer model of these differences is not tenable, and we have argued that one should take the nature of the behaviour into account in making predictions and especially the outcome of such behaviours for both actor and "receiver".

We have also argued that even when cross-cultural interaction is limited to single interaction or to indirect information, attribution theory is applicable. In particular, it appears to be reasonable to assume that causal schemata such as discounting may play an important role because they can enhance the observer's social identity along positively valued dimensions.

A second important consideration which arises from an attributional view of ethnic stereotypes is that it shows clearly why reality and stereotypes become indistinguishable, when only in-group consensus exists. The implications of this confounding effect for trying to influence ethnic stereotypes are obvious, but it is less easy to say how this difficulty may be overcome. One solution may perhaps be found in a more detailed analysis of stereotypes, as we have suggested in the last part of our chapter. If stereotypes are experienced as valid representations of reality one can consider the question: to what extent are heterostereotypes accurate representations of autostereotypes? Any discrepancies which one discovers here can be decomposed along the lines suggested, which would give us a much better insight into the specific nature of particular stereotypes.

So far it appears that there is very little research aimed at trying to analyse inter-group relations and ethnic stereotypes from an attributional point of view. We hope that the various suggestions we have made in this chapter will lead to more research of this kind, because the few studies which are available have already led to some interesting and unexpected results.

Notes

1. This chapter was made possible in part by a Social Science Research Council grant to the second author.
2. We would like to point out that this chapter is itself the product of cross-cultural inter-action between the authors, since one of them is English and the other Dutch. True to our theory of social attribution, each of us is therefore happy to accept personally any credit for the good points of this chapter, and to blame any errors on the other.
3. The reaction of the King of Kerman in Marco Polo's travels is therefore a rather enlightened one which, in an essentially scientific way, goes beyond the facile person attribution by looking for possible situational differences between Kerman and Persia.
4. One of us who has now spent a few years in England as a Dutchman is regularly con-fronted with compatriot tourists visiting Oxford, whose behaviour he is sometimes inclined to regard as "typically Dutch", attributing it to such national characteristics as "uncouth, loud, etc.". Of course, he is willing to admit that his own behaviour may be seen in the same way by Englishmen.
5. It is important to point out here that Kelley's use of the concept of consensus is very confusing because it refers both to consensus among observers' judgements and uniformity of observed behaviour in actors. In our previous analysis the consensus criterion referred to observed uniformity of behaviour. In this analysis we are discussing agreement among observers.
6. This interpretation does not follow strictly from LeVine and Campbell's stereotype theory, but it can be derived from their general idea that stereotypes reflect both projec-tive factors and real differences. If one assumes that the possible tendency of the hetero-stereotype to resemble the autostereotype of the in-group can be interpreted as the projective element in the heterostereotype, and the tendency of the heterostereotype to resemble the autostereotype of the out-group can be seen as the reality component, one can test the hypothesis of LeVine and Campbell by comparing the heterostereotype of the out-group with the in-group and out-group autostereotypes.
7. Mann and Taylor also varied the social class of the described actors, but we will ignore that aspect of their study because we are mainly interested in cultural inter-group relations.
8. It is not entirely clear from the report by Mann and Taylor which traits were actually used, because they mention the first four trait dimensions in the procedure section of their article (p. 6) but discuss at length in the results section the trait sociable—nonsociable (pp. 8—9) which is not mentioned before. Our analysis is simply based on the results section, and ignores this small contradiction.

References

ADORNO, T. W., FRENKEL-BRUNSWIK, E., LEVINSON, D. J. and SANFORD, R. N. (1950) *The Authoritarian Personality*. Harper, New York.

AMIR, Y. (1969) Contact hypothesis in ethnic relations. *Psychological Bulletin*, 71, 319—42.

AMIR, Y. (1976) The role of intergroup contact in change of prejudice and ethnic relations, *Towards the Elimination of Racism* (Edited by KATZ, P. A.). Pergamon, New York.

BILLIG, M. (1973) Normative communication in a minimal intergroup situation. *European Journal of Social Psychology*, 3, 339—43.

BILLIG, M. (1976) *Social Psychology and Intergroup Relations*. Academic Press, London.

CAMPBELL, D. T. (1967) Stereotypes and the perception of group differences. *American Psychologist*, 22, 817—29.

CRONBACH, L. J. (1955) Processes affecting scores on "understanding of others" and "assumed similarity". *Psychological Bulletin*, 52, 177—93.

DESCHAMPS, J. C. (1973—74) L'attribution, la catégorisation sociale et les représentations intergroupes. *Bulletin de Psychologie*, 27, 710—21.

DOISE, W. (1978) *Groups and Individuals: Explanations in Social Psychology*. Cambridge University Press. Cambridge.

DUNCKER, K. (1945) On problem-solving. *Psychological Monographs*, 58, (5; whole no. 270).

EISEN, S. V. (1979) Actor—observer differences in information inference and causal attribution. *Journal of Personality and Social Psychology*, 37, 261—72.

EYSENCK, H. J. and EYSENCK, S. B. G. (1969) *Personality Structure and Measurement.* Routledge & Kegan Paul, London.

FESTINGER, L. (1954) A theory of social comparison processes. *Human Relations*, 7, 117—40.

FINCHAM, F. D. and JASPARS, J. M. F. (1980) Attribution of responsibility: from man-the-scientist to man-as-lawyer, *Advances in Experimental Social Psychology*, vol. 13 (Edited by BERKOWITZ, L.). Academic Press, New York.

HEIDER, F. (1944) Social perception and phenomenal causality. *Psychological Review*, 51, 358—74.

HEIDER, F. (1958) *The Psychology of Interpersonal Relations.* Wiley, New York.

HEWSTONE, M., FINCHAM, F. and JASPARS, J. (1981) Social categorization and similarity in intergroup behaviour: a replication with "penalties." *European Journal of Social Psychology*, 11, 101—7.

HEWSTONE, M. and JASPARS, J. Intergroup relations and attribution processes, *Social Identity and Intergroup Behaviour* (Edited by TAJFEL, H.). Cambridge University Press/ Maison des Sciences de l'Homme, Cambridge/Paris. In press (a).

HEWSTONE, M. and JASPARS, J. Explanations for racial discrimination: the effect of group discussion on intergroup attribution. *European Journal of Social Psychology.* In press (b).

HULL, C. L. (1952) *A Behavior system: An Introduction to Behaviour Theory Concerning the Individual Organism.* Yale University Press, New Haven.

HUSBAND, C. (1977) News media, language and race relations: a case study in identity maintenance. *Language, Ethnicity and Intergroup Relations* (Edited by GILES, H.). Academic Press, London.

JONES, E. E. (1979) The rocky road from acts to dispositions. *American Psychologist*, 34, 107—17.

JONES, E. E. and DAVIS, K. E. (1965) From acts to dispositions: the attribution process in person perception. *Advances in Experimental Social Psychology*, vol. 2 (Edited by BERKOWITZ, L.). Academic Press, New York.

JONES, E. E. and NISBETT, R. E. (1972) *The Actor and the Observer: Divergent Perceptions of the Causes of Behaviour.* General Learning Press, New Jersey.

KATZ, D. and BRALY, K. (1933) Racial stereotypes of 100 college students. *Journal of Abnormal and Social Psychology*, 28, 280—90.

KELLEY, H. H. (1967) Attribution theory in social psychology. *Nebraska Symposium on Motivation*, 15, 192—238.

KELLEY, H. H. (1972) *Causal Schemata and the Attribution Process.* General Learning Press, New Jersey.

KELLEY, H. H. (1973) The processes of causal attribution. *American Psychologist*, 28, 107—28.

KELLEY, H. H. and MICHELA, J. L. (1980) Attribution theory and research, *Annual Review of Psychology*, vol. 31 (Edited by ROSENZWEIG, M. R. and PORTER, L. M.).

LAY, C. H., ZIEGLER, M., HERSHFIELD, D. L. and MILLER, D. T. (1974) The perception of situational consistency in behaviour: Assessing the actor—observer bias. *Canadian Journal of Behavioural Science*, 6, 376—84.

LENAUER, M., SAMETH, L. and SHAVER, P. (1976) Looking back at oneself in time: another approach to the actor—observer phenomenon. *Perceptual and Motor Skills*, 43, 1283—7.

LEVINE, R. A. and CAMPBELL, D. T. (1972) *Ethnocentrism: Theories of Conflict, Ethnic Attitudes and Group Behaviour.* Wiley, New York.

MANN, J. F. and TAYLOR, D. M. (1974) Attribution of causality: role of ethnicity and social class. *Journal of Social Psychology*, 94, 3—13.

MCARTHUR, L. A. (1972) The how and what of why: some determinants and consequences of causal attributions. *Journal of Personality and Social Psychology*, 22, 171—93.

MICHOTTE, A. E. (1946) *La perception de la causalité.* J. Vrin, Paris. (Translation: *The Perception of Causality.* Basic Books, New York, 1963.)

MIKES, G. (1966) *How To Be An Alien.* Penguin, Harmondsworth.

MONSON, T. C. Implications of the traits vs. situations controversy for differences in the attributions of actors and observers, *Attribution Theory and Research: Conceptual, Developmental and Social Dimensions* (Edited by JASPARS, J., FINCHAM, F. and HEWSTONE, M.). Academic Press, London. In press.

MOSCOVICI, S. (1961) *La psychanalyse, son image et son public* (2nd edition 1976). Presses Universitaires de France, Paris.

MOSCOVICI, S. and FARR, R. M. (Editors). *Social Representations.* Cambridge University Press/Maison des Sciences de l'Homme, Cambridge/Paris. In press.

NISBETT, R. E., CAPUTO, C., LEGANT, P. and MARACEK, J. (1973) Behaviour as seen by the actor and as seen by the observer. *Journal of Personality and Social Psychology,* 27, 154–64.

RIESMAN, D., GLAZER, N. and DENNEY, R. (1955) *The Lonely Crowd.* Yale University Press, New Haven.

SARTRE, J. P. (1954) *Réflexions sur la question juive.* Gallimard, Paris.

SNYDER, M. L., STEPHAN, W. G. and ROSENFIELD, D. (1976) Egotism and attribution. *Journal of Personality and Social Psychology,* 33, 435–41.

SPENCE, K. (1956) *Behavior Theory and Conditioning.* Yale University Press, New Haven.

STEPHAN, W. (1977) Stereotyping: role of ingroup–outgroup differences in causal attribution of behavior. *Journal of Social Psychology,* 101, 255–66.

STORMS, M. D. (1973) Videotape and the attribution process: reversing actors' and observers' points of view. *Journal of Personality and Social Psychology,* 27, 165–75.

TAJFEL, H. (1970) Experiments in intergroup discrimination. *Scientific American,* 223 (5), 96–102.

TAJFEL, H. (1974) Social identity and intergroup behaviour. *Social Science Information,* 13, 65–93.

TAJFEL, H. (Editor) (1978) *Differentiation Between Social Groups: Studies in Inter-group Behaviour.* Academic Press, London.

TAJFEL, H. and BILLIG, M. (1974) Familiarity and categorisation in intergroup behaviour. *Journal of Experimental Social Psychology,* 10, 159–70.

TAJFEL, H., FLAMENT, C., BILLIG, M. and BUNDY, R. P. (1971) Social categorization and intergroup behaviour. *European Journal of Social Psychology,* 1, 149–78.

TAJFEL, H. and TURNER, J. C. (1979) An integrative theory of intergroup conflict, *The Social Psychology of Intergroup Relations* (Edited by AUSTIN, W. G. and WORCHEL, S.). Brooks/Cole, Monterey, Calif.

TAYLOR, D. M. and JAGGI, V. (1974) Ethnocentrism and causal attribution in a South Indian context. *Journal of Cross-Cultural Psychology,* 5, 162–71.

TAYLOR, D. M. and SIMARD, L. M. (1977) Ethnic identity and intergroup relations. Paper presented at the Canadian Ethnic Studies Association National Conference on Emerging Ethnic Boundaries, Quebec.

TRIANDIS, H. C. and VASSILIOU, V. (1967) Frequency of contact and stereotyping. *Journal of Personality and Social Psychology,* 7, 316–28.

TURNER, J. C. (1975) Social comparison and social identity: some prospects for intergroup behaviour. *European Journal of Social Psychology,* 5, 5–34.

TURNER, J. C. (1978) Social categorization and social discrimination in the minimal group paradigm, *Differentiation Between Social Groups* (Edited by TAJFEL, H.). Academic Press, London.

TVERSKY, A. and KAHNEMAN, D. (1974) Judgment under uncertainty: heuristics and biases. *Science,* 185, 1124–31.

VAN KNIPPENBERG, A. (1978) Status differences, comparative relevance and intergroup differentiation, *Differentiation Between Social Groups* (Edited by TAJFEL, H.). Academic Press, London.

VAN KNIPPENBERG, A. and WILKE, H. (1979) Perceptions of collégiens and apprentis re-analysed. *European Journal of Social Psychology,* 9, 427–34.

WARNAEN, S. and JASPARS, J. Intergroup relations, social identity and self-evaluation: a field study in Indonesia, *Social Identity and Intergroup Behaviour* (Edited by TAJFEL, H.). Cambridge University Press/Maison des Sciences de l'Homme, Cambridge/Paris. In press.

Part III

Outcomes of cross-cultural interaction

STEPHEN BOCHNER

THE FINAL section of the book deals with some of the outcomes of cross-cultural contact. Depending on one's point of view, two broadly opposing sets of outcomes can be predicted, and indeed both have been found to occur. The optimists argue that if culturally diverse people could only be brought into contact with one another, they would develop mutual understanding, tolerance and respect. This belief is the main justification for the many cultural exchange schemes operating throughout the world, at some expense to the taxpayers who provide the scholarships, fellowships, university places and other forms of training and hospitality. The pessimists, on the other hand, point to the frequent instances where contact between different cultures leads to increased suspicion, hostility and often war.

There is experimental and real-life evidence for both forms of outcomes. Some contact situations promote mutual understanding leading to inter-group harmony, whereas other types of contact increase hostility and lead to poor inter-group relations. A great deal of the research effort in the field has been devoted to identifying those contact situations which are systematically related to either improving or destroying inter-group harmony, and most of the preceding chapters have made reference to this literature. The present section examines in some detail the effects of contact in two particular fields: the overseas academic sojourn and tourism.

Furnham and Bochner extend social skills theory to an analysis of cross-cultural interaction. They suggest that for persons proceeding to an unfamiliar culture, the mundane, everyday inter-personal encounters with members of the host society, e.g. in the streets, shops, factories and bars, are often a major source of stress, due to the person not knowing the rules and conventions that apply to these episodes in the receiving culture. In other words, the sojourner can be regarded as a person who is socially unskilled in the new environment, a paradoxical condition for many visitors who may be highly skilled in the ways of their own society. This formulation provides a much more precise and operationally definable account of the sojourn experience, than the rather vague notions of culture shock, culture fatigue and role shock usually employed to describe difficulty in a foreign country. The formulation also has quite precise implications for culture training, leading to a three-stage programme in which specific social skills deficits are diagnosed, followed by a training sequence, and ending with an evaluation of the degree of acquisition achieved.

The second half of Furnham and Bochner's chapter describes an original experiment generated by the social skills model, illustrating how this approach leads to a better understanding of the effects of contact on the participants; in turn suggesting specific interventions to increase the likelihood that both host and visitor will emerge from the contact with a positive rather than a negative regard for each other.

The final chapter, by Pearce, reviews the growing literature on the effect of cross-cultural contact in the realm of tourism. The chapter is organized around two themes: the impact of tourism on the visited people, and the effect of inter-cultural contact on the tourists. The author shows that the maximum impact is on host countries that are small, unsophisticated and isolated. There is also evidence that, contrary to popular belief, the tourists are affected by their experience; but as in the case of other sojourners, whether they develop positive or negative attitudes towards their hosts will depend on the same set of conditions prevailing in other forms of inter-ethnic contact. This finding places tourism within the general framework of cross-cultural interaction, and provides further evidence for the generality of the principles accounting for the outcomes of inter-group contact.

7

Social difficulty in a foreign culture: an empirical analysis of culture shock

ADRIAN FURNHAM and STEPHEN BOCHNER

Introduction

THIS CHAPTER deals with cross-cultural contact in international educational exchange. In particular, theory and research pertaining to the social difficulties of overseas students will be reviewed, and an original experiment described. Although international education is only one of many forms of cross-cultural contact, it is a very important meeting ground. What distinguishes overseas study from other kinds of interchange is its relatively benign character, although there have always been political overtones associated with exchange schemes (Bochner, 1979); in the nature of its participants, who have generally been young and members of the elite; and its implicit values, encouraging the students to transcend cultural and national boundaries, or at least make an attempt to do so in the interests of creating a scholarly or scientific network to further the expansion of knowledge in their particular area of expertise (Useem, Useem and McCarthy, 1979).

Like most other instances of contact, educational exchange has an ancient tradition. People preoccupied with contemporary race relations tend to ignore that since the dawn of time, individuals brought up in one culture have travelled to other lands, there to trade, teach, learn, convert, succour, settle or conquer. Cross-cultural education is no exception. As Brickman (1965) has shown, the idea of studying abroad is as old as recorded history.

The highly visible foreign scholar, constituting 10 per cent or more of the student population on many campuses throughout the western world (Bochner and Wicks, 1972), suggests to the casual observer that international education is a modern phenomenon, characteristic particularly of the post-colonial era. This is not so. Thus during the reign of the Emperor Asoka the Great of India (273–232 B.C.), the University of Taxila became a major international institution, attracting students from all over Asia Minor, and requiring its graduates to travel abroad following the completion of their courses. In China the emperors of the T'ang Dynasty (620–907) fostered international education. Alexander the Great provided for a kind of Rhodes Scholarship in his will. The early Roman emperors encouraged foreign teachers to come to Rome. In the Middle Ages the European university, essentially an international institution of higher learning, came into existence. In modern times, particularly in the period after the Second World War to the present, governments and foundations have supported a huge movement of students and scholars across cultural boundaries (e.g. Bochner and Wicks, 1972; Fulbright, 1976; Klineberg, 1970a, b, 1976), but the phenomenon is not new, nor are the psychological problems associated with it.

Similarly, migration has an ancient tradition, of which perhaps the most dramatic example is the settling of the so-called New World by immigrants from Europe and Asia within the space of three or four centuries. International trade and technical assistance have also long been part of the world scene. The novel *Shogun* (Clavell, 1975), set in the first Elizabethan era, raises issues identical to those being debated today, such as the effect of multinational corporations, the diffusion of innovations, modernization, and industrialization (e.g. Kumar, 1979).

Psychology, being a young science, is a relative newcomer to the commentary on cross-cultural contact. However, it has made up for its belated and piecemeal entry by a burgeoning research output, much of which has been reviewed elsewhere in this volume. The general theme running through the psychological literature is that life was not meant to be easy for the sojourner in foreign lands. This view of the matter was established by the early writers, many of whom concentrated on the more noxious aspects of cross-cultural contact. Perhaps the best-known pioneer in this area was Stonequist (1937), who published an influential book called *The Marginal Man,* dealing with the problems encountered by persons caught between two cultural systems, not belonging to or accepted by either group.

The next wave of empirical research dealing with the difficulties of the cross-cultural sojourner was stimulated by the post-Second World War boom in student exchanges. The most important studies were undoubtedly those supported by the Social Science Research Council, and published by the University of Minnesota Press, inquiring into the adjustment problems of foreign students in the United States (Bennett, Passin and McKnight, 1958; Lambert and Bressler, 1956; Morris, 1960; Scott, 1956; Selltiz *et al,* 1963; Sewell and Davidsen, 1961).

At about the same time, two new concepts were introduced into the literature, both with negative connotations for the psychological welfare of the sojourner. The first was the notion of culture shock (Oberg, 1960), or the idea that entering a new culture is potentially a confusing and disorienting experience. This concept has been widely used (and misused) to "explain" the difficulties of the cross-cultural sojourn, and we shall return to it later in the present chapter. The second concept was the notion of the U-curve of adjustment, or the idea that cross-cultural sojourners progress through three main phases: an initial stage of elation and optimism, followed by a period of frustration, depression and confusion, which then slowly turns into feelings of confidence and satisfaction (Coelho, 1958; Deutsch and Won, 1963; Du Bois, 1956; Gullahorn and Gullahorn, 1963; Jacobson, 1963; Lysgaard, 1955; Selltiz and Cook, 1962; Sewell, Morris and Davidsen, 1954).

Another major research effort came about due to problems encountered by the Peace Corps movement in the 1960s. Thousands of young American volunteer workers went abroad to teach and provide medical, technical and welfare assistance to the less fortunate peoples of the world. A condition of the Peace Corps programme was that the volunteers had to adopt a lifestyle similar to that of the indigenous folk among whom they were working. Not surprisingly, many of these young Americans found the experience bewildering, and quite a few succumbed and had to be repatriated. When these problems became evident the Peace Corps asked for professional advice, and many psychologists, usually with a clinical background, became involved in research and therapy (Guthrie, 1975; Guthrie and Zektick, 1967; Harris, 1973; Smith, 1966; Textor, 1966). This programme also marks the first major attempt to prepare people for work and study in other cultures. Whereas most of the previous research was concerned with describing the difficulties of the sojourner, developing theories to account for these difficulties, and testing hypotheses about the determinants of these stresses, the Peace Corps psychologists had a practical problem on their hands: how to alleviate the stress being experienced by many of their current volunteers, and how to inoculate future Peace Corps workers against "culture shock".

A similar need arose in the private sector, with the increase in multinational trade during the post-war reconstruction period. Companies found that their overseas operations were being hampered because their staff were not coping with unfamiliar social and business practices (Fayerweather, 1959; Skinner, 1968; Triandis, 1967; Wilson, 1961). Experts engaged in technical assistance, and military personnel, experienced similar problems (Boxer, 1969; Brislin, 1979). Applied social psychologists responded by devising various cross-cultural training and orientation programmes, of which a very good example are the culture assimilators produced at the University of Illinois (Fiedler, Mitchell and Triandis, 1971; Foa and Chemers, 1967; Triandis, 1975). An excellent review of cross-cultural training methods has recently been published by Brislin and Pedersen (1976).

In summary, the sojourn literature has a distinct clinical flavour. The problems of the sojourner tend to be conceptualized within a medical model. Sojourners who experience difficulties are considered to have suffered a breakdown in their normal healthy psychological functioning, and require therapy and counselling. For example, an influential recent book has the title *Counseling Across Cultures* (Pedersen, Lonner, and Draguns, 1976) reinforcing this view, and many clinically oriented psychologists have extended and applied traditional psychotherapeutic models and techniques to problems connected with adjusting to a new culture.

A contrary view has been proposed by Bochner, briefly touched on in Chapter 1, and more fully developed in a recent book (Bochner, 1981). This view states that the major task facing a sojourner is not to adjust to a new culture, but to learn its salient characteristics. In particular, if the sojourner is to work effectively in the new setting, and lead a relatively stress-free and fulfilling life, the person must acquire the social skills of the host culture, especially knowledge necessary to negotiate everyday social encounters with members of the receiving society. Several consequences flow from adopting a culture learning model of the cross-cultural sojourn:

(1) Failures and problems experienced by the sojourner need not be regarded as symptoms of some underlying pathology, but rather due to a lack of the necessary cultural skills and knowledge. Consequently, remedial action does not involve seeking out conflicts, "making the unconscious conscious", giving reassurance, systematic desensitization, or any of the other techniques that have been applied to this area. Rather, remedial action involves imparting appropriate knowledge and skills, and this may be achieved by using standard social skills training methods such as instruction, modelling, role-playing, video-feedback and homework (Argyle, 1979).

(2) "Adjusting" a person to a culture has connotations of cultural chauvinism, implying that the newcomer should abandon the culture of origin in favour of embracing the values and customs of the host society. On the other hand, learning a second culture has no such ethnocentric overtones. There are many examples in life when it becomes necessary to learn a practice even if one does not approve of it, and then abandon the custom when circumstances have changed. Americans will find that they have to stand much closer to an Arab during interaction in the Middle East than they would with fellow-Americans at home. Japanese must learn to have more eye-contact with westerners during conversation than is customary in their own culture. Australians in Great Britain of necessity have to learn to drink warm beer, a habit they discard as soon as they depart. An English gentleman in Japan will learn to push and shove his way onto the Tokyo subway, but resume his normal queuing practice after returning home. The posession of a particular skill by itself carries no value judgement — the act attracts notice only when the appropriate skill is not available, or the skill is used in inappropriate circumstances.

In summary, there is a good deal of truth in the assertion that life was not meant to be easy for the cross-cultural sojourner. However, there is little utility in thinking of sojourners as mentally confused people needing therapy and "adjustment". Rather, sojourners lack certain vital skills and knowledge, and can therefore be thought of as selectively ignorant, and in need of education and training, particularly in relation to everyday social encounters with members of the host culture, in the homes, market-place, factories, offices and playing fields of the receiving society.

To date, the social skills model has been developed and used primarily in connection with the problem of intra-cultural social inadequacy. The present chapter extends this model to account for the social incompetence of the cross-cultural sojourner. The next section will briefly review the social skills model as it has been developed at Oxford University for work within English society. Then the model will be extended to include cross-cultural social inadequacy. The final part of this chapter describes an experiment that was generated by the extension of the social skills model to the sojourning foreign student.

Social skills, inadequacy and cross-cultural competence

It was Argyle and Kendon (1967) who first suggested that it may be useful to construe the behaviour of people interacting with each other, as a mutually organized, skilled performance. Inter-personal difficulties occur when this performance breaks down, falters, or indeed cannot be successfully initiated in the first place. The model has implicit in it several reasons for, and explanations of, unsatisfactory inter-personal encounters, amongst them the following: (a) the individual's goals may be inappropriate or unattainable in the given situation; (b) the individual may fail to perceive or attend to some of the messages and behaviours being emitted by the other person; (c) some of the other person's behaviour and messages may be misinterpreted, or given the wrong attribution (Jones, 1976); (d) the individual may not know how to respond adequately, or make responses which in the circumstances are judged as inappropriate or inadequate by the other person.

Although the social skills model is not without its problems (Pendleton and Furnham, 1980; Yardley, 1979), it has stimulated a great deal of research (for recent reviews see Argyle, 1979; Gambrill, 1977). In particular, a considerable amount of work has gone into the assessment and treatment of social inadequacy (Sundberg, Snowden and Reynolds, 1978; Trower, Bryant and Argyle, 1978). Socially inadequate individuals are people who have failed to learn a wide range of inter-personal skills, due to poor child—parent and peer group relationships, and because of other forms of social and physical deprivation. Such individuals are incompetent in, or incapable of, certain verbal exchanges; they are unable to accurately interpret or perform non-verbal signals; they have not mastered the social conventions of the society at large, and may also be unaware of many of the rules of social behaviour pertaining to their own particular subgroup. Thus it could be said that socially inadequate individuals are often like strangers in their own land and culture. Some of the specific behaviours which the socially incompetent perform unsatisfactorily, include expressing attitudes, feelings and emotions; adopting the appropriate proxemic posture; understanding the gaze patterns of the people they are interacting with; carrying out ritualized routines such as greetings, leave-taking, self-disclosure, making or refusing requests; and asserting themselves. All of these elements of social interaction have been shown to vary across cultures (Furnham, 1979; Hall, 1959; Hall and Beil-Warner, 1978; Leff, 1977).

Turning this argument around, it follows that people who are new to a culture or subculture will not have been socialized in the rules and routines of behaviour pertaining to that society, and will therefore at least initially be socially unskilled in their new environment. Individuals in this predicament include foreign students, visiting academics, businessmen and diplomats. Many of these people tend to be highly skilled in the verbal and non-verbal facets of interaction of their own society, and find their inadequacy in the new culture particularly frustrating and embarrassing. Ordinary everyday situations such as attending parties, making contact with the opposite sex, ordering meals, shopping, even using the bathroom, all activities which hitherto presented no problems, suddenly become major obstacles.

The social skills model as it is being extended here has clear implications for the understanding and management of cross-cultural incompetence. The theoretical guidelines for remedial action are quite clear: First, it is necessary to identify the *specific* social situations which trouble that particular sojourner, and then give the individual *specific* training in those skills that are lacking. This raises the more fundamental question whether such knowledge can be imparted in the first place. After all, it is possible that social skills, like virtue, do not readily lend themselves to being taught. Fortunately, the evidence, based on intracultural studies, i.e. where the subjects are incompetent in their culture of origin, generally supports the efficacy of remedial training. For example (Argyle, 1979), at least seven social skills are capable of being developed in lacking individuals. They are:

(1) Perceptive skills: co-ordinating verbal and non-verbal behaviour, encouraging the speaker, and giving appropriate feedback.
(2) Expressive skills: speaking loudly and clearly, with the appropriate emotional tone in the voice.
(3) Conversation skills: appropriate timing, speaker exchanges, topics, and self-disclosure.
(4) Assertiveness: standing up for one's own rights without aggression or undue passivity.
(5) Emotional expression: the expression of a full range of appropriate emotions in various situations.
(6) Anxiety management: coping with social anxiety during moments of stress, such as in decision-making, or when being the focus of attention.
(7) Affiliative skills: being able to express feelings of warmth, affection, and sexuality where appropriate.

Other research (e.g. Pendleton and Furnham, 1980; Trower, Bryant and Argyle, 1978) also supports the feasibility of the social skills training method for same-culture or subculture clients, and there is no reason to suppose that the procedure would not work with persons from one society learning the social customs of another, quite different, culture. However, this proposition still awaits empirical verification.

Cross-cultural misunderstanding, social skills and culture shock

Earlier we listed two advantages of construing the foreign sojourn as a culture-learning problem rather than employing psycho-dynamic explanations: the first was that no value-judgements were being made about the relative merit of the two societies; the second was that the culture-learning model had obvious implications for remedial action. This latter element of the model was the topic of the preceding section, where the problem was spelled out as consisting of a deficit in specifiable social skills, skills that are known to be capable of being taught to receptive individuals.

A third advantage in analysing cross-cultural misunderstanding from the perspective of the culture-learning/social skills model is that it leads to quite precise operational definitions of the concept, as will be shown in the next section by comparing the social skills approach with the culture shock formulations. Labels such as culture shock, culture fatigue or culture strain (Guthrie, 1966) are rather loose, tend to refer to hypothetical intrapsychic events which have not been subjected to independent, objective verification, and yet are often used as explanatory principles (Bochner, Lin and McLeod, 1980). In contrast, the social skills model stays very close to its data, and its conclusions rest on information about how particular groups experience specific situations in particular host societies. The generality of the model is achieved by relating such empirical outcomes to the underlying principle that smooth social interaction requires a basic, mutual understanding by the participants of the rules, roles and goals of the social episode they are engaged in (Harre, 1977).

Culture shock

The term "culture shock", like that of jet lag, is now part of the popular vocabulary. It was initially introduced by Oberg (1960), and referred to the distress experienced by the sojourner as a result of losing all the familiar signs and symbols of social interaction.

These signs or cues include the thousand and one ways in which we orient ourselves to the situations of daily life: when to shake hands and what to say when we meet people, when and how to give tips, how to give orders to servants, how to make purchases, when to accept and when to refuse invitations, when to take statements seriously and when not. Now these cues which may be words, gestures, facial expressions, customs, or norms are acquired by all of us in the course of growing up and are as much a part of our culture as the language we speak or the beliefs we accept. All of us depend for our peace of mind and our efficiency on hundreds of these cues, most of which we do not carry on the level of conscious awareness (p. 177).

In a largely anecdotal article Oberg mentions at least six aspects of culture shock:

(1) strain due to the effort required to make necessary psychological adaptations;
(2) a sense of loss and feelings of deprivation in regard to friends, status, profession and possessions;
(3) being rejected by and/or rejecting members of the new culture;
(4) confusion in role, role expectations, values, feelings and self-identity;
(5) surprise, anxiety, even disgust and indignation after becoming aware of cultural differences;
(6) feelings of impotence due to not being able to cope with the new environment.

Other writers have added their own interpretations to the condition. Hall (1959) defined culture shock as the removal or distortion of many of the familiar cues of one's environment, and their substitution by other cues which are strange. Smalley (1963) proposed four stages of culture shock, a formulation that appears to be a combination of the culture shock notion with the U-curve of adjustment hypothesis. The four phases are:

(1) fascination with the new culture, yet being faced with various barriers preventing social interaction with host nationals;
(2) hostility and frustration with aspects of the new culture, and a possible emphasis on the superiority of the original culture;
(3) improvement and adjustment with an expression of humour and decreased tension;
(4) biculturalism where the sojourner develops a full understanding of host cultural norms.

Smalley (1963) emphasized the importance of language differences in culture shock. However this view neglects the important role played by non-verbal communication (Argyle, 1975).

Byrnes (1965) talked of role shock, referring to unsuccessful relationships with co-national and equal-status peers, as well as with higher-status host nationals. Guthrie (1966) used the term culture fatigue to describe the continuous minute adjustments required for day-to-day living in a foreign culture.

Cleveland, Mangone and Adams (1960), in an anecdotal report of Americans abroad, describe some of their problems in China and Japan:

There is the protocol of where to sit, when to leave, how long to carry on the small talk before the real subject of conversation is broached — matters which certainly arise in American social intercourse, but in a more muted and subtle way. To Americans there seems to be an exaggerated insincere obsequiousness in other societies, the bowing and scraping, the flowery introductions and leave-takings, the endless formal handshaking (p. 37).

Numerous writers have noted the shock and surprise that travellers experience when they become aware of ethnic or colour differences, especially if they come from racially homogeneous or segregated societies. Tajfel and Dawson (1965) performed a content analysis of essays written by seventy-three foreign students in Britain. They found that the variables affecting adaptation to British society include skin colour, country of origin, language, social structure and previous experience with British behaviour patterns. Racial prejudice and discrimination featured prominently in the essays of the students. Many had been badly prepared by misleading information from expatriates or by information services. They had particular difficulty in obtaining and negotiating lodgings, starting and maintaining opposite-sex relationships, and securing employment.

Carey (1956) described the social adaptation of colonial students in Britain, paying attention also to the reactions of host nationals to the visitors. Because of their excessively optimistic expectations these students often became disappointed, a feeling which was exacerbated by accommodation problems and British prejudice.

> To a great extent, colonial students in London find that their contacts with British people are restricted to relationships of a "formal" kind. Various organizations try to introduce them to Londoners, but with relatively little success. In the formal context of official introductions both groups tend to regard each other as stereotypes, and the relationships that ensue are generally not what the students desire (p. 164).

Carey noted that the British make only the roughest of distinctions between the various groups of colonial students, a finding similar to that reported by Hodgkin (1972) in Australia, where overseas students from the many diverse cultures of South-East Asia tend to be placed together in one category, the "Asian", by members of the host culture.

Singh (1963) interviewed over 300 Indian students in Britain, asking them about their friends, their relations with the opposite sex, their leisure time activities and their adjustment, He found that nearly half of the sample experienced difficulties that they had not anticipated. These related mainly to loneliness, home-sickness, lack of training in looking after themselves, food difficulties, and worries about domestic problems back home. Nearly half the students had academic problems, mainly due to language problems, particularly in oral expression, the higher standard of British universities, and difficulties in teacher—student relationships. Academic difficulties were significantly negatively correlated with adjustment. Adjustment was related to place of residence (students had more difficulty at Oxbridge than provincial universities), social class (upper-class students were better adjusted than middle-class students), duration of stay (a U-shaped curve of up to 3 years, with high adjustment in the initial and last phases and comparatively low adjustment in the middle), and social skills (there was a positive correlation between social skill and adjustment). Singh concluded:

> . . . the survey has shown that it may be misleading to consider the Indian students as an undifferentiated group. Their problems of adjustment to different spheres of life — social, personal and academic — depended on various factors such as social class, age, personality traits, level of study, type of university, and duration of stay in this country. It is important to emphasize this point since most of the previous studies of foreign students have overlooked the differences between them (p. 117).

The bulk of the literature on international student experiences has concerned itself with the impact of Western culture on sojourners from the less-developed parts of the world. However, a few reports do exist that have looked at how students from the so-called Third World fare in a nation that is itself under-developed, and there are also some investigations of Western students in Third World countries. These studies have come up with results identical to those pertaining to Asian and African students in the West. Thus Zaidi (1975), in a survey of foreign Muslim students in Pakistan, reported widespread social isolation, with only a very few of these students having any personal relationships with local families. In a study of American students in Taiwan, Yeh *et al.* (1973) found that social relationships between the visitors and their hosts were seen by both groups as being superficial, limited and unsatisfactory.

After a very thorough review of the literature on coping with unfamiliar cultures, Taft (1977) offers a framework for analysing adaptation to new cultures. He identified four major aspects of the adaptation process, the first two involving dynamic processes and the second two involving the acquisition of competence in culturally appropriate behaviour and culturally defined roles and attitudes.

Though Taft does not refer to *social* skills *per se,* he clearly supports a skill-based explanation for cultural coping. He concludes:

> Specifically it is suggested that the effect of all culture contact situations that evoke in individuals the need to cope with an unfamiliar culture can be analysed in terms of employment of new cognitive, dynamic and performance mechanisms by the participants and their development of new coping repertoires (p. 151).

In order to comprehend how and why certain problems arise, it is useful to consider the culture from which the visitor originates. Watson (1977) showed that it is necessary to study the social system of the migrant's home country in order to comprehend his or her adjustment difficulties. Such comparative studies, where the sending and receiving societies are contrasted, are relatively rare in the literature.

In summary, the extent and duration of what has been described as culture shock, is dependent on conditions that can be classified into three broad categories:

(1) *Cultural differences.* The quality, quantity and duration of social difficulty appears to be a function of the differences between the foreigner's culture of origin and the receiving society (Glaser, 1979; Porter, 1972; Stewart, 1966). This difference is of course multidimensional and it is possible that the two cultures may be very similar on one factor (e.g. sex role relationships) and very different on others (e.g. non-verbal communication).

(2) *Individual differences.* Large individual differences exist in the ability of people to cope with new environments. Demographic and personality variables such as age, sex, cognitive ability, socioeconomic class and education may all be relevant. It has often been said, for example, that younger, more intelligent and better-educated people should adjust faster to host cultural patterns than older, less intelligent and less-educated individuals. However, there is very little empirical evidence regarding the role of personality factors in culture learning (Taft, 1981).

(3) *Sojourn experience.* The quality of learning a new culture is dependent on the experiences a person has in it, especially at the beginning of the visit. If sojourners are carefully introduced into a new society by close, sympathetic host culture friends, the evidence indicates that they may encounter fewer problems than if they are left to fend for themselves (Selltiz and Cook, 1962; Shattuck, 1965). Certain racial characteristics may also act either to the foreigner's advantage or disadvantage. Finally, the treatment that sojourners receive from the host culture is to some extent contingent on how they conduct themselves, particularly in the early stages of the visit.

There is little doubt that culture shock exists, and plays a major role in cross-cultural contact. The evidence indicates that when people move from one culture to another they frequently find the experience bewildering, confusing, depressing, anxiety-provoking, humiliating, embarrassing and generally stressful in nature. After a period the majority of the sojourners begin to cope with their new environment, and lead effective and satisfying lives. This in essence is the content of the culture shock/U-curve hypothesis, and in a descriptive sense quite accurate. The limitation of the "culture shock" formulation lies in its simplistic theoretical foundation, its non-specific nature and its lack of clear implications for remedial action, i.e. how to reduce culture shock.

To the extent that the culture shock hypothesis has a theoretical base, it is to suppose that the problems of the sojourner stem from the absence or distortion of familiar cues. However, this hypothesis is much too broad, since the lack of familiarity could be within any one or all of the aspects of the new society, including its physical, technological, climatic, political, legal, educational and sociocultural fields. The hypothesis makes no differential predictions about the relative importance of these various areas. Therefore the culture shock hypothesis cannot be used to generate culture training schemes, since it would be necessary to teach a sojourner literally everything about a new culture in order to alleviate that person's culture shock; an impractical idea. A corollary is that it is strictly speaking not possible to conduct research on the determinants of culture shock, since it is conceived as the function of an infinite number of antecedent variables.

However, the ideas underlying the notion of culture shock are valuable, but they need to be formulated so as to lead to specific predictions, testable hypotheses, and soundly based training programmes. The evidence suggests that at the core of what has been labelled "culture shock" is the reaction of sojourners to problems encountered in their dealings with host members. It follows that a major if not critical determinant of second-culture coping, is the skill with which a sojourner can enter into a relationship with a host person, maintain that relationship, and draw it to a mutually satisfactory conclusion. This formulation overcomes many of the objections raised earlier in connection with the traditional culture shock hypothesis. The present approach states that culture shock occurs within a specific domain, namely in the social encounters, social situations, social episodes, or social transactions between sojourners and host nationals. The present approach generates specific and testable hypotheses regarding the main determinants of culture shock, namely the lack of requisite social skills with which to negotiate these situations. The present formulation also provides specific implications for research and remedial training, namely the need to identify which social situations, in which sojourner culture—host culture combination, are the most troublesome; and to devise training techniques to teach those specific skills. Once these cultural skills have been mastered it is assumed that the sojourner will be able to acquire the second culture with a minimum of "shock".

However, the social skills are seldom taught or acquired in formal training courses. They are acquired informally (or not at all), within behaviour settings that can vary from the benign and helpful to the vicious and hostile. The evidence, some of which was reviewed earlier, indicates that the quality of the sojourn experience is a vital factor in accelerating or inhibiting culture learning. However, the literature is vague with respect to the empirical ingredients that enter into the quality of the sojourn experience. The list is over-inclusive, and contains everything from the behaviour of landladies (Krutli, 1972), accommodation and food (Wicks, 1972), the availability of sexual outlets, loneliness and homesickness (Sunder Das, 1972), to the already mentioned experiences of discrimination (Lawson, 1972; Tajfel and Dawson, 1965) and status loss (Morris,

1960). On reflection, the "quality of the sojourn experience" variables are all linked to the kinds of social networks that the sojourners have been able or unable to establish. In the next section a social networks analysis of the sojourn experience will attempt to unify the scattered and disparate findings in this area, and suggest specific hypotheses about the determinants of some of the sojourn patterns reported in the literature. The chapter ends with the account of an experiment that arose out of the ideas being expressed here.

Social networks of sojourners

Klineberg (1970a, b) has noted that there is often limited personal contact between foreign students and host nationals. Richardson (1974) has shown that there is a difference in the friendship patterns of satisfied as opposed to dissatisfied British immigrants in Australia, the dissatisfied migrants having more compatriot and fewer host national friends. Selltiz and Cook (1962) found that sojourners who reported having at least one close friend who was a host member, experienced fewer difficulties than sojourners with no host culture friends. Shattuck (1965) reports that sojourners found personal, informal orientation much more effective than institutionally sponsored assistance. In a study carried out in Australia, Au (1969) found that the degree of personal contact between Chinese—Malaysian students and host nationals was positively related to the students' attitude toward Australia.

Recently, Bochner and his co-workers (Bochner, Buker and McLeod, 1976; Bochner, McLeod and Lin, 1977; Bochner and Orr, 1979) have shown that sojourning overseas students tend to belong to three social networks:

(1) A primary, monocultural network consisting of close friendships with other sojourning compatriots. The main function of the co-national network is to provide a setting in which the sojourners can rehearse and express their culture of origin.

(2) A secondary, bicultural network, consisting of bonds between sojourners and significant host nationals such as academics, landladies, student advisers and government officials. The main function of this network is to instrumentally facilitate the academic and professional aspirations of the sojourner.

(3) A third network is the foreign student's multicultural circle of friends and acquaintances. The main function of this network is to provide companionship for recreational, non-culture and non-task oriented activities.

Social network theory has clear implications for the acquisition of the social skills of a second society: culture learning will be a positive function of the number of host culture friends an overseas student has, in particular the extent to which the student has been able to gain membership in suitable bicultural social networks. The advantage of this formulation is that it leads to testable hypotheses about the nature and effects of the "quality of the sojourn experience". The main prediction is that sojourners with appropriate host culture friends will learn the skills of the second culture more easily than sojourners whose friends are all compatriots. If such a hypothesis is confirmed, the results contain obvious implications for remedial action, for example suggesting the creation of housing conditions that will increase the likelihood of the development of suitable bicultural bonds.

In the next section an experiment will be described in which the social skills and social network hypotheses were combined, and applied to an analysis of the coping behaviour of a large group of foreign students in Britain. A major purpose of the presentation is to provide a practical illustration of the kind of empirical work the model can generate. As the study is a cross-cultural extension of current work in the social psychology of stress, a brief review of theory and research in this area will precede the description of the experiment.

Stressful social situations

The distinctive feature of the social psychological approach is to view stress as emanating from the behaviour setting, i.e. that there exist stressful *situations*. This formulation owes its direction to the Person X Situation debate in social psychology (Endler and Magnusson, 1976), and to the pioneering work of Endler and Hunt (1968) in identifying commonly occurring social situations that elicit stress and anxiety. The emphasis on situational determinants of social anxiety has in turn stimulated research on developing means to reduce it, of which by far the most elaborated method is social skills training (Priestley *et al.*, 1978; Trower, Bryant and Argyle, 1978).

Argyle, Furnham and Graham (1981) have proposed a method for studying everyday social situations, and have shown that such situational analyses can lead to improved inter-group relations. Considerable effort has gone into developing new and reliable scales for measuring anxiety and social difficulty, these scales being for the most part situation-based in that subjects are required to report their reactions to anxiety-provoking social encounters (Mellstrom, Zuckerman and Cicala, 1978; Spielberger, 1972).

Hodges and Felling (1970) asked 228 students to rate forty items selected *a priori* to measure eight different areas of potentially anxious aspects of college life. Factor analysis revealed factors labelled physical danger, pain and squeamishness, anxiety from classroom participation and speech, social and academic failure, and dating. The results showed that females tended to be more apprehensive than males in situations involving physical danger and pain, but that males are just as likely as females to indicate social anxiety in situations involving speech, social and academic failure, and dating. In a similar study of university students, Bryant and Trower (1974) asked 223 students to rate the degree of difficulty they felt in thirty specified situations. Situations demanding complex levels of interaction, often with members of the opposite sex, and where close bonds had not been established, were most stressful. The dominant factor to arise out of a principal components analysis was a general factor of social difficulty roughly describable as actively seeking out relative strangers, particularly of the opposite sex.

A few studies have looked specifically at social difficulty in different cultures. Rim (1976) compared the social difficulty of groups of Israeli and British students. British students found it more difficult to approach others, take initiative in conversation, go to parties, meet people they did not know well, go out with or be in a group of people of the opposite sex, and get to know someone in depth. Israeli students on the other hand found it more difficult to go into pubs, make decisions affecting others, and go into restaurants and cafés. Furnham (in press) found that matched groups of European, Indian and African nurses in South Africa had a different pattern of social difficulty associated with everyday social situations.

Magnusson and Stattin (1978) compared responses to seventeen hypothetical anxiety-provoking situations in schoolchildren from Sweden, Japan and Hungary. They found both significant national and sex differences. Japanese and Hungarian pupils reported higher anxiety than Swedish pupils, and girls scored higher than boys in Sweden and Hungary, yet there were no Japanese sex differences. The situations were divided into three categories: ego threat, anticipation threat and inanimate threat, and the analysis revealed that apart from Japan—Hungary differences on ego threat and inanimate threat, all the other differences were significant. It was concluded that the cross-cultural description of anxious behaviour is enhanced by separating situational and reactional aspects, and by making a cross-cultural description of profiles of reactions across different kinds of anxiety-provoking situations.

Despite advances in the operationalization and measurement of anxiety, and of some cross-cultural comparisons, very little empirical work seems to have been done on everyday social situations involving people from different cultures, or "ethnic encounters" (Van der Kolk, 1978).

The experiment: an empirical analysis of culture shock

This study had two aims: the first was to map out empirically the nature and extent of social difficulties that various groups of foreign students experience in England. The second was to test two specific hypotheses:

(1) That the degree of difficulty experienced by sojourners in negotiating specific everyday social situations in England, is related to differences between the sojourner's culture and British society; the greater the disparity the more severe the difficulties encountered.
(2) That the social relations of foreign students in Britain follow a pattern similar to that found in Australia and the United States, namely that the

students belong to two networks, a co-national network whose function is culture rehearsal, and an instrumental network consisting of bonds with "useful" host nationals.

The experiment is the first to combine the social skills model and its technology, with the culture learning model and its procedures.

Overview of method

Overseas students were given a questionnaire which contained forty statements describing various everyday social situations. The respondents indicated the amount of difficulty they experienced in each situation. A control group of British students were also given the questionnaire. The data were subjected to cluster and factor analyses, and comparisons were made between the two main groups (experimental and control), as well as between various subgroups within the foreign student contingent. These operations spoke to the first hypothesis.

The foreign students were also given a questionnaire in which they indicated who their best friends were; and a further instrument in which they listed their preferred companion for eleven specific activities. These data were used to speak to the second hypothesis.

Subjects

The experimental group

The subjects were all students at English Language schools in London, Oxford and Cambridge. The following criteria were used to include subjects in the study: The Ss were between 16 and 30 years of age; single; had completed secondary education; were from the upper and middle ranges of the socioeconomic spectrum, specifically from categories 1 to 4 on the Hall Jones scale (Oppenheim, 1973); at the time of testing had been in Britain between 1 and 5 months, and had *not* been to Britain on more than two earlier occasions; and had *not* stayed in Britain for more than 9 months on any previous visits. Approximately 400 foreign language students from fifty-one countries were tested. Of these, 150 students satisfied the inclusion criteria, and the data to be reported below are based on this selected group.

Subgroups within the experimental group

The 150 experimental subjects were divided into three subgroups, according to the geographic region from which they originated. The three regional groupings were northern Europe, southern Europe, and the East respectively, with equal numbers of males and females occurring in each of the three subgroups. There is some precedent for grouping cultural groups by their physical location in the world (e.g. Berry and Annis, 1974; Boldt, 1978; Cattell, Breul and Hartman, 1951; Porter, 1972; Stewart, 1966) on the assumption that societies in physical proximity to each other are likely to have had similar linguistic, religious and cultural roots, and may therefore share many common characteristics. This assumption is of course not always warranted, and there are many examples that contradict it. Furthermore, because societies are multifaceted, two countries may be similar in some essential respects, and quite different in other significant areas. Some countries, although geographically literally poles apart, may be very similar due to a shared colonial heritage. Nevertheless, the groupings made in the present study have a degree of face validity, since the regions can be classified without too much strain along three crucial dimensions: religion, language and climate/ecology. Northern Europe tends to be Protestant, many of its languages are related and mutually intelligible, particularly in Scandinavia, and the climate has quite extreme and distinctive seasons, including a severe winter. Southern Europe tends to be Catholic, its major languages – French, Spanish and Italian – have common forms, and the climate is milder. The Eastern countries are non-Christian. The Near East tends to be Moslem, Arab-speaking, and arid. The Far East is not so easy to classify, since several major religions and linguistic traditions flourish there.

To supplement the classification based on *a priori* grounds, the grouping of subjects into the three categories: northern Europe, southern Europe, and the East was tested empirically, and the results of this analysis will be presented below.

The control group

Fifty British students at the Oxford Polytechnic served as the control group. They were matched with the experimental group on the basis of age, marital status, educational attainment, and socioeconomic status (S.E.S.). All subjects had spent at least the previous 10 years in England.

Instruments

"Social situations questionnaire"

CONTENT AND DERIVATION

The questionnaire consisted of forty statements referring to commonly occurring social situations that previous work had identified as being potentially stressful, not just for foreign students but for people in general. The list of situations was adapted from a scale developed by Trower, Bryant and Argyle (1978), and from interviews with over fifty foreign language students, not subsequently appearing in the present study. In these pilot interviews, students from many different countries were asked to identify those commonly occurring social situations that they had found particularly difficult to negotiate in Britain.

ADMINISTERING THE SOCIAL SITUATIONS QUESTIONNAIRE

Subjects were instructed to read each item, and then indicate how much difficulty, if any, they experienced in these situations since arriving in England. It was stressed that their answers were to relate to their experiences in Britain, not their home country. "Having difficulty" was defined as feeling anxious, uncomfortable, frightened, embarrassed or uneasy. Subjects were asked to give their responses on a six-point scale: never experienced, no difficulty, slight difficulty, moderate difficulty, great difficulty, and extreme difficulty. The forty items are presented in Table 14.

The "Best Friends Check List"

The "Best Friends Check List" is presented in Table 15. The instructions stressed that the subjects should think of *actual* and not just hypothetical people presently residing in England. By using the pretext of preserving the anonymity of the subjects' friends, it was possible to plausibly elicit the real matter of interest — the nationality of the friends. The check list was adapted from a similar instrument devised by Bochner, McLeod and Lin (1977). The best friends technique goes back at least to Dimock (1937), who asked adolescents to name the ten best friends in their club. Being a friend of a particular person, or having a particular person for a friend, has been used in many studies as an index of group membership (Cartwright and Zander, 1960), and the concept "friendly" occupies the 19th rank on Anderson's (1968) likableness rating of 555 personality-trait words.

The "Companion Check List"

The "Companion Check List" is presented in Table 16. Subjects were asked to indicate who their preferred companion was for each one of the 11 activities. It was again emphasized that Ss should think of actual and not just hypothetical persons presently residing in England. Subjects were not to reveal the names of these companions, but merely to list their age, sex, nationality, and occupation. As in the case of the previous check list, the experimenters were interested mainly in the nationality of the companions.

The Booklet

The three instruments (the Social Situations Questionnaire, the Best Friends

TABLE 14   *The Social Situations items*

1. Making friends of your own age.
2. Shopping in a large supermarket.
3. Going on public transport (trains, buses, tubes).
4. Going to discotheques or dances.
5. Making British friends of your own age.
6. Making close friends from other countries of your own age.
7. Going to a small private party with English people.
8. Going out with somebody who you are sexually attracted to.
9. Being with a group of people of your age, but of the opposite sex.
10. Going into restaurants or cafés.
11. Going into a room full of people.
12. Being with older English people.
13. Meeting strangers and being introduced to new people.
14. Being with people that you don't know very well.
15. Approaching others — making the first move in starting up a friendship.
16. Making ordinary decisions (plans) affecting others (what to do in the evenings).
17. Getting to know people in depth (well, intimately).
18. Taking the initiative in keeping the conversation going.
19. People standing or sitting very close to you.
20. Talking about yourself and your feelings in a conversation.
21. Dealing with people staring at you.
22. Attending a formal dinner.
23. Complaining in public — dealing with unsatisfactory service at a shop where you think you have been cheated or misled.
24. Seeing a doctor.
25. Appearing in front of an audience (acting, giving a speech).
26. Being interviewed for something.
27. Being the leader (chairman) of a small group.
28. Dealing with people of higher status than you.
29. Reprimanding a subordinate — telling off someone below you for something that they have done wrong.
30. Going to a social occasion where there are many people of another national or cultural group to yourself.
31. Apologizing to a superior if you have done wrong.
32. Understanding jokes, humour and sarcasm.
33. Dealing with somebody who is cross and aggressive (abusive).
34. Buying special goods (medicines, books, electrical goods, etc.).
35. Using public and private toilet facilities.
36. Waiting in a Q [queue].
37. Getting very intimate with a person of the opposite sex.
38. Going into pubs.
39. Going to worship (church, temple, mosque).
40. Talking about serious matters (politics, religion) to people of your own age.

TABLE 15 *The Best Friends Check List*

Who are your three best friends in England? Could you please think of all the people whom you know in England, and from this group select the *three* persons who are your best friends. To preserve the anonymity of your friends, please *do not* give their names — just describe them using the categories provided in the table below. Remember that we would like you to think of three *ACTUAL* persons who are your best friends.

Characteristics of my best friends	MY BEST FRIENDS		
	1	2	3
Age			
Sex			
Nationality			
Occupation			
Lives Where? (College, Digs, Host Family)			

Check List, and the Companion Check List), together with an instructions sheet, were stapled together to form a booklet. The booklet was labelled as originating from the Department of Experimental Psychology at Oxford University. The instructions sheet stressed the anonymity and confidentiality of the exercise. It also included a section containing several demographic questions, the answers to which provided the basis for selecting the subjects for inclusion in the study, and for classifying the foreign students into their national categories.

Procedure

Foreign students

All of the 400 foreign students were tested at their English language schools, during class-time. The booklet was distributed to the students by their own teachers, who were carefully instructed by the first author in how to admini-ster the questionnaire. The teachers went through the questionnaire with their students line by line, making sure that all the subjects understood the task. Because of the care taken with administering the questionnaire, the procedure took about an hour to complete. At the end of the session both the teacher and the students were debriefed as to the purpose of the experiment.

The schools keep a record of their students' command of English, based on an objective language proficiency test. These data were used to include in the study only those students who had a reasonable grasp of English. This screening had the dual purpose of ensuring that the subjects would be able to follow the

TABLE 16   *The Companion Check List*

Individuals seem to prefer the company of different sorts of people for different kinds of activities. Below is a list of some typical everyday activities. What kind of person do you prefer to do these things with in England? Think of an actual person who would be most appropriate as a companion for each activity, and then describe that person using the categories in the table. The list of activities has been arranged in alphabetical order.

Activity/situation	AGE	SEX	Descriptive characteristics of preferred companion NATIONALITY	OCCUPATION
1. Seek help for an *academic problem*				
2. Go to a *disco* or party				
3. Visit a *doctor*				
4. Seek help for a *language problem*				
5. Go to the *movies* (films)				
6. Go out with a person of the *opposite sex*				
7. Seek help for a *personal problem*				
8. Go into a *pub*				
9. *Shopping*				
10. *Sightseeing*				
11. Attend a place of *worship*				

experimental task; and to rule out the possibility that any social difficulties these students might experience would be due to a total inability to communicate linguistically with their hosts. As it turned out, there was no shortage of subjects possessing a substantial grasp of English, since a great many of the students attending these schools do so in order to improve rather than acquire language skills.

English students

The control group of fifty English, Oxford Polytechnic students were tested by the first author, again in their classrooms. These subjects completed only the "Social Situations Questionnaire", a task that took about 20 minutes, and were then debriefed as to the purpose of the experiment. The primary purpose of including these students in the study was to provide a baseline regarding the level of difficulty experienced by young host culture members in each of the 40 situations.

Results and Discussion

The results will be presented in three sections. In the first section, data will be discussed relating to the classification of the foreign students into three regional groupings. The second section contains various sets of results pertaining to social difficulty. The analyses had the following aims: to describe the nature and extent of social difficulties typically experienced by foreign students in Britain; to test the hypothesis that foreign students experienced greater social stress than comparable host nationals; and to test the hypothesis that the bigger the difference between the sojourner's culture and the host society, the greater the social difficulty experienced. The third section contains data relating to the social networks and preferred companion patterns of the foreign students, testing the hypothesis that the students would belong to two major networks, a compatriot "culture rehearsal" network, and a set of utilitarian bonds with useful host nationals.

Classifying the nationalities into three groups

The 150 foreign students in the study, on whom the data are based, came from twenty-nine different countries. The countries were classified by the authors into three groups, on *a priori* grounds according to similarities in religion, language and climate. The classification is shown in Table 17. For the sake of convenience, the three categories have been given the geographic labels of northern Europe, southern Europe and the East respectively. As Table 17 indicates, this is not literally true with respect to the countries placed in the southern European region, as the division includes several South American. nations. However, all of the South American countries represented in the study have close historic links with southern Europe.

Students from countries in the three regions were deemed to be located on a continuum of cultural distance from British society, northern Europeans being considered as "near", southern Europeans as "intermediate", and subjects from the East being considered as being culturally "far" from their hosts. The aim of the present analysis was to provide empirical support for the theoretical classification presented in Table 17.

The 150 foreign students were clustered in terms of their scores on the forty items on the "Social Situations Questionnaire". Three clusters emerged from this

TABLE 17   *Theoretical classification of countries*
along a continuum of cultural distance from
British society

Regional Classification and Distance		
Northern Europe (Near)	Southern Europe (Intermediate)	The East (Far)
Belgium	Argentinia	Algeria
Denmark	Brazil	Eygpt
France	Columbia	India
Germany	Greece	Iraq
Holland	Italy	Iran
Luxembourg	Portugal	Indonesia
Norway	Sardinia	Japan
Sweden	Spain	Korea
Switzerland	Venezuela	Libya
		Saudi Arabia
		Thailand

analysis. Then each student was assigned two scores: either a 1, 2 or 3 depending on which cluster the subject fell into *after* the cluster analysis; and either a 1, 2 or 3 depending on whether the subject had been theoretically classified as culturally "near", "intermediate" or "far" *prior* to the cluster analysis. The two sets of scores were then correlated. In effect, the three empirically derived clusters were correlated with the three hypothetical, theoretically derived clusters. A coefficient of +0.67 ($p < 0.001$) was obtained, providing good empirical support for the rational basis of the classification, and justifying the use of these categories in subsequent analyses of the data.

Social difficulty

Several analyses of the data were performed. The results were initially submitted to a general analysis, more in the nature of an inspection, which revealed that the pattern in the data was consistent with the central hypotheses. Subsequently, more refined and sophisticated analyses were performed to verify the hypotheses, and to shed light on some of the subtler aspects of the findings.

Overall patterns in the data

The design of the study is presented in Table 18, and the subsequent results are based on the 200 subjects depicted in the table.

The 150 overseas students were placed into their respective regional groups. A mean difficulty score was computed for each student, consisting of the sum of the subject's scores on all of the statements in the social situations questionnaire divided by 40, the number of items. Then, an average score was computed

TABLE 18   *The design of the study: number, sex, and culture distance of the subjects*

Sex	Culture			
	Near	Intermediate	Far	Hosts
Male	25	25	25	25
Female	25	25	25	25

for each of the three groupings (near, intermediate and far). The same operation was carried out with respect to the fifty control subjects, producing a mean score for that group. The four means were then ordered in terms of their magnitude, and these data are presented in Table 19. Since the larger the score the greater the difficulty, the order of mean difficulty in the four groups, from least to most, is "near", "host", "intermediate" and "far". A multiple analysis of variance over the four groups revealed that the trend was significant ($f = 2.77$; $p < 0.05$). These data provide initial confirmation that social difficulty is a positive function of culture distance. However, the location of the "host" group in the second rather than the lowest rank is not altogether consistent, and this discrepancy prompted an analysis based on comparing individual items across the four groups.

TABLE 19   *Mean difficulty scores in the four groups, ranked by magnitude of difficulty**

Near	Host	Intermediate	Far	f	p
1.33	1.60	1.90	2.11	2.77	0.05

* The higher the score the greater the difficulty.

Planned contrasts for each item were performed on all possible comparisons. Table 20 lists the number of items that produced a significant contrast at 0.05 or greater in the expected direction, i.e. according to the original hypothesis predicting the order of magnitude of social difficulty to be host, near, inter-

TABLE 20   *Planned contrasts: number of items* that were significant, at 0.05 or better, in the predicted direction*

	Host	Near	Intermediate	Far
Host		1	19	26
Near			31	33
Intermediate				10
Far				

* Total number of items = 40.

mediate and far. Table 21 lists the number of items that produced a significant contrast at 0.05 or greater in a direction contrary to the hypothesis.

TABLE 21   *Planned contrasts: number of items* that were significant, at 0.05 or better, in a direction contrary to the expected one*

	Host	Near	Intermediate	Far
Host		11	0	0
Near			0	0
Intermediate				0
Far				

* Total number of items = 40.

Leaving aside the host national group for the moment, these data clearly indicate that culture distance and social difficulty in the host culture are strongly related. Every one of the significant contrasts between the foreign groups is in the expected direction, and the number of significant contrasts increases with increasing culture distance. Thus thirty-one of the items discriminated between the near–intermediate groups, increasing to 33 in the near–far comparisons. Ten intermediate–far items significantly discriminated between these two groups, providing further justification for ordering the nationalities into three categories according to their theoretical distance from the host culture. Finally, an inspection of the array of significant comparisons indicates that only two statements (items 2 and 39, "shopping" and "worship" respectively), did not produce at least one significant contrast in the expected direction. This provides empirical support for the validity of the questionnaire as a measure of social difficulty.

Turning now to the host group data, these suggest that the English students were between the near and intermediate groups in the amount of social difficulty reported. Specifically, the data indicate that the host students experienced marginally more social difficulty than the near group, but significantly less difficulty than the intermediate and far groups respectively. These data are consistent with previous findings that British students, particularly undergraduates, have interpersonal problems over a wide spectrum of social situations (Bryant and Trower, 1974). However, previous research was unable adequately to interpret these findings, since an appropriate comparison point was lacking. With the availability of a cross-cultural reference point, a much clearer picture emerges. The present data confirm previous research that the social difficulties of students have two main determinants (Bochner, 1972). One component is related to their transition from the role of adolescent to that of becoming adult members of the community. Presumably this problem is inherent in the maturational process and therefore a universal aspect of growing up. The second component is peculiar to sojourning students, and relates to the difficulties encountered in learning a second culture, the difficulty increasing with the divergence of the host society from the culture of the sojourner.

Social difficulty as a function of culture distance

The previous analysis provided general support for the existence of a positive relationship between culture distance and social difficulty, clearing the way for a more precise test of the hypothesis. The results to be presented now are based on data from the 150 foreign students, reflecting a 3 × 2 factorial design (3 levels of culture distance and 2 levels of sex) with 25 subjects in each cell.

Overview of analysis

The data were submitted to a factor analysis, which produced six factors. Factor scores were then calculated for each subject on each factor, resulting in the forty scores of each participant being reduced to six. Six two-way analyses of variance were then performed, testing the effect of the independent variables of culture distance and sex of subject on each of the six factors respectively.

FACTOR ANALYSIS

The data were submitted to a principal components and varimax factor analysis, revealing six factors with an eigen-value of 1.5 or more, together accounting for 44 per cent of the variance. The factors, their interpretation, and the items on which they loaded, are presented in Table 22. Similar factors have been found in previous studies of social skill deficit (Trower, Bryant and Argyle, 1978) providing further justification for regarding second-culture learning as a social skills problem.

The first factor, which accounted for nearly 18 per cent of the variance, covered two themes: formal situations where there is often a status difference; and situations where the person is in the focus of attention. Both of these involve some understanding of the rules, conventions and etiquette of the host culture.

The second factor, which accounted for approximately 8 per cent of the variance, involved managing or initiating friendships, and understanding others. Many students in the pilot stage reported on the coldness and stand-offishness of English people, and their loneliness at being deprived of close friends. The third factor, which we have labelled "public rituals", is often anecdotally quoted as being a source of cross-cultural misunderstanding and difficulty (Mikes, 1966). Only two items loaded on this factor.

The fourth factor was concerned with initiating and maintaining contact, and involves self-presentation and self-disclosure, processes that have some degree of culture specificity. The fifth factor involved making public decisions. It is interesting to note the importance of shopping in this factor; students in the

TABLE 22   *The six factors, their interpretation, and loadings*

Factor 1   Formal relations/focus of attention

Variance   17.9%

Eigen-value   7.16

Items		Loading
25	Appearing in front of an audience	0.72
28	Dealing with people of higher status than you	0.70
27	Being the leader of a small group	0.68
24	Seeing the doctor	0.64
29	Reprimanding a subordinate	0.64
22	Attending a formal dinner	0.61
26	Being interviewed for something	0.60
17	Getting to know people in depth	0.45
23	Complaining in public	0.44

Factor 2   Managing intimate relationships

Variance   7.3%

Eigen-value   2.93

Items		Loading
32	Understanding jokes, humour, sarcasm	0.72
18	Taking the initiative in keeping the conversation going	0.70
15	Approaching others – starting up a friendship	0.55
1	Making friends of your own age	0.43

Factor 3   Public rituals

Variance   5.6%

Eigen-value   2.25

Items		Loading
36	Waiting in a queue	0.76
35	Using public and private toilet facilities	0.63

Factor 4   Initiating contact/introductions

Variance   4.8%

Eigen-value   1.92

Items		Loading
11	Going into a room full of people	0.76
13	Meeting strangers and being introduced to new people	0.59
4	Going to discotheques or dances	0.54
14	Being with people that you don't know very well	0.51
38	Going into pubs	0.40

Factor 5   Public decision-making

Variance   4.6%

Eigen-value   1.85

Items		Loading
2	Shopping in a large supermarket	0.79
3	Going on public transport (trains, buses, tubes)	0.57
16	Making ordinary decisions affecting others	0.52

Factor 6   Assertiveness

Variance   3.9%

Eigen-value   1.56

Items		Loading
10	Going into restaurants or cafés	0.63
21	Dealing with people staring at you	0.62
33	Dealing with somebody who is cross and aggressive	0.57

pilot stage often reporting confusion as to where and how to purchase certain goods, especially food and medicines. The sixth factor was clearly one of assertiveness in the face of rudeness or hostility. It is possible that the dress or racial characteristics of students from more exotic cultures may occasion public attention that the student is unable to cope with. Furnham (1979) has shown that assertiveness is a culturally specific variable.

ANALYSES OF VARIANCE

Six two-way analyses of variance were performed; one on each set of factor scores. The results of these analyses are presented in Table 23. Only three of the analyses produced a significant main effect. In each case the effect was due to the culture variable, and the differences were in the predicted direction. Thus the data confirmed that sojourners from more distant cultures had greater difficulty in negotiating social situations in the areas of formal relations, intimate relations and initiating contact respectively, than sojourners from cultures nearer to the host society. The only other significant effect was a culture by sex interaction on Factor 5, which is difficult to interpret.

The clearest, most unequivocal, and strongest trends were apparent on Factors 1 and 2, which together account for about a quarter of the variance, and load on 33 per cent of the items. All these items refer to personal interactions and relationships with other people, and the data therefore provide further support for the view that the social networks of the sojourner play a crucial role in acquiring the skills of a second culture.

THE MOST DIFFICULT SOCIAL SITUATIONS

The previous analyses were based on differences in social difficulty between various groups. It is possible that these comparisons may have obscured any items that all foreign students scored highly on. Consequently, a mean difficulty score for each item was computed, based on the responses of the 150 overseas students. The situations were then ranked according to the amount of difficulty reported. The ten most difficult situations are presented in Table 24, in their corresponding rank order. This procedure revealed several items that did not appear in the previous analyses, in particular the two statements that ranked highest "making British friends", and "dealing with someone who is cross". The list further confirms that the main area of difficulty of sojourners in Britain is in establishing and maintaining close intimate contact with host nationals.

Summary of social difficulty results

The following conclusions can be drawn from the data:

(1) The regional and geographic origins of sojourners can be used to indicate

TABLE 23 *Mean factor score values[a] and analyses of variance of the factor scores*

Factor 1   Formal relations/focus of attention

		Mean CULTURE			*Source*	*f*
		Near	Inter-mediate	Far		
SEX	Male	−0.38	0.05	0.18	Culture	12.40***
	Female	−0.60	0.10	0.66	Sex	0.46
					Interaction	1.79

Factor 2   Managing intimate relationships

		Mean CULTURE			*Source*	*f*
		Near	Inter-mediate	Far		
SEX	Male	−0.46	0.12	0.44	Culture	10.93***
	Female	−0.49	0.06	0.32	Sex	0.20
					Interaction	0.02

Factor 3   Public rituals

		Mean CULTURE			*Source*	*f*
		Near	Inter-mediate	Far		
SEX	Male	−0.04	0.17	0.04	Culture	0.73
	Female	−0.17	−0.15	0.07	Sex	0.36
					Interaction	0.42

Factor 4   Initiating contact/introductions

		Mean CULTURE			*Source*	*f*
		Near	Inter-mediate	Far		
SEX	Male	−0.38	0.27	0.33	Culture	5.88**
	Female	−0.36	0.17	−0.06	Sex	1.04
					Interaction	0.69

Factor 5   Public decision-making

		Mean CULTURE			*Source*	*f*
		Near	Inter-mediate	Far		
SEX	Male	−0.05	−0.21	0.37	Culture	1.46
	Female	−0.23	0.22	−0.07	Sex	0.21
					Interaction	3.52*

Factor 6   Assertiveness

		Mean CULTURE			*Source*	*f*
		Near	Inter-mediate	Far		
SEX	Male	−0.26	−0.12	0.04	Culture	0.77
	Female	0.13	−0.07	0.20	Sex	1.68
					Interaction	0.41

*** $p < 0.001$; ** $p < 0.01$; * $p < 0.05$.
[a] The higher the score the greater the difficulty.

TABLE 24   *The ten most difficult social situations, in descending order of difficulty for foreign students*

	Questionnaire item	Mean	
		Foreign students	British students
5	Making British friends of your own age	2.66	1.22
33	Dealing with somebody who is cross, aggressive	2.44	1.90
15	Approaching others – starting up a friendship	2.43	1.92
25	Appearing in front of an audience (acting, speaking)	2.32	2.76
17	Getting to know people in depth, intimately	2.27	1.58
32	Understanding jokes, humour, sarcasm	2.23	1.26
21	Dealing with people staring at you	2.21	1.92
18	Taking the initiative in keeping the conversation going	2.20	1.78
14	Being with people that you don't know very well	2.16	1.96
23	Complaining in public – dealing with unsatisfactory service	2.10	2.14

the cultural distance of visitors from their hosts, at least in relation to Britain as the receiving society.

(2) The Social Situations Questionnaire developed for the present study is a valid measure of social difficulty.

(3) The difficulties of sojourners can be explained most parsimoniously in terms of the social skills model. At the same time, extending the model cross-culturally makes the results of intra-cultural studies of social skill deficit more interpretable, by providing a wider point of reference.

(4) The greater the disparity between the host society and the sojourner's culture, the greater the degree of difficulty experienced in negotiating everyday social situations.

(5) Few sex differences in difficulty were found, further emphasizing the importance of the situation as a source of social stress.

(6) The most difficult social situations encountered by foreign students in Britain all revolved around establishing and maintaining personal relationships with host nationals.

The social networks of foreign students in Britain

One of the implications of the preceding analysis is that the sojourn experience may be critically influenced by the nature and quality of the social relations between visitors and their hosts. Very few studies can provide direct evidence regarding the actual social networks of foreign students. The present investigation did collect such data, which will now be discussed. All of the analyses, to be reported below, were based on responses of the 150 foreign students.

Friendship patterns

The data from the "Best Friends Check List" were analysed by tabulating the nationality of the best friends of the respondents into the following four categories: (a) co-national/co-language; (b) non-host, non-co-national; (c) host; and (d) no friends. The resulting frequencies were then expressed as percentages of total friends, and these data are presented in Table 25. The results indicate

TABLE 25   *Friendship networks, expressed
as percentages of total friends, in descending
order of salience*

Category	Percentage
Co-national/co-language	39
Non-host, non-co-national	38
Host	18
No friends	5
Total	100

that the most salient network is the compatriot one, followed by bonds with other, non-compatriot foreigners. Close links with British people accounted for only 18 per cent of the friendships reported. These data are consistent with similar studies conducted in the United States and Australia (Bochner, 1981). There is little doubt that the students who participated in the present study were socially isolated from the host society, in part due to their physical isolation in residential language schools. This creates a vicious circle, since the lack of English friends renders the host society relatively inaccessible, thereby reducing opportunities for learning the social skills of that culture, in turn resulting in even fewer intimate contact with British people.

Preferred culture of companion

Data from the "Companion Check List" were analysed by tabulating the nationality of the preferred companion of each respondent for each activity. Three categories were used: whether the preferred companion belonged to the co-national/co-language group; whether the companion was a host national; or whether the companion was a fellow-foreigner. The resulting frequencies were expressed as a percentage of the total number of companions for each activity, and are presented in Table 26. The main purpose of this procedure was to examine the quality of the relationships with host nationals. Consequently, the activities in Table 26 have been arranged in a descending order of preference for host national companions. Only in two of the activities do the students clearly prefer to have a host national companion. These activities are: seeking help for an academic problem, and seeking help for a language problem.

TABLE 26   *Nationality of preferred companion, expressed as a percentage of the total number of companions for each activity, arranged in decreasing order of preference for a host-national companion*

Check List number	Activity	Host	Co-national Co-language	Other
4	Help with language problem	70	10	20
1	Help with academic problem	56	17	27
3	Visit a doctor	23	27	50
7	Help with a personal problem	21	37	42
5	Going to movies (films)	19	30	51
8	Going to pubs	19	37	44
10	Sightseeing	18	26	56
6	Opposite-sex outing	15	24	61
2	Going to discotheques	12	36	52
9	Shopping	9	33	58
11	Worship	8	28	64

For the other nine activities, host nationals lag far behind co-nationals and other foreigners as desired companions. The two activities in which host nationals are sought out are both formal, utilitarian transactions that require a minimum of personal involvement.

Taken together, the data on the quality of the social relations of foreign students in Britain indicate that in general the sojourners have only very limited contact with host culture members, and the contacts that do become established, tend to be formal and utilitarian rather than personal in nature. The relatively high number of intimate contacts with non-compatriot fellow-foreigners reflects the cosmopolitan environment of the language school where these students spend their days, and the common predicament of being a foreigner in Britain, a condition which seems to transcend differences in language, customs, and religion.

Conclusion

There are many theoretical and practical advantages in regarding the "culture shock" phenomenon as a problem in culture learning. The present analysis, supported by empirical evidence, indicates that the stress experienced by sojourners is largely due to their lacking the requisite social skills with which to negotiate specific social situations. The situations which are particularly troublesome are the ones that involve personal and/or intimate contact with members of the host culture. Further evidence, based on an analysis of the social networks of the students, indicates that in fact the sojourners have very few host culture friends, and the limited contacts that they do have tend to be maintained for purely utilitarian reasons. Taken together, these data suggest that foreign students are not in a very good position to acquire the social skills appropriate to their new culture, since they are being denied the services of informal culture guides and trainers due to the paucity of their links with host members.

However, the distancing of the foreign student from the host culture may be a two-way process. There is no doubt that part of the problem is due to the insensitivity, indifference, and perhaps even hostility of host members towards the strangers in their midst. But there is some indication that the sojourners for their part tend to seek out host nationals only for utilitarian purposes, preferring to engage in more intimate activities with co-nationals and fellow-foreigners. To what extent these preferences stem from rebuffs experienced at the hands of host culture members, remains a topic for further research. The consequences for social skills acquisition, however, are clear-cut: by not performing everyday, informal activities in the presence of sympathetic English companions, these foreign students are cut off from an important source of culture training.

The most important practical implication of the social skills approach to "culture shock" is in providing a sound theoretical base for culture training, together with a proven technology. A three-stage culture training process is indicated, starting with the diagnosis of specific social skills deficits, followed by a training sequence, and ending with an evaluation of the degree of acquisition achieved. The "Social Situations Questionnaire" provides an appropriate general diagnostic instrument, capable of being used, or adapted for use, in many host cultures with many categories of visitors originating in almost any country in the world. Training programmes can be tailor-made to the specific deficits of particular visitors in particular cultures; or the programme can be made to cover the most commonly occurring situations in the target group, as revealed by empirical inquiry.

Apart from its versatility and adaptability, the social skills approach to culture learning has other advantages. Results may be obtained relatively quickly, compared with methods such as those employed by psychodynamically oriented therapists. Also, by emphasizing the acquisition of skills, the approach asserts that cross-cultural incompetence is due to inadequate or absent learning rather than being inherited or the manifestation of unresolved childhood conflicts. This construction of the problem takes away some of the stigma of being socially incompetent in a new culture, implying as it does opportunities for making up lost ground rather than genetic inferiority or psychopathology, in turn increasing the likelihood that persons will seek or accept remedial treatment.

The training technology is currently available, and being successfully used with various groups socially unskilled in the ways of their own culture. Curricula for cross-cultural training programmes are not generally available, and would need to be carefully established, drawing heavily on the services of cultural anthropologists and bicultural individuals familiar with the respective host and visitor cultures. However, by linking the learning procedures to specific social situations in natural settings, many of the ambiguities that bedevil other, more loosely structured, orientation programmes can be avoided.

Finally, the success of the training programme, and the appropriateness of its contents, can be assessed by comparing the behaviour of the trainees before and after the course, in those social situations covered by the curriculum. The generality of the model renders social skills-based culture training procedures equally appropriate in many diverse situations, ranging from teaching foreign students how to cope with British culture, to British businessmen learning the social skills of Indonesian society.

According to Brislin (1979) there are five types of cross-cultural orientation programmes: self-awareness training, in which persons learn about the cultural bases of their own behaviour; cognitive training, in which people are given information about another culture; attribution training, which features the characteristic explanations of social behaviour from another culture's standpoint; and behaviour modification and experimental learning exercises. To some extent, the social skills approach touches on aspects of all of these orientations, but always in the context of emphasizing that culture training should be directed towards the everyday, mundane social encounters of the popular culture. In this regard the approach differs from some other training programmes, with their predilection for the strange or exotic in the target culture, and their often superficial treatment of the inter-personal side of the sojourn.

Culture training is unlikely to succeed if it is portrayed as an initiation into the unfathomable mysteries of an alien and inscrutable society. It is far more effective to remind and reassure sojourners that they are engaged in learning to negotiate ordinary situations, very similar in function to those they would be dealing with in their own culture, even though the form may be somewhat different. It was Boas (1911) who first introduced the principle of the psychic unity of mankind to anthropology, an idea which has equal application to the field of culture learning, with its emphasis on the similarities that unite, rather than the differences that separate, human beings and their societies.

References

ANDERSON, N. H. (1968) Likableness ratings of 555 personality-trait words. *Journal of Personality and Social Psychology*, 9, 272–9.

ARGYLE, M. (1975) *Bodily Communication.* Methuen, London.

ARGYLE, M. (1979) New developments in the analysis of social skills, *Non-verbal Behaviour* (Edited by WOLFGANG, A.). Academic Press, London.

ARGYLE, M., FURNHAM, A. and GRAHAM, J. A. (1981) *Social Situations.* Cambridge University Press, Cambridge.

ARGYLE, M. and KENDON, A. (1967) The experimental analysis of social performance,

Advances in Experimental Social Psychology, vol. 3. (Edited by BERKOWITZ, L.). Academic Press, New York.

AU, D. S. C. (1969) The influence of contact with host nationals on foreign students' attitudes. Unpublished B.A. Honours thesis, University of New South Wales, 1969.

BENNETT, J. W., PASSIN, H. and MCKNIGHT, R. K. (1958) *In Search of Identity: The Japanese Overseas Scholar in America and Japan.* University of Minnesota Press, Minneapolis.

BERRY, J. W. and ANNIS, R. C. (1974) Ecology, culture and psychological differentiation. *International Journal of Psychology,* 9, 173–93.

BOAS, F. (1911) *The Mind of Primitive Man.* (Reprint: Free Press, New York, 1965.)

BOCHNER, S. (1972) Problem in culture learning, *Overseas Students in Australia* (Edited by BOCHNER, S. and WICKS, P.). The New South Wales University Press, Sydney.

BOCHNER, S. (1979) Cultural diversity: implications for modernization and international education, *Bonds Without Bondage: Explorations in Transcultural Interactions* (Edited by KUMAR, S.). The University Press of Hawaii, Honolulu.

BOCHNER, S. (Editor) (1981) *The Mediating Person: Bridges Between Cultures.* Schenkman, Cambridge, Mass.

BOCHNER, S., BUKER, E. A. and MCLEOD, B. M. (1976) Communication patterns in an international student dormitory: a modification of the "small world" method. *Journal of Applied Social Psychology,* 6, 275–90.

BOCHNER, S., LIN, A. and MCLEOD, B. M. (1980) Anticipated role conflict of returning overseas students. *Journal of Social Psychology,* 110, 265–72.

BOCHNER, S., MCLEOD, B. M. and LIN, A. (1977) Friendship patterns of overseas students: a functional model. *International Journal of Psychology,* 12, 277–94.

BOCHNER, S. and ORR, F. E. (1979) Race and academic status as determinants of friendship formation: a field study. *International Journal of Psychology,* 14, 37–46.

BOCHNER, S. and WICKS, P. (Editor) (1972) *Overseas Students in Australia.* The New South Wales University Press, Sydney.

BOLDT, E. D. (1978) Structural tightness and cross-cultural research. *Journal of Cross-Cultural Psychology,* 9, 151–65.

BOXER, A. H. (1969) *Experts in Asia: An Inquiry into Australian Technical Assistance.* Australian National University Press, Canberra.

BRICKMAN, W. W. (1965) Historical development of governmental interest in international higher education, *Governmental Policy and International Education* (Edited by FRASER, S.). Wiley, New York.

BRISLIN, R. W. (1979) Orientation programs for cross-cultural preparation, *Perspectives on Cross-cultural Psychology* (Edited by MARSELLA, A. J., THARP, R. G. and CIBOROWSKI, T. J.). Academic Press, New York.

BRISLIN, R. W. and Pedersen, P. (1976) *Cross-cultural Orientation Programs.* Gardner Press, New York.

BRYANT, B. M. and TROWER, P. E. (1974) Social difficulty in a student sample. *British Journal of Education Psychology,* 44, 13–21.

BYRNES, F. C. (1965) *Americans in Technical Assistance: A Study of Attitudes and Responses to their Role Abroad.* Praeger, New York.

CAREY, A. T. (1956) *Colonial Students.* Secker & Warburg, London.

CARTWRIGHT, D. and ZANDER, A. (1960) Group cohesiveness: Introduction, *Group Dynamics: Research and Theory, 2nd edition* (Edited by CARTWRIGHT, D. and ZANDER, A.). Harper & Row, New York.

CATTELL, R. B., BREUL, H. and HARTMAN, H. (1951) An attempt at a more refined definition of the cultural dimensions of syntality in modern nations. *American Sociological Review,* 17, 54–68.

CLAVELL, J. (1975) *Shogun.* Atheneum, New York.

CLEVELAND, H., MANGONE, G. J. and ADAMS, J. G. (1960) *The Overseas Americans.* McGraw-Hill, New York.

COELHO, G. V. (1958) *Changing Images of America.* The Free Press, Glencoe, Ill.

DEUTSCH, S. E. and WON, G. Y. M. (1963) Some factors in the adjustment of foreign nationals in the United States. *Journal of Social Issues,* 19 (3), 115–22.

DIMOCK, H. (1937) *Rediscovering the Adolescent*. Association Press, New York.

DU BOIS, C. (1956) *Foreign Students and Higher Education in the United States*. American Council on Education, Washington, D.C.

ENDLER, N. S. and HUNT, K. MCV. (1968) S—R inventories of hostility and comparisons of the proportions of variance from persons, responses, and situations for hostility and anxiousness. *Journal of Personality and Social Psychology*, **9**, 309—15.

ENDLER, N. S. and MAGNUSSON, D. (1976) *Interactional Psychology and Personality*. Wiley, New York.

FAYERWEATHER, J. (1959) *The Executive Overseas: Administrative Attitudes and Relationships in a Foreign Culture*. Syracuse University Press, Syracuse.

FIEDLER, F. E., MITCHELL, T. and TRIANDIS, H. C. (1971) The culture assimilator: an approach to cross-cultural training. *Journal of Applied Psychology*, **55**, 95—102.

FOA, U. G. and CHEMERS, M. M. (1967) The significance of role behavior differentiation for cross-cultural interaction training. *International Journal of Psychology*, **2**, 45—57.

FULBRIGHT, J. W. (1976) The most significant and important activity I have been privileged to engage in during my years in the Senate. *The Annals of the American Academy of Political and Social Science*, **424**, 1—5.

FURNHAM, A. (1979) Assertiveness in three cultures: multidimensionality and cultural differences. *Journal of Clinical Psychology*, **35**, 522—7.

FURNHAM, A. Social difficulty in three cultures. *International Journal of Psychology*. In press.

GAMBRILL, E. (1977) *Behavior Modification*. Jossey-Bass, San Francisco.

GLASER, W. A. (1979) Experts and counterparts in technical assistance, *Bonds Without bondage: Explorations in Transcultural Interactions* (Edited by KUMAR, K.). The University Press of Hawaii, Honolulu.

GULLAHORN, J. T. and GULLAHORN, J. E. (1963) An extension of the U-curve hypothesis. *Journal of Social Issues*, **19** (3), 33—47.

GUTHRIE, G. M. (1966) Cultural preparation for the Philippines, *Cultural Frontiers of the Peace Corps* (Edited by TEXTOR, R. B.). The M.I.T. Press, Cambridge, Mass.

GUTHRIE, G. M. (1975) A behavioral analysis of culture learning, *Cross-cultural Perspectives on Learning* (Edited by BRISLIN, R. W., BOCHNER, S. and LONNER, W. J.). Wiley, New York.

GUTHRIE, G. M. and ZEKTICK, I. N. (1967) Predicting performance in the Peace Corps. *Journal of Social Psychology*, **71**, 11—21.

HALL, E. T. (1959) *The Silent Langauge*. Doubleday, Garden City, N.Y.

HALL, J. and BEIL-WARNER, D. (1978) Assertiveness of male Anglo and Mexican—American college students. *Journal of Social Psychology*, **105**, 175—8.

HARRE, R. (1977) The ethogenic approach: theory and practice. *Advances in Experimental Social Psychology*, vol. 10 (Edited by BERKOWITZ, L.). Academic Press, New York.

HARRIS, J. G., JR. (1973) A science of the South Pacific: analysis of the character structure of the Peace Corps Volunteer. *American Psychologist*, **28**, 232—47.

HODGES, W. and FELLING, J. (1970) Types of stressful situations and their relation to trait anxiety and sex. *Journal of Consulting and Clinical Psychology*, **34**, 333—7.

HODGKIN, M. C. (1972) The cultural background of Southeast Asian students in Australia. *Overseas Students in Australia* (Edited by BOCHNER, S. and WICKS, P.). The New South Wales University Press, Sydney.

JACOBSON, E. H. (1963) Sojourn research: a definition of the field. *Journal of Social Issues*, **19** (3), 123—9.

JONES, E. E. (1976) How do people perceive the causes of behavior? *American Scientist*, **64**, 300—5.

KLINEBERG, O. (1970a) Psychological aspects of student exchange, *Students as links between Cultures* (Edited by EIDE, I.). UNESCO, Paris.

KLINEBERG, O. (1970b) Research in the field of educational exchange, *Students as Links between Cultures* (Edited by EIDE, I.). UNESCO, Paris.

KLINEBERG, O. (1976) *International Educational Exchange: An Assessment of its Nature and Prospects*. Mouton, Paris.

KRUTLI, A. H. (1972) Accommodation and housing. *Overseas Students in Australia* (Edited by BOCHNER, S. and WICKS, P.). The New South Wales University Press, Sydney.

KUMAR, K. (Editor) (1979) *Bonds Without Bondage: Explorations in Transcultural Interactions.* The University Press of Hawaii, Honolulu.

LAMBERT, R. D. and BRESSLER, M. (1956) *Indian Students on an American Campus.* University of Minnesota Press, Minneapolis.

LAWSON, A. R. (1972) Pacific Islands students in Australia, *Overseas Students in Australia* (Edited by BOCHNER, S. and WICKS, P.). The New South Wales University Press, Sydney.

LEFF, J. (1977) The cross-cultural study of emotions. *Culture, Medicine and Psychiatry,* **1**, 317–50.

LYSGAARD, S. (1955) Adjustment in a foreign society: Norwegian Fulbright grantees visiting the United States. *International Social Science Bulletin,* **7**, 45–51.

MAGNUSSON, D. and STATTIN, H. (1978) A cross-cultural comparison of anxiety responses in an interactional frame of reference. *International Journal of Psychology,* **13**, 317–32.

MELLSTROM, M., ZUCKERMAN, M. and CICALA, H. (1978) General vs. specific traits in the assessment of anxiety. *Journal of Consulting and Clinical Psychology,* **46**, 423–31.

MIKES, G. (1966) *How To Be An Alien.* Penguin, Harmondsworth.

MORRIS, R. T. (1960) *The Two-way Mirror.* University of Minnesota Press, Minneapolis.

OBERG, K. (1960) Cultural shock: adjustment to new cultural environments. *Practical Anthropology,* **7**, 177–82.

OPPENHEIM, A. (1973) *Questionnaire Design and Attitude Measurement.* Heinemann, London.

PEDERSEN, P., LONNER, W. J. and DRAGUNS, J. G. (Editor) (1976) *Counseling Across Cultures.* The University Press of Hawaii, Honolulu.

PENDLETON, D. and FURNHAM, A. (1980) Skills: a paradigm for applied social psychological research, *Analysis of Social Skill* (Edited by SINGLETON, W., SPURGEON, P. and STAMMERS, R.). Plenum, New York.

PORTER, R. E. (1972) An overview of intercultural communication. *Intercultural Communication: A Reader* (Edited by SAMOVAR, L. A. and PORTER, R. E.). Wadsworth, Belmont, Calif.

PRIESTLEY, P., MCGUIRE, J., FLEGG, D., HEMSLEY, V. and WELHAM, D. (1978) *Social Skills and Personal Problem Solving.* Tavistock, London.

RICHARDSON, A. (1974) *British Immigrants and Australia: A Psychosocial Inquiry.* ANU Press, Canberra.

RIM, Y. (1976) A note on personality, psychosocial disturbance and difficulties in social groups in two cultures. *Interpersonal Development,* **6**, 91–5.

SCOTT, F. D. (1956) *The American Experience of Swedish Students: Retrospect and Aftermath.* University of Minnesota Press, Minneapolis.

SELLTIZ, C., CHRIST, J. R. HAVEL, J. and COOK, S. W. (1963) *Attitudes and Social Relations of Foreign Students in the United States.* University of Minnesota Press, Minneapolis.

SELLTIZ, C. and COOK, S. W. (1962) Factors influencing attitudes of foreign students toward the host country. *Journal of Social Issues,* **18** (1), 7–23.

SEWELL, W. H. and DAVIDSEN, O. M. (1961) *Scandinavian Students on an American Campus.* University of Minnesota Press, Minneapolis.

SEWELL, W. H., MORRIS, R. T. and DAVIDSEN, O. M. (1954) Scandinavian students' images of the United States: a study in cross-cultural education. *Annals of the American Academy of Political and Social Science,* **295**, 126–35.

SHATTUCK, G. M. (1965) *Between Two Cultures: A Study of the Social Adaptation of Foreign Students to an American Academic Community.* Department of Rural Sociology, Cornell University, Ithaca, N.Y.

SINGH, A. K. (1963) *Indian Students in Britain.* Asia Publishing House, Bombay.

SKINNER, W. (1968) *American Industry in Developing Economies: The Management of International Manufacturing.* Wiley, New York.

SMALLEY, W. (1963) Culture shock, language shock, and the shock of self-discovery. *Practical Anthropology*, **10**, 49–56.

SMITH, M. B. (1966) Explorations in competence: a study of Peace Corps teachers in Ghana. *American Psychologist*, **21**, 555–66.

SPIELBERGER, C. (1972) Conceptual and methodological issues in research on anxiety, *Anxiety: Current Trends in Theory and Research* (Edited by SPIELBERGER, C.). Academic Press, New York.

STEWART, E. C. (1966) The simulation of cultural differences. *Journal of Communication*, **16**, 291–304.

STONEQUIST, E. V. (1937) *The Marginal Man.* Scribner, New York.

SUNDBERG, N., SNOWDEN, L. and REYNOLDS, W. (1978) Toward assessment of personal competence and incompetence in life situations. *Annual Review of Psychology*, **29**, 179–221.

SUNDER DAS, S. (1972) The psychological problems of the Eastern student. *Overseas Students in Australia* (Edited by BOCHNER, S. and WICKS, P.). The New South Wales University Press, Sydney.

TAFT, R. (1977) Coping with unfamiliar cultures, *Studies in Cross-cultural Psychology*, vol. 1 (Edited by WARREN, N.). Academic Press, London.

TAFT, R. (1981) The role and personality of the mediator, *The Mediating Person: Bridges Between Cultures* (Edited by BOCHNER, S.). Schenkman, Cambridge, Mass.

TAJFEL, H. and DAWSON, J. L. (Editor) (1965) *Disappointed Guests.* Oxford University Press, London.

TEXTOR, R. B. (Editor) (1966) *Cultural Frontiers of the Peace Corps.* The M.I.T. Press, Cambridge, Mass.

TRIANDIS, H. C. (1967) Interpersonal relations in international organizations. *Organizational Behavior and Human Performance*, **2**, 26–55.

TRIANDIS, H. C. (1975) Culture training, cognitive complexity and interpersonal attitudes, *Cross-cultural Perspectives on Learning* (Edited by BRISLIN, R. W., BOCHNER, S. and LONNER, W. J.). Wiley, New York.

TROWER, P., BRYANT, B. and ARGYLE, M. (1978) *Social Skills and Mental Health.* Methuen, London.

USEEM, J., USEEM, R. H. and MCCARTHY, F. E. (1979) Linkages between the scientific communities of less developed and developed nations: A case study of the Philippines, *Bonds Without Bondage: Explorations in Transcultural Interactions* (Edited by KUMAR, K.). The University Press of Hawaii, Honolulu.

VAN DER KOLK, C. (1978) Physiological reaction of Black, Puerto-Rican and White students in suggested ethnic encounters. *Journal of Social Psychology*, **104**, 107–14.

WATSON, J. L. (1977) Introduction: Immigration, ethnicity, and class in Britain, *Between Two Cultures: Migrants and Minorities in Britain* (Edited by WATSON, J. L.). Blackwell, Oxford.

WICKS, P. (1972) International houses, *Overseas Students in Australia*. (Edited by BOCHNER, S. and WICKS, P.). The New South Wales University Press, Sydney.

WILSON, A. T. M. (1961) Recruitment and selection for work in foreign cultures. *Human Relations*, **14** (1), 3–21.

YARDLEY, K. (1979) Social skills training: a critique. *British Journal of Medical Psychology*, **52**, 55–62.

YEH, E. K., MILLER, M. H., ALEXANDER, A. A., KLEIN, M. H., TSENG, K. H., WORKNEH, F. and CHU, H. M. (1973) The American student in Taiwan. *International Studies Quarterly*, **17**, 359–372.

ZAIDI, S. M. H. (1975) Adjustment problems of foreign Muslim students in Pakistan, *Cross-cultural Perspectives on Learning* (Edited by BRISLIN, R. W., BOCHNER, S. and LONNER, W. J.). Wiley, New York.

8

Tourists and their hosts: some social and psychological effects of inter-cultural contact

PHILIP L. PEARCE

Introduction

THERE are several reasons for believing that tourist—host contact is a special form of cross-cultural interaction. Typically, tourists stay in the visited communities for very short and carefully structured periods of time. Their travel motivations set them apart from other inter-cultural sojourners and their affluence compared to the locals is pronounced. These characteristics generate at least two unique features of tourist—host inter-cultural liaison. Firstly, tourists, as opposed to immigrants, students and foreign workers do not have to adapt to the local community. For example the tourist is granted immunity from local legal and cultural restrictions and can traverse the landscape in a small cultural bubble of his own nationality (Barthes, 1973; Waters, 1966). Although tourists may experience culture shock, this experience is often confined to the initial stage of that process (Gullahorn and Gullahorn, 1963; Taft, 1977), and may indeed be stimulating and exciting to the traveller, since it can fulfil his sensation-seeking motivations (Mehrabian and Russell, 1974). Secondly, the tourist's affluence, even when he is a relatively young drifter—nomad (Cohen, 1973), locates him in a peculiar sociological niche, that of the stranger or adventurer (Simmel, 1950), and thus he has the opportunity to observe and scrutinize the visited community. In this chapter it will be demonstrated that effects of tourist—host contact are mediated by the tourists' affluence, motivation, transience and sociological status in the host community.

Definition of the tourist

While it is possible to distinguish such general and unique properties of tourist—local interaction, it is apparent that there are many kinds of tourists and tourist–host contact. The fundamental concern of this chapter is with the mutuality of tourist–local influence and it is therefore necessary to specify the multiple meanings inherent in the term "the tourist". Economic and political concerns define tourists as persons crossing international boundaries for set periods of time (Burkart and Medlik, 1974; McIntosh, 1972), but a more satisfactory definition for psychological inquiry is an experiential one (cf. Cohen, 1972, 1974, 1979). Here any person outside of the home area and travelling for leisure can be defined as a tourist. Thus a person may feel like and be a tourist on a factory tour in his own home town. For the present purposes the economic and experiential dimensions will in general coincide, since the effects of mutual tourist–local influence will be reviewed on an international scale. The interpretation of the varied effects of mutual tourist–local influence in this chapter will also be closely related to two motivational categories of tourists. A useful and parsimonious distinction which can be made concerning tourist motivation for the present analysis is the dichotomous one of "interested in the local people"–"interested in recreational tourism". This follows two of the categories of tourism types – ethnic tourism and recreational tourism – outlined by Smith (1978) and is sufficiently comprehensive to categorize many types of tourists and tourism studies.

Direct and indirect contact effects

As suggested before, the principal concern will be with the social and psychological effects of tourist–host contact. It will be argued that there are two sources of social influence generating these effects. Direct person-to-person encounters may change attitudes, opinions and feelings of self-esteem, while less direct influences may operate through larger economic and cultural changes in a community. For example, indirect contact effects may result from the building of large tourist hotels which create more working opportunities for women than men. This in turn can produce social sex role conflicts in traditional communities (Young, 1973). On the person-to-person level the ability of taxi-drivers to exploit their foreign customers may result in financial and psychological satisfaction for the locals. The tourists, however, may use such instances of exploitation to construct a negative stereotype of the local people. Feldman (1968), in studying helping behaviour, observed these kinds of biases with Parisian taxi-drivers and American tourists. It will be argued that the majority of tourist effects on the local people are of an indirect nature while the effects of contact on the tourists themselves are more immediate and direct. The direct and indirect effects of tourists on the host community and the hosts on the tourists will now be considered in turn.

The effects of tourists on the visited people

Direct contact influences for isolated and poor communities

Direct contact between the tourists and the local people of Third World and poor communities often generates discord, exploitation and social problems. Admittedly, some studies have demonstrated that previously marginal members of local communities profit from the tourist presence. For example, Smith (1978) observes that older Eskimos, who have resisted previous American acculturation attempts and who have overtly retained their traditional crafts, are in a position to capitalize on their skills. Reiter (1978), in studying a remote French Alpine community, has observed that when the local people have decided to join the "tourist boom" the traditional power of the community leaders may be strengthened. As Smith (1978) and Taft (1981) both observe, local individuals in direct contact with tourists may gain considerable upward mobility, but may need special bilingual skills and charismatic, tolerant personalities to be successful. But if a few local people profit, the majority of Third World hosts appear to lose.

Studies in Tonga (Urbanowicz, 1977, 1978) note that tourists from large cruise ships produce crowded conditions in the small towns and that Tongan children beg from the visitors at major tourist attractions. In addition prostitution and homosexuality are seen as a response to the visits of the cruise ships (both to serve the crew members and some tourists) while the quickly generated tourist dollars in the port towns produce drunkenness and crime on a new scale.

Such observations are not limited to tiny Pacific islands (cf. Nicholls, 1976). For instance, Mexican border towns have numerous prostitution bars for American tourists, while the Seychelles islands, promoted to tourists as "islands of love" because of their traditionally uninhibited sexual standards, now have "rampant" and "ferocious" rates of venereal disease (Turner and Ash, 1975). Similarly Bangkok and Hong Kong have reputations for prostitution and the availability of drugs in response to the needs of Japanese, American and Australian tourists.

While such social patterns are clearly an economic response to the needs of tourists, direct social and psychological contact effects which are of a non-economic nature may also be discerned. The simple process of tourists observing or watching the local people can have profound effects. Certain cultural and economic day-to-day activities of ethnic groups seem to appeal to tourists and are promoted as tourist attractions. For example, Smith (1978) demonstrates that tourists in Alaska frequently stroll along the beaches as fishermen and hunters return to butcher their kill. Tourist expectations, at least expectations of the "interested in local people" style, are fulfilled because the visitors are able to watch the "living culture". But the local people feel insulted, and tire of answering endless questions about their procedures. Smith reports that the locals resent the tourists photographing their activities and in time erected barricades to prevent the would-be photographers. In a final attempt to regain their privacy taxis were hired to haul the seals and other game to the Eskimos' homes, where the slaughtering could proceed.

Further evidence that tourist curiosity and simple passive observation results in a loss of privacy, and feelings of conspicuous and confused embarrassment, is cited by Greenwood (1978). In the Basque town of Fuenterrabia a yearly ritual procession, the Alarde, commemorates the town's sense of solidarity and group spirit. This public festival recalls a seventeenth-century victory by the town's citizens over the French. The ritual was traditionally performed for the community itself and participation in the event was a spontaneous and unstructured affair with little distinction between performers and onlookers. Tourist promotion of the Alarde in the late 1960s resulted in a vast increase in the number of onlookers without any enduring relationship to the community. Greenwood records that the effect of this invasion was stunning. As soon as the Alarde emerged as a public show to be performed for outsiders, it became difficult to get participants to appear in it. This predicament prompted payment for performance, but to little avail. In the process of packaging the festival as a cultural commodity, its essential ritual meaning for the local people was lost. Acccording to Greenwood the result is a confused and discontented community.

There is evidence too that the local people come to see themselves in some of the ways the tourists view them. Tourists come to Tahiti partly because of its reputation for beautiful women. Petit-Skinner (1977) argues that the psychological relationship of the married or courting couple in Tahiti is affected by the tourists' perception of and behaviour towards Tahitian females. The modern Tahitian male has been forced into a subservient role, which contrasts with the traditional values of Tahitian society where men are dominant and powerful in community life.

This change of roles is due to the attention lavished on the attractive Tahitian women by tourists, and the governmental policy of employing women as tourist guides to show the visitors Tahitian life. Tahitian women and men, Petit-Skinner argues, are beginning to see themselves as others do.

For some small, technologically unsophisticated communities direct contact with tourists, if the latter come in small, manageable numbers, can be psychologically beneficial to the hosts. Boissevain (1979) notes that young people living on the Mediterranean island of Gozo welcome connections and friendships with tourists. They see such contacts as a chance to broaden their horizons and feel flattered that the visitors have chosen their island in preference to the larger more industrialized Malta. The sheer number of tourists involved in visiting an area would seem to be an important factor affecting the outcome of direct tourist—host contact.

For example, other evidence indicates that the hosts may develop negative ethnic attitudes towards tourists. A study of the small Spanish Catalan community of Cape Lloc by Pi-Sunyer (1978) found that stereotypes of the numerous English, French, German, Italian, Portuguese and American tourists had developed. In common with other stereotype research, Pi-Sunyer establishes that while the original image may have held some "kernel of truth" with respect to a few tourists, in time the stereotype is automatically applied to all group members (cf. Campbell, 1967). Thus the Catalans see the French as pushy and bad-mannered, the Germans as stingy, the English as arrogant, and the Italians as untrustworthy.

It would appear that a familiar cycle of inter-group contact lies behind the ethnic attitudes expressed in these two studies. As the number of tourists increases the easy-going, rewarding tourist—host contacts diminish. Negative aspects of some tourists are noted, and this crystallizes into a stereotype which is then uniformly applied. Now tourists are no longer seen as possibly rewarding individuals, and the path is open for the over-pricing of goods, victimization and even aggression (Tajfel and Billig, 1974; Wilder, 1978; Zimbardo, 1969). The only way to prevent this cycle of stereotyping would appear to be a carefully controlled governmental programme monitoring tourist numbers in small communities.

Indirect contact effects for isolated and poor communities

Many of the social and psychological contact effects on the local people are of a less direct nature and not all such effects are negative. One of the strongest arguments for the view that tourism can provide social benefits to Third World or technologically unsophisticated communities, is that it can revitalize ethnic arts and traditions. Thus Waters (1966) claims, somewhat eulogistically:

> this cultural renaissance is taking place all the way from the grass roots at the village level to the top councils of national governments. . . . With a modest amount of help, the native craftsman practising a dying art finds a new demand for his product and then employs young apprentices, thus teaching his trade to a new generation (p. 116).

McKean (1978) adopts a more cautious stance but he does observe that much of the literature on the effects of tourism contains a "pessimistic hand-wringing for the return of the good old days". McKean notes that all cultures undergo transition processes and argues that tourists may fortify selected aspects of a culture through conserving, reforming and re-creating certain traditions. This is illustrated in Balinese society where the demand for modernization can, ironically, be achieved through the perpetuation of ancient traditions. The tourists' desire to view Balinese culture has led to what McKean terms cultural involution, the increased elaboration of established forms and practices. As a consequence, Balinese cultural expressions, such as wood-carvings, monkey-dances and dragon and witch displays are now more widespread than they were a decade ago.

Furthermore, the dancing and craft skills are now included in the school curriculum. While it is no doubt a peculiar sight of cultural syncretism to see young Balinese dancers, clad in traditional costume, driving their Japanese 250cc motorbikes on the way to performing a legendary opera, McKean argues that the identity of such young modern Balinese is sharpened by the mirror of tourism.

Mackenzie (1977) discussing the "airport art" of Samoa, also suggests that certain local practices, such as body tattooing, are again increasing as a way of consciously expressing Samoan identity. Positive and profitable effects of tourist interest in the Cuna people and their culture have also been recorded in Latin America (Swain, 1978) although the economic dangers inherent in relying principally on ethnic tourism are noted.

While ethnic art can be a source of local identity, self-esteem, and psychological satisfaction, it is not always seen as thriving under the influence of tourist interest. Graburn (1976) argues that tourists encourage a junk market of inexpensive souvenir art forms. While Navajo jewellery, Maori wood-carving and Kenyan face-masks are of undoubted quality and embody the best traditional skills, numerous wooden figures or paintings of Raquel Welch and John Wayne trivialize the local people's skills. This shift from the sacred to the profane in cultural crafts represents one instance of what Lambert has termed the coca-colonization of the world (Lambert, 1966).

One feature of selling local culture to the tourists is often overlooked. Many cultures attach enormous symbolic and spiritual importance to their ceremonies and art objects. Furthermore an adequate interpretation of these symbolic meanings may require considerable anthropological knowledge on the part of the consuming tourist. Without an understanding of the cosmological significance of cultural activities such as Aboriginal corroborees or Indonesian burials, tourists will merely see these events as "quaint" or "pretty" customs (Crystal, 1978; Pittock, 1967). This not only trivializes the local event, it also wastes an opportunity for the tourist to appreciate the ethnocentrism of his own culture. Worst of all, the more extreme forms of tourist exploitation of local cultural products may make a sacrilege of former religious symbols by marketing them *en masse* (Mackenzie, 1977). This may literally endanger the lives of women and young children of the ethnic groups for whom such objects are traditionally taboo and where sighting these items should be punished by death.

The wider picture of the indirect effects of tourist impact on local people is expressed in a number of diverse ways. Changes in language use, environmental impacts and alterations to employment patterns have all been observed in response to the influx of tourists. For example, White (1974) demonstrates that the decline of the native language in eastern Switzerland, Romansch, coincided with the growth of tourism. This relationship holds not only for the region as a whole but is repeated within the local districts or communes, those localities with greater tourist development suffering the fastest rate of language decline. Environmental effects wrought by tourist density, souvenir-hunting and the infrastructure built to serve tourist needs often damage the recreational settings of the local people (Bosselman, 1979; Cohen, 1978). Farrell (1977) argues that uncritical attitudes to environmental issues in hotel-building in Hawaii have resulted in tourist ghettos. Such areas are a maze of hotels, apartments and condominiums and these high-rise structures can so disrupt the ecology of a beach-front environment that the foreshore is permanently damaged or eroded, thus being less attractive both for the locals and the tourists (Campbell, 1972; Goldstein, 1977; Roy, 1977).

Increasing economic dependence upon tourism may alter the job structure and roles of a community, sometimes creating more new jobs for women than men (cf. Lundberg, 1972; Petit-Skinner, 1977). Furthermore, many of these jobs are menial and underpaid which promotes local frustration and alienation (Kent, 1977). The combined effects of such negative tourist influences have led researchers to postulate empirical indices of tourist–host friction. For example, Hills and Lundgren (1977) propose an irritation index which they describe as a composite of the myriad forms of friction tourists produce for their hosts. While the researchers do not adequately specify how to evaluate and measure the tourist impact, they do specify some common sources of irritation. They note that in the Caribbean, shop attendants serve tourists first and locals last; inflation due to the tourist presence makes locals pay more for food; access to beaches is cut off by tourist hotels; local commuting time increases; and the crowding of beaches and parks makes traditional, spontaneous cricket games dangerous. A more systematic treatment of the concept of an irritation index for tourist–host relations would facilitate assessment of tourist impacts and could assist planning for tourist numbers. The development of such a scoring system would also have applicability in studies of the social impact of economic change such as mining and transport corridors on traditional communities (cf. Berger, 1977; Lysyk, 1977; Reser, 1979).

Bryden (1973) suggests that there are two concepts which help to explain the growth of local resentment. He emphasizes the relative deprivation of the local people compared to the tourist; and he suggests that the tourists form a reference group for the visited community by providing tangible evidence of the relative affluence of other nations. Bryden supports this argument by noting that the consumption patterns of the local people tend to move in the direction of the tourists' consumer lifestyle. This may include dietary changes as well as more conspicuous signs such as purchasing American cars (cf. Veblen, 1970).

Bryden's analysis, and the pattern of findings concerned with tourist impact on the local people, indicate that this form of ethnic contact is strongly influenced by the economic status of the participants, as well as being conditioned by the tourists' length of stay and motivations for travelling (Amir, 1969). But tourists do not only travel to Third World countries. An ethnic contact situation in which there is greater equivalence of economic status might be American tourists in Sweden, Australians in South Africa or Belgians in Britain.

Direct contact effects for technologically advanced communities

The negative effects of direct and indirect tourist contact on the local people in technologically advanced countries would seem to be reduced, although not eliminated. For example, in 1978, the English Tourist Board sampled Londoners' attitudes to tourists in their city and found a highly favourable set of reactions. Only 8 per cent of Londoners in the survey thought the city should cut down on its number of tourists, and only 14 per cent said they suffered personally from tourists in such spheres as overcrowding of transport and shops. Many Londoners expressed the view that they would like more opportunities to get to know tourists and that the large numbers visiting London gave them a sense of pride in their city. The residents of Soho, South Kensington and Greenwich, who have greater contact with tourists, had greater reservations about increasing tourist numbers in the city, but they too reported a sense of satisfaction with the tourist presence, because they were able to use tourist entertainment facilities. Rothman (1978), using a similar survey methodology, reports a study of resident reactions to domestic tourists in small coastal towns in the United States. The findings parallel very closely those obtained by the English Tourist Board (1978) in relation to Londoners' reactions. In the two Atlantic coast towns studied by Rothman tourists were seen as expanding commercial and municipal services and offering the prospect, which was sometimes realized, of long-term friendships with outsiders. Some negative impacts of tourism included litter, traffic congestion, inflation and noise, but many residents reported being able to cope adequately with these disruptive influences.

The theme that in advanced societies direct contact between tourists and hosts can result in important friendships, is given a special emphasis in Israel. Cohen (1971) reports that friendships between Arab youths and tourist girls are sociologically important for this traditionally marginal Arab subgroup. Girls from western and northern European countries apparently do not share the local Jewish girls' prejudice against Arab males, and are willing to be escorted around the city, talk about their own societies and occasionally offer sexual favours. These contacts considerably enhance the Arab boys' self-esteem and offer, somewhat remotely, a chance for the Arab youths to escape their troubled Israeli existence, where their insecure status, lack of education and restricted job opportunities afford little prospect for the future. While Cohen considers such solutions to be largely illusory, he observes that direct contact with the tourist girls is at least alleviating the "system-generated" tension for some Arab youths.

Indirect contact effects for technologically advanced societies

A final note in this section on the tourists' impact on local communities concerns the indirect influences of the tourist presence in advanced societies.

Tourists assist considerably in financing theatres, restaurants and major sporting events in London (British Tourist Authority, 1972a). It has been estimated that more than 4 million tourists attend London art galleries and museums, that 2¼ million theatre tickets are sold to tourists in any one year and that up to 1 million visitors attend music performances. Although these facilities would probably exist irrespective of tourist financial help (Young, 1973), the social life of the host culture is considerably strengthened by the tourist presence. Similarly the maintenance of great houses, the continued existence of zoos, national parks and wildlife reserves all owe some measure of their success to tourist incomes. For many aspects of cultural life, then, the indirect effects of tourists when they visit affluent countries assist the local people.

Although the social environment of the visited community is often preserved, the physical environment of the receiving country is frequently molested. Bosselman (1979) notes that the ancient skyline of Jerusalem has been invaded by tourist hotels, while Cohen (1978) records a multitude of environmental sins foisted upon the locations tourists visit. Included in this list are the massive ecological changes wrought by such operations as Disneyworld (Lundberg, 1972); and the entire transformation of towns and cities such as Palma in Majorca and Hawaii's Waikiki (Cohen, 1978). Young (1973) suggests that giant hotels are a particularly undesirable accretion to a city's architectural heritage because they are of economic necessity multi-storeyed, and therefore frequently in discord with the local setting.

Although the number of sociological and psychological studies reporting tourist impact on advanced societies is rather meagre, a number of countries seem to hold a set of assumptions concerning such impacts. For instance, Turner and Ash (1975) observe that Intourist, the Russian travel organization, exerts enormous control over foreign tourists' experiences. Implicit in this structuring of the tourists' experience is the notion that direct tourist–host contact would be prejudicial to the correct perspective of one or both contact parties. Similarly Ritter (1975), discussing the attitudes of Islamic countries towards foreign tourists, observes that Saudi Arabia, Libya, Iraq and a number of southern Arab states are frankly not interested in having non-Islamic visitors. Again it appears that tourists are viewed as agents of cultural change, with the dress of women, the use of alcohol and the mixing of the sexes being particularly sensitive areas of potential influence.

Summary: tourist impact on the local people

In summary, tourists appear to have maximum social and psychological impact on their hosts when the host communities are small, unsophisticated and isolated. This impact may be a powerful one, either in direct inter-personal encounters or in subtle, indirect influences on the visited community. When the receiving society is technologically more advanced and the affluence gap between tourists and hosts narrower, the contact experience has less impact. In this instance, tourists may develop friendships with the hosts, and the visitors can sustain local social institutions as well as prompting pride in the visited community. The negative effects are not restricted to inter-personal friction, but also include indirect stress to the hosts through noise, pollution and environmental degradation.

The effects of inter-cultural contact on the tourists

There are two views concerning the effects of the travel experience on the tourists themselves. On the one hand international travel is said to promote tolerance and understanding of other cultures. Another view is that "we travel not that we may broaden and enrich our minds, but that we may pleasantly forget they exist" (Huxley, 1925). This perspective considers the tourist experience to be shallow and inconsequential and hence very unlikely to leave any lasting impression on the traveller (Barthes, 1973; Turner and Ash, 1975). A proper account of tourist–host contact must provide evidence to distinguish between these two perspectives. Two kinds of evidence are relevant here. There are large-scale national surveys of tourists' post-travel attitudes; and smaller psychological studies of particular instances of travel as a form of ethnic contact. Both these types of evidence will be discussed.

Large-scale surveys of tourist attitudes

In a series of representative large-scale surveys conducted by the British Tourist Authority (BTA), overseas visitors were asked about their attitudes to holidays in Britain. The responses differed according to the tourists' country of origin. Thus, Americans commented on the polite and helpful nature of the British people and greatly praised the country's cultural association and scenery (BTA, 1972a). Canadian tourists to Britain were impressed by the country's historical and cultural associations, while other favourable comments were directed towards the courtesy of the people and the country's scenery and landscape (BTA, 1972b). Studies of European tourists in Britain indicated a wide diversity of motivations for travelling, but many of the wealthier Dutch, German and French travellers praised the interesting cities and museums while remaining rather neutral towards the British people and their way of life (BTA, 1972c). Not all such surveys indicate clear images of Britain after holidaying there. Twenty-five per cent of Brazilian visitors, including Britain on their trips around Europe, were unable to name anything particularly attractive about their visit (BTA, 1973).

Similar research was conducted by Shipka (1978) with regard to America as a holiday destination for Europeans. Some improvements in how Americans were perceived included the perception that Americans were friendlier than imagined, the country safer than its image connoted, and that prices were not exorbitant. This large-scale survey work provides some general evidence that many travellers form clear images of the countries they visit. However, to understand precisely how these images alter a more systematic measurement and comparison of pre- and post-travel attitudes is required.

Social psychological studies of tourist attitude change

Studies of stereotyping and ethnic contact in social psychology have general implications for a model of tourist attitude change following inter-cultural experiences. Since the bulk of the contact research is concerned with overseas students and their images of the visited nationalities, only selected studies will be reviewed here in detail. As discussed elsewhere in this volume (see Bochner, Chapter 1), ethnic contact research has provided a number of guidelines or rules for assessing contact situations. These rules will be reviewed later in the synthesis section of this chapter where they will be applied both to the tourists' effects on the local people and the influence on the tourists themselves.

An early study of the effects on tourists of inter-cultural contact is provided by Smith (1955, 1957). Young Americans who spent a summer touring Europe were sent a mail questionnaire, both before and after their travels. The questionnaire contained ethnocentrism, fascism and conservatism scales. A stay-at-home group of similar students served as controls. Behavioural indices (such as gifts and correspondence to Europe) were also used to assess the effect of the trip on the students' attitudes. Smith reported few attitudinal changes on the scales used, and concluded that deeply rooted attitudes were not affected by the travel experience. For the few subjects who did change their attitudes Smith argued, following interviews with the travellers, that the change took place due more to peer conformity pressures than to some functional personality need of the individual. The brief European excursion had fostered some contacts with the hosts, since most travellers exchanged correspondence and gifts. A follow-up study revealed that in a few cases these relationships persisted for up to 4 years, but only where intense personal relationships had been established (Smith, 1957). It can also be claimed from this research that travel may operate as a "sleeper" effect, since 4½ years later many of Smith's subjects were less ethnocentric and authoritarian. The difficulty of such an interpretation lies in distinguishing the travel effects from the larger social and cultural changes of opinion taking place in the American community in the same time-period. In addition, many of these students may have had additional travel experiences and cross-cultural contacts in the intervening years. These kinds of methodology problems have been underestimated in evaluating the effects of cross-cultural experience (cf. Bochner, Lin and McLeod 1979).

Further ethnic contact research of attitude change among travellers has been conducted by Triandis and his colleagues (Triandis, 1972; Triandis and Vassiliou, 1967). As well as providing some useful conceptual distinctions, this programme of work, and the study of Triandis and Vassiliou in particular, highlights some of the problems of research in this field. Triandis and Vassiliou studied three groups of Americans who had varying contact with Greeks, and three Greek groups with differing contact experiences with Americans. These groups were principally Greek students and American military personnel, and the inter-cultural experiences involved travelling and meeting the other nationality in their own country. The researchers distinguished heterostereotypes (images of another nationality) from autostereotypes (images of one's own nationality). They predicted, according to an unequal status assessment of the contact situation, that Americans would devalue Greeks but not themselves, while Greeks would see Americans more positively but the Greek autostereotype would suffer. This status interpretation held for the American sample but not for the Greek students in America, who managed to evaluate Americans more positively, without denigrating themselves.

The problems raised by this study are of a general and pervasive nature in studying traveller's attitudes and responses to inter-cultural contact. Firstly, it is usually difficult to obtain strictly comparable groups in this kind of work. The findings may be equally well explained by the nature of the samples of students and servicemen chosen. Secondly, the effects of sensitizing the travellers to the researchers' hypotheses frequently appears in such studies. A stay-at-home control group of similar educational and socioeconomic status is a basic prerequisite for evaluating travel effects (cf. Campbell and Stanley, 1966). Another contribution of the Triandis and Vassiliou paper is to show how important the tourists' motives are in trying to understand inter-cultural contact, enabling the researcher to clarify the purpose of the contact and hence its meaning for the participants.

Another study more directly concerned with assessing tourists' attitudes to the visited nationality was conducted amongst British tourists visiting either Greece or Morocco (Pearce, 1977a). The tourists studied were young members of cheap package tours on 2–3-week tours of either country. A set of questions concerning their travel motivations revealed that they were predominantly interested in relaxing, drinking and having a good time with fellow-travellers in novel, sunny settings, and that they were not particularly motivated by a desire to meet the local inhabitants and study their culture. A group of control subjects who were interested in travel but could not join these particular groups for time-scheduling reasons were used to assess test sensitization and measurement effects in the questionnaire. Four aspects of the tourists' attitudes to the local people were tested by comparing their responses 1 week before the overseas holidays, and 1 week after the tourists had returned to Britain. The four central questions were as follows:

(1) Would the travellers change their overall evaluation of the visited nationality?
(2) What beliefs (if any) about the visited nationality would change due to the travel experience?

(3) Would the tourists have more confidence in their beliefs after their holidays?
(4) Would the tourists begin to differentiate the visited community by noticing social class, ethnic and racial groups, rather than responding to the community as a whole?

The results for the tourists to Greece and the tourists to Morocco were somewhat different but a number of changes were recorded for both tourist groups, while the non-travelling control group showed no significant changes in any of the four areas under review. This lack of change in the control group strengthens the view that the effects obtained are due to travelling as opposed to questionnaire sensitization. To appreciate the results obtained in the study of travellers to Greece and Morocco a preliminary methodological issue must be discussed.

Many studies of attitude change and inter-cultural contact use a list of beliefs or scales describing the hosts, and evaluate changes along these scales. This approach is adequate provided the appropriate scales have been chosen. In order to ensure that all relevant dimensions were employed in the second part of the study, a multidimensional scaling analysis of stereotyped descriptions of Moroccans and Greeks was initially undertaken. This provided a two-dimensional picture of fifty stereotyped adjectives, and twenty such terms were then chosen to sample the full range of meaning inherent in the semantic space describing these national groups. For the tourists to Greece the results showed that the travellers saw the Greeks as less suave, more religious and less affluent than they did prior to their holidays. An unexpected effect was obtained in the belief statements, where the British tourists also changed one of their beliefs about their fellow-countrymen during the same period. The returning tourists saw

TABLE 27   *Travellers' changes in beliefs about their hosts and their own nationality (after Pearce, 1977a)*

Travellers to Greece Post-travel changes in beliefs about		Travellers to Morocco Post-travel changes in beliefs about	
The Greeks	Own nationality	The Moroccans	Own nationality
Suave* (–)†		Tense (+)	Tense (–)
Religious (–)		Greedy (+)	
Poor (+)	Poor (–)	Mercenary (+)	
Rich (–)		Poor (+)	Poor (–)
		Rich (–)	
		Conservative (+)	
		Talkative (+)	
		Musical (+)	

 * All items reported here were shown to be significantly different in the post-travel testing from the pre-travel testing using *t*-test for related samples at the 0.01 level of significance.

 † The sign (–) refers to a perceived decrease in the characteristic and the sign (+) refers to a perceived increase in the post-travel belief statement.

the British people as more affluent than they did before the holiday experience. The effect of a direct comparison with the visited country may well have been responsible for this change. This kind of change of belief by comparison with a new external standard of reference has parallels in the psychological principle of perceptual adaptation level (Helson, 1948).

The pattern of findings for the tourists to Morocco had some rather different features. The Moroccans were evaluated less favourably on the global score of liking following the tourists' holidays. The beliefs which changed between the two testing periods were that the Moroccans were poorer than imagined, more conservative, more talkative, more musical, more tense, and exhibited more mercenary and greedy characteristics than envisaged. The tourists to Morocco also changed some of their perceptions of the British after travelling. Their fellow-countrymen were now seen as less tense and more affluent than prior to

TABLE 28   *Travellers' changes in evaluation of their hosts.*

(a) *Travellers to Morocco evaluating the Moroccans*

| Sample | No. of cases | Mean (0–100) | s.d. | Difference | | t value related samples | d.f. | p |
				Mean	s.d.			
Pre-travel	31	63.5	18.5	7.7	11.5	3.71	30	<.05
Post-travel	31	55.8	22.5					

(b) *Travellers to Greece evaluating the Greeks*

| Sample | No. of cases | Mean (0–100) | s.d. | Difference | | t value related samples | d.f. | p |
				Mean	s.d.			
Pre-travel	41	90.5	7.1	3.0	9.32	2.06	40	<.05
Post-travel	41	93.5	5.1					

the travel experience. Again the notions of a new standard of reference and social comparison might be suggested as the bases for this change. The finding that tourists can make some small-scale re-evaluations of their own countrymen after travelling abroad parallels findings for students living abroad, who also alter their perceptions of home (Herman and Schild, 1960; Riegel, 1953; Useem and Useem, 1967).

Another aspect of the Pearce study related tourists' changes in beliefs about the local people to the confidence with which these beliefs were initially held. It was demonstrated, both for the tourists to Greece and Morocco, that the travellers' initial confidence in their beliefs influenced the changes which occurred, since the beliefs which were most likely to change were those which were held less confidently. Overall, though, the tourists' confidence in their views about the Greeks and Moroccans increased. This provides some empirical support for the familiar phenomenon of the returning tourist brashly asserting that he or she now knows all about the locals and the country in question (cf. Lundberg, 1972).

The notion was not supported that the tourist is a kind of amateur ethnographer collecting information and forming differentiated hypotheses, albeit somewhat unsubtle ones, about the local people (cf. MacCannell, 1976). The two groups of tourists did not perceive significantly more cultural subgroupings (such as Berbers and French in Morocco, or Turks and Cypriots in Greece) following their travel experiences. However, this does not directly contradict MacCannell's assertion that the analogy of tourist as an amateur scientist (cf. Kelly, 1955) is appropriate for some tourists, since it must be recalled that the motivational structure of the British travellers under review belonged to the category of relaxation tourism outlined earlier. Indeed it can be argued that the changes in beliefs of the tourists in this study are linked to their relaxation tourism motivation, since many of the changed beliefs might be considered to deal with the specifics of the inter-cultural transactions (such as shopping, food and accommodation) in which such tourists participate. A listing of the beliefs which did change — they include the adjectives mercenary, greedy, poor, tense and religious — can be considered, in part, to support this view. However, it will require other studies of different kinds of tourists to investigate adequately MacCannell's proposal that tourists are seeking to collect information about the sociological structure of the visited societies.

Other impacts of contact on the tourist

In the preceding sections the principal focus has been upon attitudinal changes which occur in tourists' views about the visited people. Other kinds of impacts on the tourists may also be discerned. Tourists are subject to particular health risks while travelling and contact with local people may have long-range effects on the tourists' physical well-being (Turner and Ash, 1975). There are also reported cases of psychiatric breakdown amongst tourists (Prokop, 1970). In studies of German tourists visiting Innsbruck, Prokop found several instances of tourist depression, alcoholism and other mental health problems, as recorded by the Innsbruck hospitals. He attributed these behaviours to the high incidence of drinking among the travellers, and argued that the release from day-to-day pressures precipitated the tourists' self-doubts and depression. It is apparent that the advertising images of stress-free holidays are considerably misplaced.

Further evidence that travelling can create problems is provided in the work on life stress by Holmes and Rahe (1967). In scaling stress-related events in an individual's life span from 0 (no stress) to 100 (maximum stress), holidays were given a score of 15. This was comparable to such events as changes in working conditions, troubles with one's boss and mortgage stresses. The figure of 15 may also be an underestimate for international travel where the tourist has to cope with an unfamiliar culture. Europeans typically report that travel is more stressful than do Americans, presumably because they experience more foreign culture contacts by travelling in other European countries (Harmon, Masuda and Holmes, 1970).

The origins of the social stresses for the tourist in his contact with the local people are numerous. The tourist has problems in locating and orienting himself in the new environment (Pearce, 1977b), and this alone has implications for the travellers' sense of security and emotional well-being (Lynch, 1960). In New York special maps are available to warn tourists of the "safe, dangerous at night and dangerous all day" areas of the city (Downs and Stea, 1977).

While the tourist is occasionally treated as a special kind of stranger in the community and is helped more by the local people (Feldman, 1968; Pearce, 1980), the social interaction between tourists and locals is another potent form of stress. The question of language is paramount here. Many tourists find that their inability to communicate with the local people is enormously frustrating, and language difficulties may generate considerable stress when sickness occurs, travel plans go astray or luggage and money are lost (Rogers, 1968; Taft, 1977). The solution for many tourists is to confine their travels to countries where their own language is understood fairly readily (Robinson, 1976).

There are also subtle differences in non-verbal communication between different cultures. For example the gestures of the locals may confuse the tourist. To the American visiting Sardinia it may be a considerable source of confusion to find that the O.K. gesture is interpreted as a symbol of homosexuality (Morris, 1978). Even the basic nodding of the head for agreement and disagreement has subtle variations. While it is apparent that many universally applicable gestures and emotional expressions exist (Argyle, 1975), some features of interaction with the hosts are likely to be subtly different for the tourists. For instance the use of space may differ. Watson and Graves (1966) found that Americans tend to think Arabs pushy and threatening because of the latter's preference for more direct, closer and intimate interaction. While specialized training procedures may help to overcome these difficulties (Collett, 1971), most tourists are probably unaware of these non-verbal cues until they are confronted with dramatic breakdowns in their interactions.

Some host cultures, finding their visitors to be difficult and socially unskilled from their own perspective, have started to produce pamphlets outlining some of the local cultural rules and norms that tourists should follow. Pacific islands have been to the fore in the understanding of interaction difficulties (Fox, 1977). For example, Fiji suggests that visiting Australians should not tip the local people, should learn the correct greeting rituals, should appreciate the polite and reciprocal bonds of friendship, and should not confuse lack of clothing with promiscuity (Fiji Visitors' Bureau, 1975). This kind of educational material is also often contained in guidebooks but the extent to which tourists follow these specific prescriptions is unknown.

General rule-breaking, on the other hand, has been recorded. Khuri (1968), in an article concerning bargaining in the Middle East, observes how tourists break fundamental rules of address, mistake the proper sequences of actions when bargaining and misconstrue Arab courtesy. Ritter (1975) notes that bikini-clad European women swimming and sunbathing are an affront to Middle-Eastern notions of women's roles in society, and contravene norms about public dress. Similarly, the clothing styles, long hair and casualness of "tourist—drifters" have aroused public censure from Singapore to Leningrad (Cohen, 1971; Turner and Ash, 1975).

The cultural mediator or "go-between"

Throughout this discussion there has been the assumption that there is direct contact between host and visitor. This is no doubt correct for many affluent individual travellers and Cohen's drifter—tourists, but the group or package tourist often experiences the visited country through the tourist guide, tour chaperone or some other mediating figure. It has been suggested that when this figure is a member of the local community he or she may well be a socially marginal figure (Smith, 1978). The effect of the tourist guide on the travellers has received little systematic attention but an important distinction may well prove to be whether the guide is seen as a member of the travel party or the host culture. One effect of the guide on the travel experience is to place the tourist in a dependent, passive, child-like state with the guide emerging as the authority figure controlling an unruly mob (Owen, 1968). This has led one tourist researcher to note that the guided tour is really a kind of sheltered adventure (Schmidt, 1975) and that, in the terms of transactional analysis, the guide is the parental figure distributing largesse. Reactions to the tourist guide as a mediator in inter-cultural contact would appear to be an interesting topic for further research. It should be observed that in the studies of tourists' attitudes reported earlier there were no officials performing the role of tourist—host mediator.

Summary: the impact of inter-cultural contact on the tourist

At the beginning of this section is was stated that one view of the tourist experience held that the contact was so superficial as to deny the possibility of attitudinal and other changes. This proposition is not supported by the present review. The research indicates that tourists can modify their perceptions of their hosts, they can re-appraise selected aspects of their fellow-countrymen, and they can emerge more confident in their beliefs about the host culture. In addition, the impact of the travel experience can alert tourists to the problems of inter-cultural interaction, through language and non-verbal communication difficulties. While research concerning the impact of inter-cultural encounters on tourists is still in its infancy, the current position is that tourists, even without the specific motivation of wanting to meet and interact with the locals, can be influenced by the contact process.

This is not to deny that some of the influences are negative, and that the host culture may be liked less, but it does suggest that travel researchers such as Hiller (1976) are correct in arguing that the effects of travelling may eventually be a force for cross-cultural understanding.

Synthesis

It was suggested in the body of this review that ethnic contact research might provide some organizing framework for the various kinds of mutual tourist—host impact discussed. Four principles which characterize contact situations are relevant to tourist—host interaction. These are the status of the participants or social comparison theory (Kelman, 1962; Morris, 1956; Selltiz and Cook, 1962; Triandis and Vassiliou, 1967), the opportunity for contact dimension (Amir, 1969; Stouffer, 1949), the intimacy of contact (Amir, 1969; Salter, 1974a; Selltiz and Cook, 1962), and the interactant's attitudes (Cook, 1962; Smith, 1955, 1957). At a general level the use of these principles as *post-hoc* explanatory devices is quite fruitful. For example, the negative effects of tourists viewing local people's activities and influencing the hosts' self-esteem derive from the unequal status of the participants, due to the tourists' relative affluence, mobility and experience with other cultures. It is the tourists who have the power in the social situation and the hosts, confronted with a new group of people for social comparison, re-align their view of the world. Bryden's (1973) analysis of tourism in the Caribbean Islands shows how the locals copy American culture as a consequence of tourist contact. This is but one example of the general trend, documented earlier in this chapter, for tourists to have powerful direct and indirect effects on the local culture, and the social comparison theory serves to integrate much of this research. Where the social comparison of the two cultures in contact is less dramatic, as was illustrated in the discussion of tourist impact in developed countries, the effects are less pronounced.

In drawing attention to the effects of the contact on the tourists themselves, Smith (1957) provided evidence that tourist—host relationships were only sustained when intimate contacts had been formed. This follows the intimacy of contact principle (Amir, 1969; Selltiz and Cook, 1962). The studies of tourists in Greece and Morocco suggested that attitudinal changes occurred as a consequence of the tourists' day-to-day encounters with the locals. Thus the attitudes of the tourists and their motivation for travelling were central to the kinds of changes reported. This supports the "interactants' attitudes" principle of Smith (1955, 1957) and Cook (1962). Both in terms of tourist influences on the local people and in the effects of the contact on the tourists themselves, these general principles of ethnic contact provide a convenient description of the forces shaping the contact outcomes.

However, providing a broad *post-hoc* description of inter-cultural contact is rather different from predicting the precise effects of particular situations. It can be argued that the above principles of ethnic contact, when critically assessed, are not very useful for explaining particular instances of tourist–host experiences. For example, should opportunity for contact be measured by the number of people encountered or those who could be encountered? Irrespective of the definition which one uses, it would be exceedingly difficult to measure this variable for a tourist sample. Furthermore, how does one distinguish between intimate and frequent contact? Earlier articles are not very informative on these matters, and they have often defined each situation individually rather than using a set of standardized dimensions. For example, the notion of intimacy has been taken as "living next door to someone" (Wilner *et al.*, 1952), "being close personal friends with outgroup members" (Goldsen, 1955) or "participating in numerous shared activities in inter-cultural societies" (Chadwick-Jones, 1962). The notion of status, too, has been interpreted in several different ways. Triandis and Vassiliou (1967) used the status of two nationalities as a whole for their criterion and employed the researchers' description of the situation as their defining principle. Others think that the views of the subjects, not the researchers, should be of paramount importance (Harré and Secord, 1972), while a further group consider only the status of the interacting individuals and not nationalities to be the key to this problem (e.g., Chadwick-Jones, 1962; Wolf, 1961). Clearly, the skill and theoretical bias of the researcher seem to play a more important role in defining the nature of the ethnic contact situation than does the use of a set of quantitative rules.

Thus it appears at this stage of tourist–local contact research that no clear-cut rules exist which will give a precise prediction. More emphasis on the attitudes and motives of the participants (an emic perspective) may result in a better framework for hypothesis-testing in this field but even here much work remains to be done. The "interested in the local people"–"interested in relaxation tourism" dichotomy suggested in this chapter may be of some use in generating predictions in future studies. There also exists a need to extend and diversify the present databank on the effects of tourist–host contact, particularly in the field of understanding tourist attitude changes, since the extant studies are few and restricted in scope. In particular, longitudinal or diachronic studies of attitude change are needed to understand the long-term effects of contact.

In conclusion it appears that research effort in this field should be directed towards a controlled assessment of short- and long-term contact effects, with particular attention to the tourists' motivation and the precise features of the contact situations. This will eventually provide a body of knowledge which can be used to test theoretical principles of tourist–host contact. For the present, the field is characterized by adequate *post-hoc* descriptions of observed social and psychological effects, but has little to offer from the point of view of *a priori* assessment and prediction. It would seem very desirable to be able to predict and explore the effects of tourist–host contact, not only from the point of view of assessing the social impacts of a multi-million dollar industry, but also to understand the interrelated phenomena of modernization, industrialization, culture change and preservation, and the leisure needs of the developed world.

References

AMIR, Y. (1969) Contact hypothesis in ethnic relations. *Psychological Bulletin,* 71, 319–42.

ARGYLE, M. (1975) *Bodily Communication.* Methuen, London.

BARTHES, R. (1973) *Mythologies.* Paladin, London.

BERGER, T. R. (1977) *Northern Frontier: Northern Homeland.* (The report of the Mackenzie Valley Pipeline Inquiry, vol. 1). James Lorimer, Toronto.

BOCHNER, S., LIN, A. and MCLEOD, B. (1979) Cross-cultural contact and the development of an international perspective. *Journal of Social Psychology,* 107, 29–41.

BOISSEVAIN, J. (1979) The impact of tourism on a dependent island: Gozo, Malta. *Annals of Tourism Research,* 6, 76–90.

BOSSELMAN, F. (1979) *In the Wake of the Tourist: Managing Special Places in Eight Countries.* The Conservation Foundation, Washington.

BRITISH TOURIST AUTHORITY (1972a) The Chicago Workshop: the United States travel market. *Research Newsletter,* 7 (Winter).

BRITISH TOURIST AUTHORITY (1972b) Attitudes to travel among affluent adult holiday-makers in Holland, Germany and France – 1972. *Research Newsletter,* 6 (Autumn).

BRITISH TOURIST AUTHORITY (1972c) The Toronto Workshop: the Canadian travel market. *Research Newsletter,* 7 (Winter).

BRITISH TOURIST AUTHORITY (1973) Travellers to the U.K. from Brazil and the Argentine – 1972. *Research Newsletter,* 10 (Autumn).

BRYDEN, J. (1973) *Tourism and Development: Case Study of Commonwealth Caribbean.* Cambridge University Press, Cambridge.

BURKART, A. J. and Medlik, S. (1974) *Tourism.* Heinemann, London.

CAMPBELL, D. (1967) Stereotypes and the perception of group differences. *American Psychologist,* 22, 817–29.

CAMPBELL, D. and STANLEY, J. (1966) *Experimental and Quasi-experimental Designs for Research.* Rand McNally, Chicago.

CAMPBELL, J. F. (1972) *Erosion and Accretion of Selected Hawaiian Beaches, 1962–1972.* University of Hawaii, Sea Grant Program, Honolulu.

CHADWICK-JONES, J. K. (1962) Intergroup attitudes: a stage in attitude formation. *British Journal of Sociology,* 13, 57–63.

COHEN, E. (1971) Arab boys and tourist girls in a mixed Jewish–Arab community. *International Journal of Comparative Sociology,* 12, 217–33.

COHEN, E. (1972) Toward a Sociology of International Tourism. *Social Research,* 39, 164–82.

COHEN, E. (1973) Nomads from affluence: notes on the phenomenon of drifter–tourism. *International Journal of Comparative Sociology,* 14, 89–103.

COHEN, E. (1974) Who is a tourist? A conceptual clarification. *The Sociological Review,* 22, 527–55.

COHEN, E. (1978) The impact of tourism on the physical environment. *Annals of Tourism Research,* 2, 215–37.

COHEN, E. (1979) Phenomenology of tourist experiences. *Sociology,* 13, 179–201.

COLLETT, P. (1971) Training Englishmen in the non-verbal behaviour of Arabs. *International Journal of Psychology*, **6**, 209—15.

COOK, S. (1962) The systematic analysis of socially significant events: a strategy for social research. *Journal of Social Issues*, **18**, 66—84.

CRYSTAL, E. (1978) Tourism in Toraja, Sulawesi, Indonesia, *Hosts and Guests* (Edited by Smith, V.). Blackwell, Oxford.

DOWNS, R. and STEA, D. (1977) *Maps in Minds*. Harper & Row, New York.

ENGLISH TOURIST BOARD (1978) Study of Londoners' attitudes to tourists. *Journal of Travel Research*, **17**, 19.

FARRELL, B. H. (1977) *The Tourist Ghettos of Hawaii*. Center for South Pacific Studies, University of California, Santa Cruz.

FELDMAN, R. (1968) Response to compatriot and foreigner who seek assistance. *Journal of Personality and Social Psychology*, **10**, 202—14.

FIJI VISITORS' BUREAU (1975) *Advice to visiting Australians*. Fiji Government Press, Suva.

FOX, M. (1977) The social impact of tourism: a challenge to researchers and planners, *A New Kind of Sugar: Tourism in the Pacific* (Edited by FINNEY, B. R. and WATSON, K. A.). The East—West Center, Honolulu.

GOLDSEN, J. (1955) Quoted in SELLTIZ, C. and COOK, S. (1962).

GOLDSTEIN, V. (1977) Planning for tourism on the island of Hawaii: the effects of tourism on historical sites and culture, *A New Kind of Sugar: Tourism in the Pacific* (Edited by FINNEY, B. R. and WATSON, K. A.). The East—West Center, Honolulu.

GRABURN, N. (Editor) (1976) *Ethnic and Tourist Arts: Cultural Expressions from the Fourth World*. University of California Press, Los Angeles.

GREENWOOD, D. (1978) Culture by the pound: an anthropological perspective on tourism as cultural commoditization, *Hosts and Guests* (Edited by SMITH, V.). Blackwell, Oxford.

GULLAHORN, J. E. and GULLAHORN, J. T. (1963) An extension of the U-curve hypothesis. *Journal of Social Issues*, **19**, 33—47.

HARMON, D. K. MASUDA, M. and HOLMES, T. H. (1970) The Social Readjustment Rating Scale: a cross-cultural study of Western Europeans and Americans. *Journal of Psychosomatic Research*, **14**, 391—400.

HARRÉ, R. and SECORD, P. (1972) *The Explanation of Social Behaviour*. Blackwell, Oxford.

HELSON, H. (1948) Adaptation level as a basis for a quantitative theory of frames of reference. *Psychological Review*, **55**, 297—313.

HERMAN, S. and SCHILD, E. (1960) Contexts for the study of cross-cultural education. *Journal of Social Psychology*, **52**, 231—50.

HILLER, H. (1976) Some basic thoughts about the effects on tourism of changing values in receiving societies. *The Travel Research Association, Seventh Annual Conference Proceedings*, pp. 199—201.

HILLS, T. and LUNDGREN, J. (1977) The impact of tourism in the Caribbean. A methodological study. *Annals of Tourism Research*, **4**, 248—67.

HOLMES, T. H. and RAHE, R. H. (1967) The Social Readjustment Rating Scale. *Journal of Psychosomatic Research*, **11**, 213—18.

HUXLEY, A. (1925) *Along the Road: Notes and Essays of a Tourist*. Chatto & Windus, London.

KELLY, G. A. (1955) *The Psychology of Personal Constructs*. Norton, New York.

KELMAN, H. (1962) Changing attitudes through international activities. *Journal of Social Issues*, **18**, 68—87.

KENT, N. (1977) A new kind of sugar, *A New Kind of Sugar: Tourism in the Pacific* (Edited by FINNEY, B. R. and WATSON, K. A.). The East—West Center, Honolulu.

KHURI, F. I. (1968) The etiquette of bargaining in the Middle East. *American Anthropologist*, **70**, 698—706.

LAMBERT, R. D. (1966) Some minor pathologies in the American presence in India. *Annals of the American Academy of Political and Social Sciences*, **368**, 157—70.

LUNDBERG, D. E. (1972) *The Tourist Business*. Institutions Volume Feeding Management Committee, Chicago.

LYNCH, K. (1960) *The Image of the City.* M.I.T. Press, Cambridge, Mass.

LYSYK, K. (1977) *Alaskan Highway Pipeline Inquiry.* Canadian Ministry of Supply and Services, Ottawa.

MACCANNELL, D. (1976) *The Tourist: A New Theory of the Leisure Class.* Schocken, New York.

MCINTOSH, R. (1972) *Tourism, Principles, Practices, Philosophies.* Grid, Columbus, Ohio.

MCKEAN, P. (1978) Towards a theoretical analysis of tourism: economic dualism and cultural involution in Bali, *Hosts and Guests* (Edited by SMITH, V.). Blackwell, Oxford.

MACKENZIE, M. (1977) The deviant art of tourism: airport art, *The Social and Economic Impact of Tourism on Pacific Communities* (Edited by FARRELL, B.). Center for South Pacific Studies, University of California, Santa Cruz.

MEHRABIAN, A. and RUSSELL, J. (1974) *An Approach to Environmental Psychology.* M.I.T. Press, Cambridge, Mass.

MORRIS, D. (1978) *Man Watching.* Jonathan Cape, London.

MORRIS, R. T. (1956) National status and attitudes of foreign students. *Journal of Social Issues,* **12,** 20–5.

NICHOLLS, L. L. (1976) Crime detection and law stabilization in tourist-recreation regions: a conference report. *Journal of Travel Research,* **15,** 18–20.

OWEN, C. (1968) *Britons Abroad.* Routledge & Kegan Paul, London.

PEARCE, P. L. (1977a) The social and environmental perceptions of overseas tourists. Unpublished D.Phil. dissertation, University of Oxford.

PEARCE, P. L. (1977b) Mental souvenirs: a study of tourists and their city maps. *Australian Journal of Psychology,* **29,** 203–10.

PEARCE, P. L. (1980) Strangers, travellers and Greyhound bus terminals: studies of small scale helping behaviours. *Journals of Personality and Social Psychology,* **38** 935–40

PETIT-SKINNER, S. (1977) Tourism and acculturation in Tahiti. *The Social and Economic Impact of Tourism on Pacific Communities* (Edited by FARRELL, B.). Center for South Pacific Studies, University of California, Santa Cruz.

PI-SUNYER, O. (1978) Through native eyes: tourists and tourism in a Catalan maritime community, *Host and Guests* (Edited by SMITH, V.). Blackwell, Oxford.

PITTOCK, A. B. (1967) Aborigines and the tourist industry. *Australian Quarterly,* **3,** 87–95.

PROKOP, H. (1970) Psychiatric illness of foreigners vacationing in Innsbruck. *Neurochirugie und Psychiatrie,* **107,** 363–8.

REITER, R. R. (1978) The politics of tourism in a French Alpine community, *Hosts and Guests* (Edited by SMITH, V.). Blackwell, Oxford.

RESER, J. (1979) Report of initial stage of the social and environmental impact assessment of uranium mining and the Arnhem highway on Aboriginal communities in the vicinity of Ramangining, Arnhem Land, N.T. Department of Behavioural Sciences, James Cook University of North Queensland.

RIEGEL, O. W. (1953) Residual effects of exchange of persons. *Public Opinion Quarterly,* **17,** 319–27.

RITTER, W. (1975) Recreation and tourism in Islamic countries. *Ekistics,* **236,** 56–69.

ROBINSON, H. (1976) *A Geography of Tourism.* McDonald & Evans, London.

ROGERS, J. (1968) *Foreign Places: Foreign Faces.* Penguin Education, Harmondsworth.

ROTHMAN, R. A. (1978) Residents and transients: community reactions to seasonal visitors. *Journal of Travel Research,* **16,** 8–13.

ROY, L. (1977) Planning for tourism on the island of Hawaii: the effects of tourism on natural resources, natural beauty and recreation, *A New Kind of Sugar: Tourism in the Pacific* (Edited by FINNEY, B. R. and WATSON, K. A.). The East–West Center, Honolulu.

SALTER, C. A. (1974a) International contact, social rewards, and attitudes toward the country visited. *Psychological Reports,* **35,** 49–50.

SALTER, C. A. (1974b) Status comparability and attitudes toward a foreign host nation: a cross-cultural study. *The Journal of Psychology,* **88,** 201–14.

SCHMIDT, C. (1975) The guided tour: insulated adventure. *The Travel Research Association, Sixth Annual Conference Proceedings,* p. 145.

SELLTIZ, C. and COOK, S. (1962) Factors influencing attitudes of foreign students toward the host country. *Journal of Social Issues*, **18**, 7–23.

SHIPKA, B. (1978) 1978 international travel outlook. *Proceedings 1978 Travel Outlook Forum.* United States Travel Data Center, Washington, pp. 133–57.

SIMMEL, G. (1950) *The Sociology of Georg Simmel* (translated by K. H. Woolf). The Free Press of Glencoe, New York.

SMITH, H. P. (1955) Do intercultural experiences affect attitudes? *Journal of Abnormal and Social Psychology*, **51**, 469–77.

SMITH, H. P. (1957) The effects of intercultural experience: a follow-up investigation. *Journal of Abnormal and Social Psychology*, **54**, 266–9.

SMITH, V. (1978) Eskimo tourism: micro-models and marginal men, *Hosts and Guests* (Edited by SMITH, V.). Blackwell, Oxford.

STOUFFER, S. A., SUCHMAN, E. A., DEVINNEY, L. C., STAR, S. A. and WILLIAMS, R. W. (1949) *The American Soldier*, vol. 1. Princeton University Press, Princeton, N.J.

SWAIN, M. B. (1978) Cuna women and ethnic tourism: a way to persist and an avenue to change, *Hosts and Guests* (Edited by SMITH, V.). Blackwell, Oxford.

TAFT, R. (1977) Coping with unfamiliar cultures, *Studies in Cross Cultural Psychology*, vol. 1 (Edited by WARREN, N.). Academic Press, London.

TAFT, R. (1981) The role and personality of the mediator, *The Mediating Person: Bridges Between Cultures* (Edited by BOCHNER, S.). Schenkman, Cambridge, Mass.

TAJFEL, H. and BILLIG, M. (1974) Familiarity and categorization in intergroup behaviour. *Journal of Experimental Social Psychology*, **10**, 159–70.

TRIANDIS, H. C. (1972) *The Analysis of Subjective Culture.* Wiley, New York.

TRIANDIS, H. C. and Vassiliou, V. (1967) Frequency of contact and stereotyping. *Journal of Personality and Social Psychology*, **7**, 316–28.

TURNER, L. and ASH, J. (1975) *The Golden Hordes.* Constable, London.

URBANOWICZ, C. (1977) Integrating tourism with other industries in Tonga, *The Social and Economic Impact of Tourism on Pacific Communities* (Edited by FARRELL, B.). Center for South Pacific Studies, University of California, Santa Cruz.

URBANOWICZ, C. (1978) Tourism in Tonga: troubled times, *Hosts and Guests* (Edited by SMITH, V.). Blackwell, Oxford.

USEEM, J. and USEEM, R. (1967) The interfaces of a binational third culture: a study of the American community in India. *Journal of Social Issues*, **23**, 130–43.

VEBLEN, T. (1970) *The Theory of the Leisure Class.* Unwin, London. (1st edition 1925.)

WATERS, S. R. (1966) The American tourist. *Annals of the American Academy of Political and Social Science*, **368**, 109–18.

WATSON, O. M. and GRAVES, T. D. (1966) Quantitative research in proxemic behaviour. *American Anthropologist*, **68**, 971–85.

WHITE, P. E. (1974) *The Social Impact of Tourism on Host Communities: A Study of Language Change in Switzerland.* School of Geography, University of Oxford; Research Paper No. 9.

WILDER, D. (1978) Reduction of intergroup discrimination through individuation of the out-group. *Journal of Personality and Social Psychology*, **36**, 1361–74.

WILNER, D. M., WALKLEY, R. P. and COOK, S. W. (1952) Residential proximity and inter-group relations in public housing projects. *Journal of Social Issues*, **8**, 45–69.

WOLF, H. E. (1961) Judgments formules sur le Francais et les Italiens par des eleves allemands. *Revue de Psychologie des Peuples*, **16**, 287–305.

YOUNG, G. (1973) *Tourism, Blessing or Blight?* Penguin, Harmondsworth.

ZIMBARDO, P. (1969) The human choices: individuation, reason and order versus deindividuation, impulse and chaos, *Nebraska Symposium on Motivation*, vol. 17 (Edited by ARNOLD, W. J. and LEVINE, D.). University of Nebraska Press, Lincoln.

Name index

Subject index

231